THE HEJAZ RAILWAY

JAMES NICHOLSON

THE HEJAZ RAILWAY

JAMES NICHOLSON

STACEY INTERNATIONAL
AL TURATH

Editor-in-Chief
Caroline Shaw

Design
Graham Edwards

Stacey International
128 Kensington Church Street
London W8 4BH
Tel: +44 (0)207 221 7166
Fax: +44 (0)207 792 9288
E-mail:
enquiries@stacey-international.co.uk
Website:
www.stacey-international.co.uk

in association with
Al-Turath
PO Box 68200
Riyadh 11527
E-mail:
al-turath@al.turath.com
Website:
www.al-turath.com

ISBN: 1900988 81X

© Stacey International 2005

The right of James Nicholson to be identified as the author of this work has been asserted by him in accordance with the Copyright, Designs and Patents Act of 1988.

CIP Data: A catalogue record for this book is available from the British Library

All rights reserved. No part of this publication may be reproduced, stored in a retrieval system, or transmitted in any form or by any means, electronic, mechanical, photocopying, recording, or otherwise, without the prior permission of the copyright owners.

Printed by Tien Wah Press, Singapore

This book is published with the kind sponsorship of Chevron Corporation

The publishers would also like to thank Axa Gulf - Norwich Union for supporting the author in his research

Photographic Credits:

Every effort has been made to contact owners of copyright material. The following photographers and institutions are gratefully acknowledged for their contributions:

Al Turath: 10*b*, 15, 37*t*
John Alexander: Cover, ii-iii, xi, xiv-xv, 9, 25, 52, 53, 55, 58, 80, 136, 157*b*, 167*b*, 169, 174, 175
Ben Ashworth: 24, back cover
Uwe Bergmann: 67
British Embassy, Saudi Arabia: 86
British Library: 60
Peter Campbell: 43, 139*b*, 160*t*, 179
Keith Costelloe: 78*tl*, 78*tr*, 78*bl*, 78*br*
Durham University: 8, 23*t*, 31*b*, 33*b*, 38, 39, 42, 79, 96, 125*t*, 139*t*, 172
Ecole Biblique et Archéologique Française (Jerusalem): 10*t*, 16, 41*t*, 89, 111
George Fishwick: 40
Imperial War Museum: 11, 12, 17*l*, 19*b*, 26, 27, 31*t*, 35, 51, 54, 56, 57, 59*t*, 61, 70, 73, 74,75, 82, 83, 85, 92, 93, 94, 95, 97, 101, 102*t*, 102b, 103, 105, 106*b*, 107, 108, 109, 112*b*, 114*t*, 115, 118, 120, 122, 123, 124, 125*b*, 126, 127, 128, 130*t*, 132*b*, 133, 135, 137, 140, 144, 145, 146, 151, 152, 153*t*, 153*b*, 154, 155, 156, 158, 159*t*,
159*b*, 161, 163*t*
Istanbul University: 21*t*, 22, 23*b*
Robert Lindsay: 32
Walter Luedin: 41*b*, 98-9, 165*t*, 173*t*
Middle East Centre, Oxford University: 164
Newcastle University: 20
Iain Nicholson: 113
James Nicholson: viii, 6t, 14, 28, 29*t*, 29*b*, 33*t*, 34*b*, 37*b*, 44, 45, 59, 62, 63, 66, 68-9, 71*t*, 77, 81*t*, 81*b*, 84, 91*t*, 91*b*, 104*t*, 104*b*, 106*t*, 110, 114*b*, 116*t*, 116*b*, 119, 121*t*, 121*b*, 129, 130, 131*t*, 131*c*, 131*b*, 134, 147, 148, 150, 157*t*, 163*b*, 165*b*, 166*t*, 166*b*, 168*t*, 168*b*, 170, 171*t*, 171*b*, 173*b*, 176, 177*t*, 177*b*
Patrick Pierard: 4, 90*t*
Public Records Office: 2, 13, 30*t*, 30*b*, 64*b*, 66*t*, 76, 117, 132*t*, 138
Kevin Ramsey: 64*t*, 64*c*
Owain Raw-Rees: 149
Royal Geographical Society: 19*t*
John Stephen: 17*r*, 72
Matthew Sutherland: 34*t*, 90*b*, 141, 142-43

Foreword

Chevron is proud of its unique and enduring association with the Kingdom of Saudi Arabia. From the first concession granted to us by King Abdul Aziz in 1933, and the first oil discovery in 1938, we have been honoured to play a leading role in the business sector of the Kingdom. Today Chevron continues to partner with Saudi Arabia to develop its business interests and to promote the economic growth and welfare of the Kingdom.

We continue to conduct business in the Kingdom through Saudi Arabian Texaco in partnerships that together generate over three hundred thousand barrels of crude oil a day, with significant other joint ventures across the Kingdom creating and marketing chemicals and petroleum products as well as providing a wide range of skills and, most significantly, the transfer of technology.

Chevron is pleased to be the sponsor of *The Hejaz Railway*. Here is a work that combines authoritative research with outstanding presentation. It gives the reader an insight into a largely neglected part of the Kingdom of Saudi Arabia's remarkable history. Much of the original rail embankment still survives today, as do the station buildings. A new initiative by the Saudi government to preserve the railway has included a major project to restore Madinah station.

Let this book be your companion and guide. It is our hope that it will entertain and inform, bringing a fascinating aspect of Saudi Arabia's cultural heritage to wider appreciation.

David J. O'Reilly
Chairman of the Board and CEO
The Chevron Corporation

Acknowledgements

A large number of people have contributed to the making of this book. In particular, I would like to thank Max Scott of Stacey International, who has steadfastly guided me through the many pitfalls of the publishing world and provided the necessary encouragement (and occasional prod) to carry through the project.

I would like to express my deep appreciation to John Alexander, who has given most generously of his time and expertise. In addition, he has very kindly permitted me unlimited access to his extensive photographic collection. I am also very grateful to Patrick Pierard, author of the guidebook *Off-Road in the Hejaz* and a leading authority on the archaeological and historical sites of the region. A delightful travelling companion, his infectious enthusiasm is matched only by his broad knowledge of his subject.

My thanks are especially due to Keith Costelloe for his advice and support, as well as providing numerous observations on the text. Proofreading was also undertaken by Ted Wynne, Megan Peterson and John Alexander, who made a number of important recommendations and suggestions. In addition, H. St John Armitage read the manuscript and kindly gave me the benefit of his vast experience of the region and its people, supplying a wealth of information on, among other things, the railway, T.E. Lawrence, the tribal system and the military campaigns. Many photographers assisted in the project. I would particularly like to thank John Alexander, Walter Luedin, Ben Ashworth, Peter Campell, Matthew Sutherland and Keith Costelloe. I am also very grateful to Roger Clark, whose unstinting help and advice with the maps and graphics was invaluable.

I would like to acknowledge the support and assistance of Dr Zahir Othman, Director of Al Turath (Heritage) in Riyadh, Saudi Arabia, Hany Anwar, the Senior Projects Coordinator, Mohammed Reda, the Information Officer and Sheikh Samad, Graphics Assistant. I am also very grateful for the help of Mohammed al Hamdan, Director General of the Project and Restoration Department at the Saudi Deputy Ministry of Antiquities.

For permission to reproduce quotations from T.E. Lawrence, I am indebted to the Trustees of *Seven Pillars of Wisdom*. I am grateful to Owain Raw-Rees for his advice on the various medals awarded for the Hejaz Railway and the First World War campaigns in the region. The generous assistance given to me by Salih Sen, second Secretary at the Turkish Embassy in Riyadh, was of enormous value. I would also like to express my thanks to R. Tourret, whose own book on the Hejaz Railway is a veritable treasure-house of railway information, Graham Edwards for his design work, Jim Stabler, author of the essential off-roaders' guide *The Desert Driver's Manual*, for information on the route, Kevin Ramsey for computer support, Caroline Shaw for editing the manuscript and Richard Morrison and Owain Raw-Rees for their backing of the project.

This book would not have been possible without the assistance of a number of individuals and institutions. In particular, I am grateful to

Professor Meral Alpay of Istanbul University, Jane Hogan and the staff of Durham University Library (Sudan Archive), Debbie Usher of the Middle East Centre at St Antony's College, Oxford University, Jean-Michel Tarragon of the Ecole Biblique et Archéologique Française, Jerusalem, Chris Coward of the Royal Geographical Society, Philip Kerrigan, Chairman of the T.E. Lawrence Society, and David Harman of the Transport Ticket Society. I also greatly appreciate the help of the staff of King Saud University Library, Riyadh; the King Fahd National Library, Riyadh; the Public Records Office, Kew; the Imperial War Museum Photograph and Document Archives, London; the British Library (Oriental and India Office Collections), London; Newcastle University (the Gertrude Bell Archive); Princeton University, U.S.A.; the Liddell Hart Centre for Military Archives, King's College, London; the Ministry of Tourism, Riyadh; and the Damascus University History and Humanities Libraries.

I am also very grateful for the warm reception and assistance given to me at so many of the working stations in Syria and Jordan. At a time of great political upheaval, the almost constant goodwill (and countless cups of refreshing sweet mint tea) I received, represented for me the triumph of a people's innate good nature and sense of hospitality over their day-to-day problems. In particular, I would like to thank the following: Younes al Nasser (Director, Planning and Statistics) and Najjah Ibrahim (Director, Public Relations) at Damascus Kanawat Station; Mohandis Mustafa Younes, Mohandis Mustafa al Jazairi and Suhail Nassir at Damascus Qadem Station and Museum; Mohandis Usama Kharaisha (Director), Odah Muhaisen (Station Master) and Saleh Subhi Shishtawi at Amman Station and Museum.

I would also like to express my appreciation to the following, who have contributed to the making of this book with help, advice or encouragement: Tom Stacey, Sir Derek Plumbly, the former British Ambassador to Saudi Arabia, Hamid Benbouazza, Robert Lindsay, Dr Iain Nicholson, Malcolm Brown, John Semple, Uwe Bergmann, Paul Catchpole, Duncan Moffat, Joseph Quinn, Leslie Barros, Dr James Nicholson, Mrs Elizabeth Nicholson, Professor Andrew Nicholson, Mahmoud Zein al Abidin, the curators and staff of Clouds Hill, Dorset, the staff of the Medain Saleh Hotel in Al Ula, Hugh Alexander, Pat Kennedy, Chris Nicholson, George Fishwick, Anthony Lyons, John Stephen, Charles Cornish, Peter Coleman, David Riley, Henry Wilson, Irene Costelloe, Jerome Burke, Kate Campbell, Philip Hitchcock, Malcolm Young, Fahd Romi, Matt White, John Slater, Michael Clifford, R.G. Watkins (Books & Prints), Axel Nelms, Bob Knox, Peter Richards, Jeremy Dent, Peter Hill and Bill Downing.

Finally, I would like to thank my wife, Teresita, and my daughter, Natasha, who have been my greatest inspiration and support, as well as my constant and most loyal travelling companions.

James Nicholson   Riyadh 2005

Preface

Some 130 kilometres north of Madinah, the crumbling earth railway embankment sweeps in a broad curve to the right, leaving the line of the new tarmac road for the first time. It was at this point that our small convoy halted. Maps were checked, GPS readings taken, and then, having moved down into 4-wheel drive, we headed out across the wide broken bed of the desert valley. Keeping the embankment in sight at all times, it was not long before a collection of small, cube-shaped structures came into view, their sharp rectangular lines silhouetted perfectly against the backdrop of a towering cliff. For most people this is the real beginning of the adventure, for while a few stations can be seen from the Madinah road, it is here, away from the rumble of trucks and the smell of gasoline, that one has the first true glimpse of how the railway must have looked nearly a century ago.

For a young British captain in March 1917, it was also a beginning. In a cold dawn breeze he scrambled up the steep hill opposite Abu Na'am Station and looked down from his vantage point on the same little cluster of buildings. Beneath him too, he could see the narrow track of a railway, twisting away into the barren hills, linking the two great Arab cities of Damascus and Madinah. Although he had already formulated a vague plan of action, he could have had no idea at that time of the extraordinary fame that his exploits along this railway would bring him.

The stirring of the cold pre-dawn air awoke me the next morning, and leaving the camp still slumbering peacefully under the rapidly fading stars, I made my way back along the embankment and across the grey pebbled floor of the valley. From the top of the same hill, I took in the hushed and motionless scene - dawn breaking as it had done for nearly a century since that day over this bleak and forgotten corner of the Hejaz. In geological terms, of course, it was only the briefest of asides, and for me too, dwarfed by the vast emptiness, the passage of time seemed to evaporate. As with so many of his descriptions of the railway, Lawrence's account of the simple dawn reveille he witnessed that morning in 1917 could bring the scene almost miraculously back to life….

'We lay like lizards in the long grass round the stones of the foremost cairn upon the hill-top and saw the garrison parade. Three hundred and ninety-nine infantry, little toy men, ran about when the bugle sounded, and formed up in stiff lines below the black building till there was more bugling: then they scattered, and after a few minutes the smoke of cooking fires went up. A herd of sheep and goats in charge of a little ragged boy issued out towards us. Before he reached the foot of the hills there came a loud whistling down the valley from the north, and a tiny, picture-book train rolled slowly into view across the hollow sounding bridge and halted just outside the station, panting out white puffs of steam.'

My own personal journey was to end, like Lawrence's, a year and a half later in Damascus. Along the way I had passed a seemingly endless line of stations just like Abu Na'am, standing very much as they had been when they were abandoned by the Turks at the end of the war. I had followed mile upon mile of the same earth embankment as it led me unfailingly through the harsh waterless terrain. And as I passed, I could not help but wonder about the men who had built this line, toiled in the dry earth with their bare hands under the same unforgiving sun, a thousand miles from home. In an attempt to tell their story my journey would also take me through some of the world's great libraries, universities, national archives and museums.

The Hejaz Railway of course has become well-known throughout much of the modern world owing primarily to the fame of one man, T.E. Lawrence. In particular the 1962 David Lean film *Lawrence of Arabia*, based on his adventures in the First World War, has provided an enduring popular image both of the man himself and the land in which his name was made. Lawrence's story, however, did not have to wait until 1962 to find a captive audience. In 1919, when the American war correspondent Lowell Thomas brought his collection of lantern slides and cinematic film to the Royal Opera House in Covent Garden, it was thought the show would last for two weeks. Six months later, several thousand people had passed through the box office to attend his lecture. Whether or not Thomas' portrayal of Lawrence was strictly accurate was not important. What mattered to a nation tired of the hideous images of the trenches was the chance to experience a different side to the war.

The contrast between the conflict in northern Europe and the one in which Lawrence played his part could not have been more striking. Apart from anything else, while the main theatre of operations on the Western Front had eventually ground to an awful stalemate, the campaign in Arabia had ended in a clear victory for the Allies. In a way too, Lawrence's fame was born out of the mud of Flanders. With the memory of the quagmire that was trench warfare still fresh in the nation's mind, the pictures of Lawrence in his flowing white robes leading his men across the clean, open expanses of the desert came as a welcome relief. The nature of desert conflict, with its lightning hit-and-run tactics, also meant that the casualties could generally be counted on one hand rather than in tens or even hundreds of thousands. When one of the regular Arab army commanders suggested to the British that they emulate the European combatants by using mustard gas, Lt Col. Dawnay, appalled by the idea, referred the matter to his senior officer, making it clear however that he was 'very much opposed to the idea of introducing western frightfulness into our very gentlemanly little war.'

Then there was the railway itself. Winding its way through some of the most dramatic desert mountain scenery in the world, it followed the centuries-old pilgrimage road into the heart of Arabia. Its construction was a tale of endurance and resolve made epic by the heat, the harsh conditions and the hostility of the tribes. In the golden age of imperial railway construction too, the sight of the great steam engines cutting through the vast, empty desert valleys, their plumes of white smoke billowing out behind them, stirred the imagination and filled the Covent Garden audiences with a wonderful sense of romantic adventure.

J.N. Lockman has written that T.E. Lawrence without his trains would be like William Tell without his apple, and indeed it is hard to imagine how his story could have developed in quite the same way had he been ambushing tanks or digging trenches in the sand. Lawrence seems to have felt something of this himself, for there is nearly always a tone of heightened excitement in his descriptions of the railway. The classic account of his wartime experiences, *Seven Pillars of Wisdom*, has some of its finest passages in bringing to life the railway, its stations, the Turkish garrisons and the old steam locomotives. The two stories, it seems to me, are bound up together, each imparting to the other something unique and strangely compelling, something that has managed to capture the public imagination for almost a century. While it is undoubtedly true that without Lawrence, the Hejaz Railway would never have enjoyed such widespread renown, I believe it is also the case that without the Hejaz Railway there may never have been a 'Lawrence of Arabia'...

James Nicholson   April 2005

For my parents
James and Elizabeth Nicholson

Contents

Foreword   v

Acknowledgements   vi

Preface   ix

1. *Introduction*   2
2. *Building the Railway - I - The Main Line*   18
3. *Building the Railway - II - The Branch Lines*   50
4. *Paying for the Railway*   62
5. *Running the Railway*   70
6. *Outbreak of the First World War*   86
7. *The War along the Railway - I - The Hejaz*   100
8. *The War along the Railway - II - Aqaba & Northwards*   120
9. *The War along the Railway - III - The Road to Damascus*   144
10. *The Railway after the First World War*   162

Appendix 1.   Restoration of Madinah Station   180

Appendix 2.   Hejaz Railway Stations   184

Chapter Notes   186

Bibliography   188

Index   190

THE HEJAZ RAILWAY

1. *Introduction*

Opposite:
Map 1 – The Hejaz Railway

Below:
The British Consul in Damascus, W. Richards, writing to his ambassador in Constantinople to express his doubts as to the feasibility of the Ottoman Hejaz Railway project.

A 'Wildly Improbable' and 'Fantastic' Scheme

In the spring of 1900 the British Consul at Damascus, W. Richards, wrote to his ambassador in Constantinople, Sir Nicolas O'Conor, with excuses for having failed to report on a proposed scheme to build a railway line from Damascus to Makkah. While admitting that rumours concerning such a plan had indeed been circulating in Damascus, he justified his neglect in passing on the information by pointing out that the venture 'seemed to me and others so wildly improbable, not to say fantastic, that I refrained from reporting on it to your Excellency.'[1]

Two months later, having studied the intended project more closely, he had found no reason to revise his opinion. Taking into consideration the great distance to be traversed, the harsh waterless terrain, the appalling working conditions, the opposition of the tribes and the overall weakness of the Ottoman Empire, he had no hesitation in confirming to Sir Nicolas that the realisation of such a scheme was viewed with 'scepticism and incredulity by all thinking men here.'[2]

Looking southwards from the fertile gardens of their green, well-watered city, the thinking men of Damascus saw only a thousand miles of predominantly barren wilderness. While there may have been sufficient water to sustain the scattered bedouin tribes, the scarcity of the precious desert commodity would undoubtedly present an enormous obstacle to a railway construction project of such a scale. The route would have to cross areas of hard volcanic rock, interspersed with vast drifts of wind-swept sand. Wadis that remained dry for years at a time could become surging boulder-strewn torrents in a matter of hours when the rains finally fell. Steep climbs would have to be negotiated and descents cut through great desert escarpments. Every yard of the way in the less populated southern reaches would have to be painstakingly surveyed before any track-laying could even be considered.

In such desolate country there would be no local workforce available. Even if one could be brought in, the conditions on the ground were so harsh that it would be difficult, if not impossible, to procure sufficient numbers of volunteers. Temperatures that could soar into the 50s centigrade in the summer months would fall below zero in winter. Food and water, fuel for

cooking and lighting, all the day-to-day provisions and medical supplies would have to be brought to the advance parties by camel. The men would be far from their families, without any form of recreation and cut off from the outside world. They would be susceptible to dysentery and disease, including the greatly-feared cholera, outbreaks of which occasionally struck the region with devastating results. The work gangs would be easy prey for the tribes of bedouin living in the country along the line, who opposed the railway, believing that the 'devil's donkey' was coming to replace the camel, whose hiring and guiding – particularly during the annual pilgrimage to Makkah – had provided one of the mainstays of their livelihood since time immemorial.

Finally, even if all these seemingly insurmountable obstacles could be overcome, there still remained the cold hard fact that Turkish finances were in an extremely precarious condition. Richards, along with all the other thinking men of Damascus, was only too aware that, at the turn of the 20th century, the once-mighty Ottoman Empire was close to bankruptcy, crippled with debt, and dependent on the great European financial lending houses to provide capital – with stringent conditions attached – for any major new development projects. Sultan Abdulhamid II's proclamation therefore, that the Hejaz Railway was to be built solely with Ottoman money, an Ottoman workforce and Ottoman raw materials and equipment, seemed to make the likelihood of a successful outcome even more 'fantastic'.

On 1 September 1908 however, the inauguration ceremony for the completed line from Damascus to Madinah was held in the latter city. Although concessions had been made in the areas of European technical expertise and equipment, the administration, financing and overall control of the project had remained wholly in Ottoman hands. Faced with increasing evidence of Western industrial might, the railway was a testimony to the Ottoman ability to compete successfully at the same level. Although for political reasons the line was never extended to Makkah, the achievement of reaching Madinah, deep within the Hejaz, was enough to confound the sceptics, who had misjudged the strength of Ottoman resolve and underestimated the will of the frail but determined Sultan.

The Political Background - The Decline of the Ottoman Empire

When Abdulhamid II became Sultan in 1876, he inherited an empire already saddled with economic problems. The Peace of Paris, which had settled the Crimean War in 1856, had put Ottoman finances under such strain that the government of the day had been forced into making a series of foreign loans at exorbitant interest rates. Twenty years later, as much as 80 per cent of state revenue was being absorbed to service the debt to foreign bondholders. Within a year of his accession, Abdulhamid's difficulties were further compounded as the empire was plunged into another, even more disastrous, war with Russia. Having advanced to the very outskirts of Constantinople,

Below:
In winter, flash floods could quickly develop, washing away large sections of the rail embankment.

Above:
Madinah Station with mountains to the north-west. The two long buildings on the right are the passengers' rest house (nearest the train) and the employees' rest house.

the Russians were able to impose extremely harsh terms on the new Sultan. At the Congress of Berlin in 1878, in addition to losing two-fifths of the empire's territory, the Ottomans had to pay a huge war indemnity of over 800 million French francs. With the already overwhelming burden of debt repayments, this obligation pushed the empire to the verge of bankruptcy.

At the heart of the empire's problems was the fact that it had been unable to keep pace with the rapid military and industrial development achieved in the West. A number of humiliating defeats had emphasised the growing disparity between European and Ottoman military strength, and led to a reform movement (the Tanzimat) intended to modernise the empire's armed forces. The reforms had been made possible by the destruction of the traditional military élite, the Janissaries, in 1826, and did go some way towards improving the army's organisation and overall capability. However, they failed to address the underlying causes of Ottoman weakness, and left the empire's institutions and social framework essentially unchanged.

Throughout the 19th century the decline in Ottoman strength, successive military defeats and the growth of nationalist sentiment in the provinces, led to a steady erosion of central control. The Sublime Porte (the Ottoman government) was forced to grant varying degrees of autonomy to a number of its subject territories, particularly in the Balkans and other parts of eastern Europe. Following the calamitous war with Russia immediately after Abdulhamid's accession, this process was accelerated, with independence being gained by Greece, Romania, Bulgaria, Serbia and Montenegro. Although they retained some limited territory in Macedonia, Albania and Thrace, for all practical purposes the Ottomans were no longer a significant

THE HEJAZ RAILWAY

Above:
The twin water tower at Abu Na'am was built with stone cladding to protect the tanks from attack.

Right:
Map 2 - Arab Territories of the Ottoman Empire, 1900. By the end of the 19th century, the loss of most of the empire's European provinces made the protection of its Arab possessions a major political concern.

power in Europe. The great empire that had once stretched all the way to the gates of Vienna had ceased to exist.

Abdulhamid II's Response to European Expansion

Following the Congress of Berlin the imperial powers, under the pretext of protecting their economic interests, began to eye the Sultan's remaining possessions. North Africa in particular became a target, with the French adding Tunisia to their previous acquisitions in Algeria, and the British occupying Egypt and the Sudan. In an attempt to confront European imperialism and save 'the sick man of Europe' from total disintegration and collapse, Abdulhamid began to formulate a set of policies aimed at safeguarding both his own rule and the empire's territories.

The loss of the European provinces greatly increased the significance of the Asian section of the empire and strengthened the Sultan's determination to hold on to his Arab possessions. The opening of the Suez Canal in 1869 had

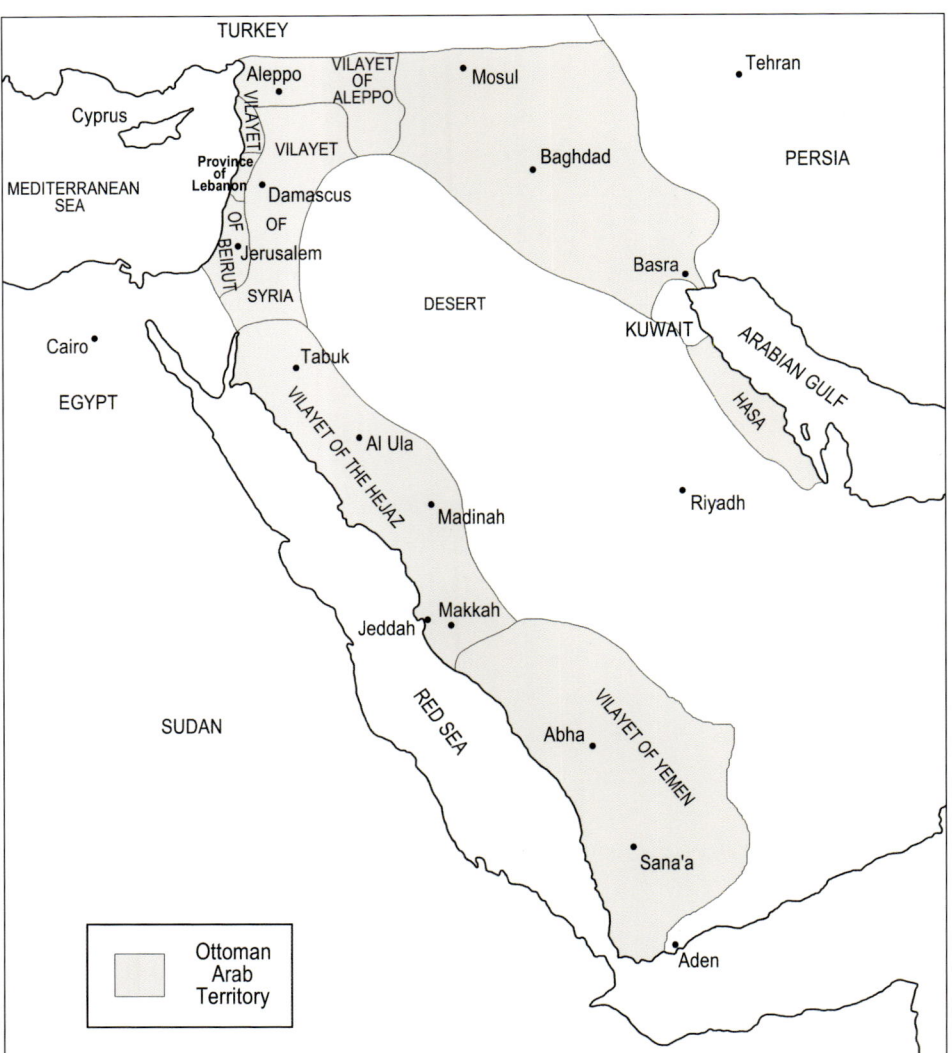

provided a quicker, more effective means of transporting Turkish troops to Yemen and the Hejaz, but the British occupation of Egypt in 1882 left the Ottomans dependent on the goodwill of the new custodians to provide continued access. With much of the empire's territory south of Damascus remaining remote and difficult to reach, it was clear that the region's transport and communication systems would have to be developed if strong central control was going to be imposed by the government in Constantinople.

At the beginning of his reign, Abdulhamid defeated the reformists under the Grand Vizier, Midhat Pasha, and dismissed the constitutional government. He replaced it with a system of strong personal rule, establishing 'a far more extensive autocracy than anything achieved previously by the greatest of Sultans.'[3] With his position at home assured, Abdulhamid took up the ideological banner of pan-Islam as a means of galvanising the majority of the empire's subjects behind his rule. The pan-Islamic movement was already popular by the time he came to power, and the suffering of Muslims after Ottoman defeats in the Caucasus and the Balkans had strengthened its appeal, providing the Sultan with a perfect instrument to deflect criticism and generate support for his policies. As well as bolstering loyalty within the empire, it gained him power and prestige in the rest of the Islamic world. With millions of Muslims under European rule in India and North Africa, this influence could be turned to good effect as a way of manipulating Western foreign policy.

Abdulhamid's espousal of the pan-Islamic movement was reflected in his promotion of the Arab section of the empire. Support was provided for the traditional religious institutions. Numerous new schools and mosques were opened, and grants and gifts were made available for charitable causes. Arabs were encouraged to play a greater role in the Ottoman military, with an increased possibility of service within their own regions. Even more significant was the number of Arab officials elevated to high office within the Sultan's ruling court hierarchy. Foremost among these was the Damascene Izzat Pasha al Abid who, as Abdulhamid's Second Secretary and Chief Adviser, was to have a major influence on the building of the Hejaz Railway.

The Sultan's standing in the Islamic world was based primarily on his position as Caliph, the leader of all the Muslims, and his ability to safeguard the annual pilgrimage to the holy city of Makkah. Ottoman control over Greater Syria (comprising modern Syria, Jordan and Palestine) was largely limited to the major towns. In the Hejaz, the Sultan's position was even more precarious. In Makkah and Madinah a dual system of government was operated, with power being shared by the Amir of Makkah, the traditional local ruler selected from members of the Hashemite family, and the Vali, the Sultan's official representative. Ottoman authority fluctuated according to the prevailing fortunes of these two leaders, but owing to the region's remoteness, could never be assured. For the same reason, Yemen and the Asir, while officially acknowledging Ottoman sovereignty, remained largely autonomous. Finally, in the mountains and desert regions of the Hejaz, the bedouin, who were nominally under the rule of the Amir of Makkah, were in practice beyond any government jurisdiction.

Above:
The Ottoman Sultan Abdulhamid II was to be the driving force behind the building of the railway.

THE HEJAZ RAILWAY

Early Railway Development in The Ottoman Empire

The Crimean War of 1854-56 demonstrated the inadequacies of the empire's transport system. At about the same time, Europe's ability to move huge troop displacements over great distances was confirming the military benefits of large-scale railway development. Sultan Abdulaziz (1861-1876) became increasingly aware of the significant political and economic advantages of establishing proper communications across the empire and decided to initiate a full programme of railway construction. The weakness of the empire's economy forced the Sultan to look to Europe for the required capital, and the West's technical expertise persuaded him to adopt a system of granting concessions to foreign companies to carry out the work. The first contract, for a 125-kilometre line between Smyrna (Izmir) and Aydin, was granted to a British company. Others quickly followed, and in 1883 Abdulaziz's ambition was posthumously fulfilled when Constantinople was connected to Vienna, Paris and London by the Orient Express. In 1888, the growing influence of good relations with Berlin was reflected in the granting of a concession to the Germans to build the Anatolian Railway, linking Constantinople to Ankara. Despite competition from the British and French, in 1903 the Germans were also awarded the right to extend the line right across northern Arabia to Baghdad.

In Syria, railway concessions were awarded both to French and British

Below:
Sketch map from an original by Meissner Pasha, the chief engineer, showing the planned location of Medain Saleh Station.

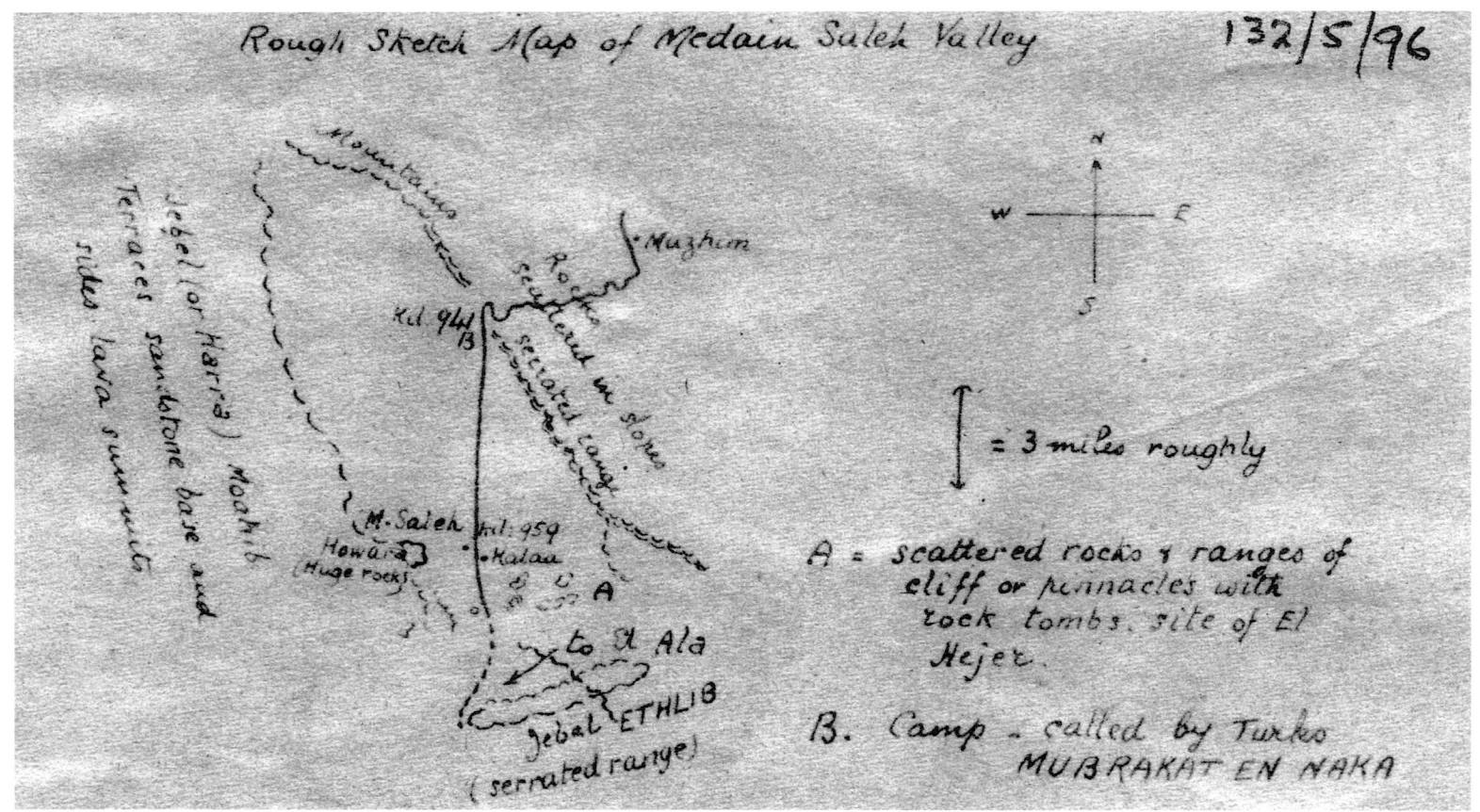

Above:
The Beirut – Damascus railway had to cross two mountain ranges within a distance of 147 kilometres. The locomotive is an S.L.M. (Swiss Locomotive and Machine Works) 2-6-0T, climbing through the Barada Gorge in the Anti-Lebanon range.

companies. Competing for the lucrative freight market to export wheat from the rich agricultural area of the Hauran, in 1891 the French began construction on a line to connect Damascus to Muzeirib. The following year, the British started work on their own concession from the Mediterranean port of Haifa to Deraa. Due to financial difficulties, progress on this line, which was eventually bought back by the Ottomans and made into the principal branch of the Hejaz Railway, petered out after only eight kilometres. In 1892, determined to acquire an outlet to the sea, the French began the construction of a railway between Beirut and Damascus.

The Damascus to Muzeirib line, less than 100 kilometres long and built over flat, straightforward terrain, was inaugurated in August 1894. The Beirut to Damascus railway however, was a very different prospect. Two mountain ranges - the Lebanon and Anti-Lebanon, reaching almost 1,500 metres above sea level - had to be traversed. To negotiate the steep gradients on the mountainous sections, a rack railway had to be employed. It was constructed using a narrow-gauge track of 1.05 metres, and required special rack-drive locomotives. Despite all the engineering difficulties, the work was completed by 1895. The Beirut to Damascus line was connected up to the French-built Homs-Hama-Aleppo railway in 1906 and the combined system was administered by the Société Ottomane du Chemin de Fer de Damas, Hama et Prolongements (D.H.P.).

THE HEJAZ RAILWAY

Above:
Muazzam Fort. Large birkas (cisterns) on the old pilgrimage route were dependent on rain water for their supply.

Right:
Land caravan making its way to Madinah. Before the Hejaz Railway was built, the journey from Damascus to Makkah took over forty days.

INTRODUCTION

The Hejaz Railway - The Birth of an Idea

The idea of continuing the development of the Ottoman rail network southwards to connect Damascus to the Holy Cities of the Hejaz must have appealed to the Sultan, as protector of the annual Haj (pilgrimage), for a number of different reasons. The railway would provide his Muslim subjects with a religious service on a truly grand scale. Prior to the 20th century, performing the Haj, one of the five pillars of Islam, was no easy requirement. The overland journey from Damascus could take more than 40 days, and the pilgrims suffered from all the hardships of the road, the extremes of temperature, disease, dysentery, a shortage of good drinking water and the constant threat of attack. Not a few of the faithful died on the journey and were buried where they fell at the side of the road.

The cost of the journey was an additional burden. Many of the pilgrims saved for years in order to be able to fulfil a lifetime's ambition. During the 19th century the numbers undertaking the Haj had declined drastically, with as few as 1,000 setting off from Damascus in 1890. The building of the railway would undoubtedly represent an achievement worthy of a great Muslim Caliph. It would provide a quicker, easier, safer and cheaper means of making the journey to Makkah, and would crown Abdulhamid's reign with a visible symbol of his piety, manifesting his concern for the Holy Places and the well-being and security of his subjects.

While the religious aspect of the railway was always the most publicised and championed, it was by no means the only motivating force behind the venture. By providing a tangible expression of his pan-Islamic policy, the Sultan knew he would also gain considerable political credibility, both among his own subjects and with the Muslims of other states. The ability to match the Europeans with a public work of monumental proportions, and without recourse to foreign borrowing, would help to restore some of the empire's former prestige and confirm Abdulhamid's legitimacy to rule over the Arab territories. At the same time, an increase in the numbers performing the Haj would in itself provide valuable extra income for Makkah and Madinah – both cities being largely dependent on the pilgrimage for revenues. As well as enabling taxes to be collected throughout the Arab provinces, it was also hoped that the line would stimulate trade, urban development, agriculture and mineral exploitation. The relative unimportance of economic factors, however, was well illustrated by the fact that the railway avoided the coastal route, preventing some of the empire's ports being linked up to the inland cities. It was decided that the strategic advantage of keeping out of range of the powerful British Navy was of greater overall significance.

For political reasons, the strategic potential of the line received little overt publicity, but it was a critical factor in the Sultan's decision to build the railway. Lessons had been learned from Europe, where in the second half of the 19th century mass armies had been deployed swiftly to the battlefront by the use of extensive rail networks. The military advantages of rapid troop mobilisation were confirmed for the Ottomans by their Constantinople to Salonica line during the successful war against the Greeks in 1897. It became increasingly evident that a railway to the Hejaz, by extending a strong

Above:
The building of the telegraph line between Damascus and Madinah proved that a construction project through the difficult terrain of the Hejaz was possible. The huge stone monoliths in the background are part of the Mabrak al Naga escarpment, north of Medain Saleh.

THE HEJAZ RAILWAY

Above:
British control of the Suez Canal made the building of a railway to the Hejaz a matter of strategic priority for the Ottoman Empire.

Opposite:
Map 3 ~ Ottoman map. Made from the sketches drawn by Mokhtar Bey during his overland pilgrimage to Makkah.

military presence into some of the most unruly and autonomous areas of the empire, would be able to strengthen the Sultan's authority internally, and at the same time establish a buttress against British and French intentions in the region. The potential to bypass the Suez Canal was considered vital in order to counter the British, who had already occupied Egypt, Sudan and Aden, and were busy forging alliances with Kuwait and the Trucial States in the Gulf.

Proposals for the Railway

The suggestion for a line to connect Damascus to the Red Sea had first been made by a German-American civil engineer, Dr Charles Zimpel, as early as 1864. Nothing came of the idea, and subsequent proposals, both official and unofficial, for a railway to the Hejaz, were received from a number of different people close to the court. Among them were Izzat Pasha, the Sultan's Second Secretary; Major Ahmed Reshid; Ahmed Izzat Pasha, the head of the Jeddah awqaf (religious endowments); Mehmet Shakir Pasha and an Austrian

INTRODUCTION

THE HEJAZ RAILWAY

engineer, Wilhelm von Pressel. Another proposal came from Mohammed Insha Allah, an Indian Muslim teacher and journalist from the Punjab. Although his first official approach was made as late as 1897, he had been advocating the idea of an Ottoman railway system free of Western influence for some time. After 1897 he stepped up his campaign for a line to the Hejaz, both in his own journal, *The Wakil*, and in the Islamic papers of Cairo and Constantinople.

As Sultan, Abdulhamid must certainly have taken the final decision as to whether such a politically significant and large-scale project would be undertaken. However, although the enterprise had many attractions, in view of his extremely cautious nature, it is likely that his decision was influenced by some of his close advisers. The pan-Islamic element of the venture would certainly have been endorsed by Abu al Hada, the Sultan's astrologer and a firm advocate of his religious policy. Others have seen the prime mover behind the scenes as the German general, Von der Goltz, who as the Sultan's chief military adviser would have emphasised the strategic potential of the line. Following the Imam Yahya's 1898 revolt in Yemen, Izzat Pasha was instructed to prepare a report on the uprising, including recommendations for its suppression. One of his suggestions was the construction of a railway line to the Hejaz. As a Damascene and a supporter of Abdulhamid's religious and political programmes of reform, Izzat Pasha would have been well placed to promote the project on all levels. Ottoman court politics however, were largely played out behind closed doors, and it is not clear whose role was the most significant in finally convincing Abdulhamid to sign the official order to start the work. What is certain is that for the next eight years, together with the Sultan himself, Izzat Pasha was to be the driving force behind the accomplishment of the project.

While the idea of the railway was still being considered, a project to build a telegraph line to the Hejaz enabled the feasibility of the project to be assessed. It was originally intended to extend as far as Yemen, but the construction never reached further than Madinah, due to opposition from the local tribes. The line was built by a special telegraph battalion under General Sadiq Pasha al Muayyad. By following the old pilgrimage road for much of the route, it was shown that a construction project through the difficult terrain and harsh conditions of the Hejaz was not an impossibility. It was recognised that the building of a railway would be a far more complex undertaking than a telegraph, but by the time General Muayyad's men had reached Madinah, the official decision to start work on the Hejaz Railway had already been taken.

Preparations for the Railway

The Sultan issued an imperial order (Iradé) on 2 May 1900, calling upon the Muslims of the world for support and financial backing. While the necessary administrative framework was being put in place, the Ottoman military engineer Mokhtar Bey was dispatched on the annual pilgrimage caravan from Damascus to Makkah to survey the route. Together with Ali Rida al Rikabi,

Below:
Water column at Hedia Station. The provision of water by train delivery was vital for the operation of the railway and the survival of the station workers and garrisons.

Above:
Hartmann 2-6-0 in the repair yard at Madinah Station. There are six derelict locomotives at the station, three Hartmanns, two S.L.M.s and one Tubize.

he produced a number of plans, diagrams and measurements detailing the path of the centuries old Haj road. From his report a more formal map was drawn up by Captain Omar Zaki and Lt. Hassan Muayin. Despite being based on the rough sketches made by Mokhtar Bey under the difficult circumstances of his journey, it was the most accurate representation of the route in existence. Not surprisingly, the major concerns highlighted by Mokhtar Bey's report were the shortage of water and the lack of security, particularly on the southern sections of the route. The main advantage of following the ancient Haj road was that, owing to the inability of camels to cross mountainous terrain, the pilgrims had been forced to find the flattest possible route. By keeping to the same track, the engineers would be able to minimise the necessity for tunnels and large bridges.

In line with the Sultan's announcement that the railway would be built without foreign involvement, Ottomans were appointed to the two principal administrative structures created for the enterprise. In Constantinople, the

THE HEJAZ RAILWAY

Above:
Al Ula Station from the west. 1909.

Central Commission was established with powers to oversee the whole project. It dealt with financial matters, supplies, contracts and appointments, and was also responsible for carrying out diplomatic negotiations and issuing official proclamations relating to the railway. Headed by Sultan Abdulhamid himself, it included such high-ranking representatives of the court and government as the Grand Vizier, the Minister of Public Works, the Minister of the Navy, the Director of Works at the Naval Arsenal and Izzat Pasha, the Sultan's influential Second Secretary.

In Damascus, a Local Commission was set up to liaise with the Central Commission and oversee the running of the project on the ground. As well as supervising the actual building work, it was responsible for local financial matters, such as the distribution of salaries and the payment of contractors. It also played an important role in channelling advice and information from the engineers at the railhead to the Central Commission in Constantinople. This enabled important decisions on areas such as the purchase of supplies and the issuing of contracts to be based on recommendations made by experts at the grass roots level. As with the Central Commission, the

INTRODUCTION

membership of the Damascus Local Commission included some of the highest-ranking dignitaries and officials in the province. The Vali of Syria, Nazim Pasha, was to remain Chairman until 1908. Other members included the Commanding Officer of the 5th Army; General Sadiq Pasha al Muayyad, the builder of the Damascus to Madinah telegraph; Vice-Admiral Hamdi Pasha, the Inspector-General of the railway; Abdulrahman Pasha Yousif, the influential leader of the Syrian pilgrimage caravan; Kazim Pasha, the Chief of Construction; and Adib Nazmi, the Secretary of the Damascus City Council.

With the administrative structure in place, supplies and materials started to arrive in Damascus. The first consignment of rails was received from the Naval Arsenal, and a staff of 12 Ottoman engineers, backed up by 30 graduates from the Royal Engineering School, was dispatched from Constantinople. The great work of construction was ready to begin. Behind the scenes at the Yildiz Palace, Sultan Abdulhamid, surrounded by a scheming court and a vast network of spies and informers, was acutely aware that the railway could alleviate some of the empire's most serious problems at a stroke. It would revitalise trade, provide a strategic line of communication with the Arab territories, establish stronger central control, bolster his pan-Islamic policy and reinforce his position as Caliph. His personal involvement and unswerving support were to be major factors behind the accomplishment of the project, and must go a long way towards explaining the ultimate success of what at the outset was considered to be a 'wildly improbable' and 'fantastic' scheme.

Left and above:
1908 and 2003. A sand dune now covers part of the rail embankment south of Abu Taqa. The track and telegraph have long since disappeared.

THE HEJAZ RAILWAY

2. Building the Railway

I - The Main Line - Damascus to Madinah

Below:
Map 4 -
"Damas Hama et Prolongements" (D.H.P.)
Muzeririb - Damascus Line

Muzeririb - Damascus Section of the Hejaz Railway

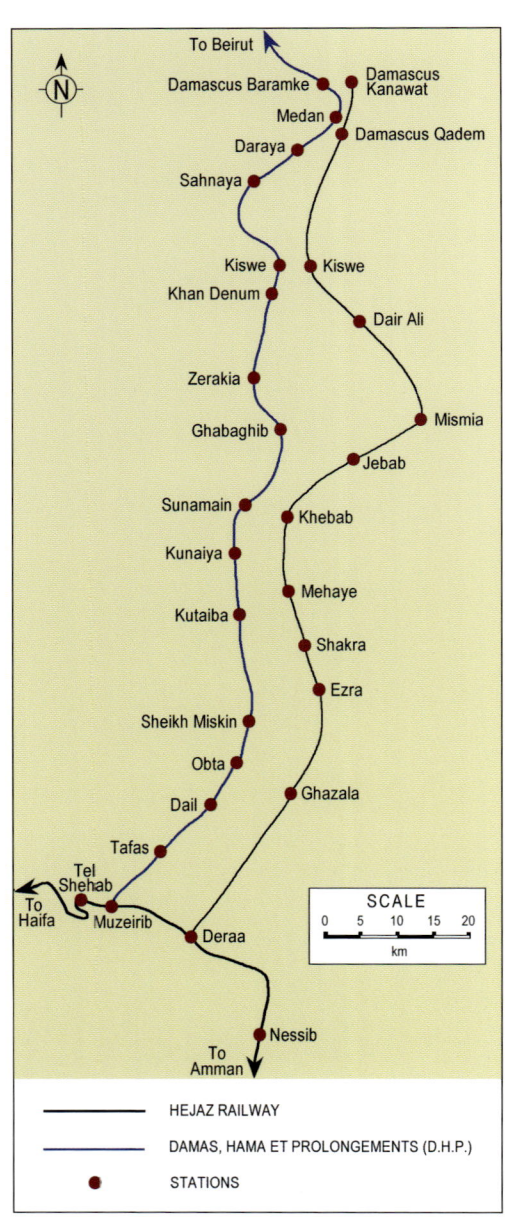

Early Decisions and Difficulties

Construction of the Hejaz Railway officially commenced on 1 September 1900, the 24th anniversary of Sultan Abdulhamid II's accession to the throne. It is often assumed that work on the line started at Damascus and proceeded southwards towards Madinah. In fact, it was originally believed that the Ottoman government would be able to purchase the French-owned D.H.P. line from Damascus to Muzeirib. Negotiations for its acquisition were opened with the company in 1900 and, in anticipation of a successful outcome, the first work was carried out to extend the track from the existing terminus at Muzeirib Station to the nearby town of Deraa. A makeshift workforce was hastily assembled and on 26 October the Vali (Governor) of Syria presided over a ceremony at Muzeirib to inaugurate the actual commencement of work.

At the beginning of December 1900 an Italian named Signor Labella arrived in Damascus as Chief Engineer for the railway, on an annual salary of 20,000 French francs. Having reviewed the situation on the ground in Muzeirib, he immediately put in a request for 7,000 workmen, stating his preference for Italians or Egyptians. Towards the end of the same month, another foreign engineer was appointed to a similar position but at the slightly higher salary of 24,000 francs. For the next eight years, Herr Heinrich August Meissner, a German previously employed by the Salonica Junction Railway, was to become the driving force behind the successful construction of the Hejaz Railway.

In order to conform to the D.H.P. Beirut-Damascus-Muzeirib line, on which supplies and rolling stock would have to be brought in, a narrow-gauge track of 1.05 metres was used. Owing to the severe flash floods that could occur during periods of rain, it was also decided that the rails would be laid on an embankment, three to four feet high. Large numbers of conscripts were drafted in to carry out the earthworks, and masons were employed to build bridges and culverts to allow the flood water to pass under the line without damaging the track.

During the first year, the work was beset by problems and progress was extremely slow. The administrative organisation was inefficient and proved

BUILDING THE RAILWAY - I. THE MAIN LINE

unable to procure the required construction materials. The original surveys for the Muzeirib area were found to be unsatisfactory and had to be re-done. Perhaps the greatest obstacle to progress however, was the appalling conditions under which the conscripts had to work. The Ottoman Chief of Construction, Mehmed Ali Pasha, with his officer staff, had little or no experience of railway construction and believed only in maintaining strict military discipline. Wages were paid in arrears, or not at all, and there were no incentives to encourage the conscripts to improve their work rate. The harsh conditions soon led to mutiny. Work was interrupted and several of the engineers fled to Egypt rather than face harsh military retribution. In the event, Mehmed Ali Pasha himself was court-martialled for his treatment of the conscripts, and in particular for failing to provide them with adequate rations. His replacement as Chief of Construction, Field Marshall Kazim Pasha, quickly obtained redress for the troops and over the next eight years was able, with Herr Meissner, to provide a stable administrative platform for the construction of the railway.

The inauguration ceremonies for newly-completed sections of line were scheduled to be held every year on 1 September, the anniversary of the Sultan's accession. On that day in 1901 the members of the Local Commission, the sheikhs, the notables and the religious dignitaries travelled by special train to Deraa, where virtually the whole population of the surrounding area of the Hauran was gathered. Prayers were said for the preservation of the precious life of his Imperial Majesty, the Sultan, and official speeches were made to praise the work carried out that year. In truth however, less than 15 kilometres of track had been completed and the Sultan was far from happy with the rate of progress. Four out of the six Ottoman

Above:
After a difficult start, Field Marshall Kazim Pasha, in overall charge of the construction project, developed a good working relationship with Meissner Pasha, the German chief of engineering.

Below:
Ceremony to inaugurate Deraa Station.

engineers employed on the line had already been summarily dismissed at the same time as Mehmed Ali Pasha. At the end of 1901, on completion of his first year's contract, the services of Labella 'by the advice of Herr Meissner'[1] were also dispensed with. The stage was now set for the sometimes rough, but long-lasting and generally successful working relationship between Meissner, in charge of engineering, and Kazim Pasha, as overall Ottoman Chief of Construction.

Western Involvement

The early construction problems made it clear to the Sultan that the original plan to build the railway using a solely Ottoman workforce would have to be sacrificed in order to achieve acceptable rates of progress. Meissner began to take on greater numbers of foreign workers, until about half his engineering team comprised Europeans. The majority of these were Germans, but there were also a few French and Belgians. It was only in the later stages of construction, when the Istanbul Engineering College and a specially-created department of the École Technique began to produce properly qualified graduates, that the balance shifted back in favour of the Turkish employees. This coincided nicely with the fact that, south of Al Ula, due to the proximity of the Islamic Holy Places, Christians were prohibited from working on the line, and an all-Muslim workforce had to be used.

Below:
The German engineer Heinrich Meissner (with the white beard) brought technical expertise and great administrative ability to the building of the railway.

Above:
Labourers engaged in the backbreaking work of building the earth embankment.

Left:
Map 5 ~ Damascus - Ma'an

THE HEJAZ RAILWAY

Above:
Train carrying wooden sleepers to the railhead south of Amman.

The general labouring was carried out by unskilled military conscripts, and foreign artisans were brought in to undertake the more difficult areas of construction such as rock cutting and the building of bridges, culverts, tunnels and stations. At various times between 450 and 600 skilled foreign workers, including Italians, Austrians, Greeks, Montenegrins, Egyptians and Syrians, were employed on this kind of work. This diversity in the workforce however, caused some serious cultural and linguistic difficulties. The Italians for example, were prized for their high quality masonry work and regarded as virtually irreplaceable, but they caused such friction with the local population that in 1902 the Vali of Syria asked for a prohibition on their employment. The British Consul in Damascus, W. Richards, reported on the situation to his ambassador: 'The Italian navvy is an excellent workman… but he has three serious defects; he drinks heavily as soon as his day's work is done, he is always ready with his knife and he is somewhat loose in his morals. If to these three factors a fourth be added viz: his absolute ignorance of the language of the country in which he is working, all the necessary elements of a serious disagreement with its inhabitants are present at one and the same time.'[2]

Heinrich Meissner - The Laying of Solid Foundations

Meissner's success with the Ottomans was based largely on his knowledge of the language and his sensitivity to Turkish culture and methods. Born in Leipzig in 1862, the son of a lawyer, he graduated with distinction from the Technical University of Dresden in 1885. He gained experience of railway construction in the European territories of the Ottoman Empire, where he learned Turkish, Italian and English. His linguistic ability, coupled with an innate sense of tact and diplomacy, enabled him to avoid the customary antagonisms that existed between foreign employees and the Ottoman authorities. According to the British military attaché in Constantinople, Lt Col. F. Maunsell, 'He has studied with the greatest care the Turkish character and always displays excellent tact in managing his superiors.'[3] To these administrative capabilities, Meissner added an iron will. Tactful and diplomatic he may have been, but he expected those in his employ to bend their backs to the task as resolutely as he himself did. W. Richards again comments, 'in addition to natural abilities of a high order and professional attainments which are evidently much above the average [he] is an energetic and keen workman and while he does not spare himself, he is not at all disposed… to allow anything like "malingering" in those who are under his orders.'[4]

Meissner's obvious abilities, together with his tact in dealing with his superiors, gained him a large degree of autonomy in the management of the construction work. Although officially under Field Marshall Kazim Pasha, the Ottoman Director of Construction, he soon had almost complete control over matters of a technical or engineering nature. In the initial stages, there were some serious disagreements between the two men, arising principally from the Field Marshall's tendency to 'interfere' in matters of engineering detail. At one point it even looked as if Meissner would resign from his post at the end of his first two-year contract. However, the growing recognition that the German was indispensable to the overall success of the project led to

Above:
European technicians were brought in to use dynamite for blasting through rock.

Below:
Workers laying the rails on sleepers.

a settlement of their differences, and a new contract was signed giving him greater independence. For his role in the construction effort, Meissner 'was awarded the rank of Mirmiran (literally 'Chief of Chiefs', a class of Pasha) by the Sultan Abdulhamid.'[5]

Meissner was able to use his growing influence to encourage the contracting-out of some sections of the work, particularly those requiring highly-skilled levels of engineering. Although the contractors used were mainly locally-based and small scale, there were some attempts by larger, foreign companies to gain access to the project. In May 1902, the Administration de Chemin de Fer Belges sent out a number of its engineers to inspect the intended route and negotiate with the High Commission on a deal to construct up to 400 kilometres (nearly a third) of the main Madinah line. Their failure to come to an agreement reflected the Commission's desire to maintain full Ottoman control over the project, rather than any financial or engineering concerns.

Meissner's presence, together with a more efficient supply network, led to faster progress during the early part of 1902. Disastrously however, in the late spring, following the great influx of pilgrims during the Haj, there was an outbreak of cholera. Many soldiers and workers succumbed to the disease and many others fled the area. Work ground to a halt, and by the time of the annual inauguration ceremony on 1 September the railway had only reached Zerqa, a small town some 20 kilometres north of Amman. In all, under 100 kilometres had been built in two years, less than a tenth of the total distance to Madinah. At this time, the Holy Cities must have seemed a long way off. Over the next few years however, with Meissner in charge of engineering, and the Sultan and his powerful Second Secretary Izzat Pasha taking a personal interest in the progress of the railway, there was to be a marked improvement in the work rate. Despite another major outbreak of cholera in 1903, from this point, the distances of line completed each year began steadily to increase.

The Line Advances

Negotiations for the purchase of the French-owned D.H.P. line from Damascus to Muzeirib had opened with great optimism. An original demand by the French for eight million francs had been dropped to five million, and the Ottomans were confident of securing further reductions. Although discussions continued sporadically for almost two years, by the end of 1902 it had become clear that the Hejaz Railway's offer of 3.5 million francs was not going to be accepted. It was therefore decided that a new line should be built, parallel to the existing D.H.P. track, straight from Damascus to Deraa without touching at Muzeirib. This section of the railway (measuring 123 kilometres) was finished in time for the inauguration ceremony of 1 September 1903, and together with the continuation of the line southwards from Zerqa to Qatrana, amounted to nearly 250 kilometres, over double the distance completed in the first two years. The section between Zerqa and Kassir represented the first major deviation from the traditional pilgrim

Below:
Jung 2-8-2 crossing rocky terrain north of Qatrana in Jordan.

Above:
A train, pulled by an H.S.P. (Haine St. Pierre) 2-8-2, on the steep section of line between Amman and Kassir.

route. It was necessitated by an ascent of 340 metres to the top of a plateau just south of Amman. The most difficult stretch, between Amman and Kassir, involved a climb of over 200 metres in just 12 kilometres. At its steepest, the gradient reached 1/50, requiring some skilled engineering work. The ascent was accomplished by means of a series of tight curves of 100 metres radius, spaced over a distance of three kilometres. A considerable amount of rock-cutting had to be carried out, and several important pieces of masonry work were undertaken, including a large, 20-metre high, double-tiered aqueduct of hewn stone, and a 140-metre long tunnel.

In general, the line followed the old pilgrim road wherever possible, and few deviations were made to bring the railway to inhabited areas. Stations were built as they were needed, and many of their names represented no more than the actual spot where they were located, with no village or even hamlet having previously existed in the area. In other places, such as Zerqa, although the station was called after the nearest settled area, the actual village of that name stood at some considerable distance from the line. Amman and Zerqa, as well as some other small villages such as Jerash, had only recently been settled by Circassian refugees from the Caucasus, fleeing the Russian advance during the disastrous war of 1876. These Circassian colonies, ranged along the edge of the desert, provided an important source of guards, who would play a significant role in protecting the work teams, and later the railway itself, from local tribes hostile to its construction.

Above:
The station buildings at Amman, the ancient city of Philadelphia. The engine is a Krauss 0-6-0T.

Early Services

As construction progressed, the completed sections of line were increasingly used both for passenger and freight services. This brought in much-needed revenue, as well as providing the railhead (the furthest point reached in construction) with materials and supplies. By the end of December 1903, the Damascus to Amman section of the line was open for traffic. Two passenger and five goods trains made the return trip each week, bringing in receipts of about T.L. 1,000 (Turkish lira) per month. (The value of the Turkish lira fluctuated throughout the period, but in 1908 one T.L. was worth about 18 shillings sterling.) According to early accounts, the running of services was still very basic 'and hours of departure and arrival of trains quite uncertain.'[6] Mr. Wilkie Young, visiting from the British Consulate in Beirut, had to wait two and a half hours at Amman before his train for Damascus departed. He blamed the lack of organisation on the fact that the administration was split between military and civilian personnel. The train he was on consisted of two third-class carriages and a luggage van, and carried about 50 passengers. The carriages were 'extremely dirty' and had no form of lighting. His journey of 222 kilometres entailed 12 hours of actual travelling, spread out over two days. He described most of the station buildings as being little more than stopping places, with sidings, a water tank and a few tents.

Arriving at Deraa just after sunset, the train halted and the passengers were left on their own to find accommodation. The railway buildings at Deraa even at this early stage were quite extensive, owing to the station's significance as the intended junction between the Haifa branch and the main line. However, Wilkie Young was unable to find a hotel, and complained that 'notwithstanding the prospective importance of the place, there is at present no accommodation whatever for travellers, and one is obliged to spend the night in a somewhat squalid encampment owned by an Italian contractor.'[7] The next morning the train left Deraa an hour before sunrise, but with 'some confusion prevailing, as the carriages were without lights; and, as far as I recollect, the same might almost be said of the station.'[8]

Manpower and Materials

The further the railway advanced into the desert, the more acute the problem of labour became. For reasons of economy, and due to the shortage of civilian volunteers, it was necessary to use large numbers of troops. At the start of operations in 1900, an Imperial Iradé had created a completely new element in the Turkish army, the Railway Battalion, formed in Damascus and composed mainly of suitably skilled artisans under the command of engineer officers. Within months it was decided to form a second force, Railway Battalion No.2. By the beginning of 1902, both these battalions of 1,200 men each were fully employed on the construction work. Their numbers

Below:
Turkish conscripts working as labourers on the railway construction, coming into Damascus in baggage cars.

THE HEJAZ RAILWAY

Above:
Many of the stations in the Hejaz were built around a narrow central courtyard with stairs to the top floor and a flat roof.

were further strengthened by 3,000 troops from various 5th Army Corps infantry regiments, also based in Damascus. Two hundred sappers and 50 telegraph specialists brought the total number of troops working on the railway at that time to 5,650.

The unskilled infantry troops were primarily employed on the earthworks, while the more competent railway battalions made the track-bed, laid the rails and undertook some minor masonry work such as the building of bridges and culverts. They also provided men for carrying out the preliminary route surveys. The sappers were detailed to the railway workshops as mechanics, metal workers and carpenters. The men of the telegraph detachment were originally used to set up the railway telegraph system. Once this had been completed, they were posted to the stations along the line as operators.

The Sultan's original plan to use materials provided solely by Ottoman factories and foundries was soon abandoned. The desire to comply with the absolute ruler's wishes however, led to a demand by the Central Commission for the Naval Arsenal in Constantinople to provide large quantities of rails and rolling stock for use on the railway. This was soon shown to be wholly unrealistic and, apart from the manufacture of some expensively-produced rails, a few first-class carriages and a mosque car, it was clear that the Naval Arsenal would be unable to meet the enormous demand for equipment generated by the railway. In its place, the Central Commission set up a system of procurement, and the required materials and rolling stock were ordered from abroad, mainly from European suppliers.

Rails and Rolling Stock

Contracts for rails were awarded to Cockerill of Belgium, Donawitz of Austria and the American Steel Trust (with rails stamped 'Maryland-USA'). In the later stages they were also supplied by a Belgian firm operating in Russia (these rails being marked 'Providence-Russe, 1906'), Dowlais of Wales and, particularly for the southern sections of the line, by the German company Gute-Hoffnung-Hutte. Although nearly all the rails have now disappeared from the defunct part of the line in modern Saudi Arabia, in places where the track does remain, the initials G.H.H. can still sometimes be seen. The single-headed steel rails measured between 27 and 30 feet in length and weighed between 30 and 38 lbs per yard. They were manufactured on the Vignoles system, invented in 1836 by Charles Vignoles. This type of flat-bottom rail incorporated a wide foot as a base, which resulted in improved track stability, reduced failures, longer life for both rails and sleepers and lower maintenance costs. They also provided greater vertical and lateral rail stiffness, the latter being particularly important for trains running over stretches of line with tight curves. They were attached to the sleepers by iron spikes (for wooden sleepers) or hexagonal nuts and bolts (for metal sleepers). At first, wooden sleepers were preferred, as they could be supplied from the empire's own forests in Anatolia, Macedonia and Syria. However, they were soon found to be unsuitable for the hot climate, because the wood shrank and split in the very high summer temperatures, causing the rails to come loose. This resulted in the carriages rolling as they passed over the unstable track. From Zerqa southwards therefore, steel sleepers were used, spaced 14 to a rail. These were mainly supplied by Cockerill and the American Steel Trust.

The most significant area of expenditure on materials was the rolling stock, and for this a number of different European suppliers were used. In the early stages of construction, a Belgian La Meuse 0-4-0T was found to lack sufficient power for the work and had to be replaced by a variety of 0-6-0Ts, two from St. Leonard (Liège, Belgium), three from La Meuse, eight from Hohenzollern (Dusseldorf, Germany) and twelve from Krauss (Munich, Germany). In 1903 Krauss also built eight of the more powerful 2-8-0s for the railway. As the construction work neared completion, 2-6-0s and 2-8-0s were the preferred choice. Fourteen 2-6-0s, manufactured in 1906 and 1907 were obtained from Germany, seven each from Hartmann (Chemnitz, Germany) and Jung (Jungenthal bei Kirchen, Germany). Twelve 1907 Jung 2-8-0s and seven 1907 Hartmann 2-8-0s were also acquired, with 15 more of the Hartmanns being made available between 1910 and 1911.

According to Lt Col. F. Maunsell, the passenger carriages used during the first years of the railway were supplied by Baume et Marpent of Haine St. Pierre, Belgium. In 1904 the railway's stock comprised one sleeper saloon, 15 mixed first- and second-class coaches and 40 third-class coaches; 56 in all. There was also a mosque car, which was one of the few pieces of rolling stock produced by the Naval Arsenal in Constantinople. At about the same time, the goods wagon stock amounted to 100 vans and 145 low-sided wagons. One important function of the low-sided wagons was the transportation and distribution of water, particularly to the stations between Qatrana and Ma'an, and later to the southern sections of the railway. The water was carried in two large iron tanks mounted at each end of the wagons. It was delivered to the various guard-houses and stations along the line, where it was stored in large barrels sunk into the ground. The goods wagons were supplied by the German companies Suddeutsche Wagon Fabrik-Kelsterbach of Frankfurt-am-Main and Gothaer Wagon Fabrik Fritz Bothmann & Gluck.

Construction

The building of the line was carried out in three separate stages - reconnoitring, surveying and construction. The distance covered in each of these three sections varied according to the terrain, but could be anything between 50 and 150 kilometres. In the first stage, the reconnoitring party pushed ahead into the desert to make a basic preliminary survey of the terrain and to carry out studies of the ground along the intended route. Using compasses and pedometers, the engineers marked out the line of the track that the surveyors and construction workers would follow. Their work could take several months and was both difficult and dangerous. In order to survive in the desert for this length of time, a full caravan had to be organised and equipped. They took with them all the supplies required for the expedition –

Above:
Damaged rail with part of an inscription dedicated to Sultan Abdulhamid II

Below:
Narrow gauge track of 1.05 metres was laid on a 1-metre high embankment.

THE HEJAZ RAILWAY

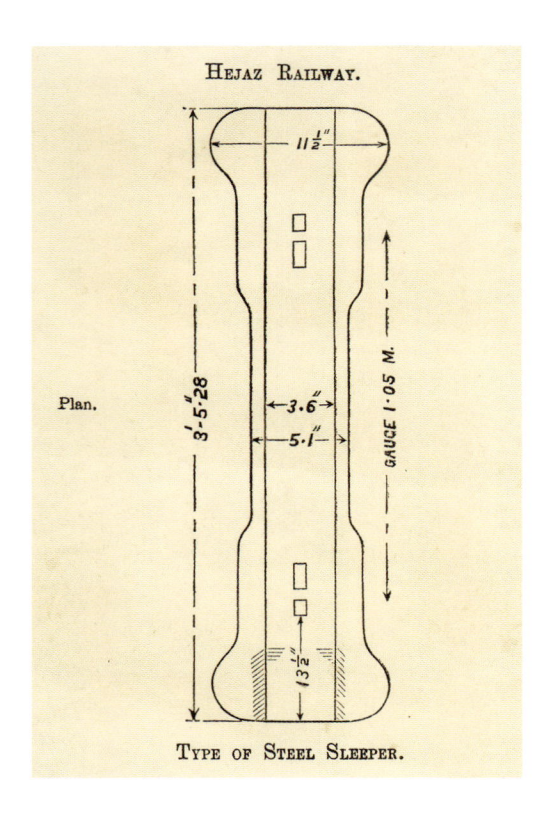

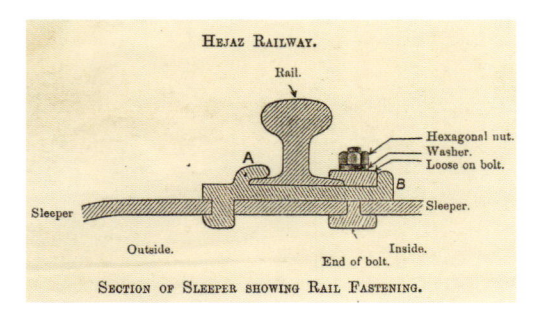

Above:
Sketches of sleeper and rail attachments made by Lt Col F. Maunsell in 1905.

food, water, tents, fuel, bedding, as well as all the necessary technical equipment. A cavalry detachment accompanied the team as protection against hostile tribes, and this too had to be fully provisioned.

One of the soldiers acted as camp cook, preparing all the food for the company during the mission. The diet was monotonous, generally consisting of tinned mutton, rice and rusk biscuits. There were no vegetables or fresh fruit. The reconnoitring team consisted of one railway engineer as expedition leader, two civil engineers, one doctor, 10 soldiers from one of the railway battalions and an escort of 20 cavalry. At the end of the expedition the results of the preliminary study were presented in a report, which together with an accompanying sketch, was passed on to the team of surveyors carrying out the second stage of the operation.

The surveying party, like the advance reconnoitring team, had to be equipped and supplied for long periods of isolation in the desert. They usually split the area covered into three equal parts of between 30 and 50 kilometres, and separate teams carried out the survey for each section. Although they did not have to travel as far from the railhead as the reconnoitring teams, they faced similar hazards and the same harsh conditions. Their job was to establish the exact route and levels of the projected railway line. Using the report and sketches provided by the preliminary survey, and with the help of a tachymeter, a small tripod-mounted telescope designed for the rapid measurement of distances and elevations, they compiled their results in the form of detailed measurements. These were then put together into a comprehensive report and submitted to the manager of the engineering works, generally located in the nearest large station to the railhead.

In the final stage, the actual work of construction was undertaken. The operation was divided into three separate fields: earthworks, masonry work and the building of the line itself. The earthworks involved making the embankment, and any rock cutting or preparatory levelling of the ground. The masonry work included bridges, dykes, tunnels, aqueducts and culverts, as well as the construction of the stations, staff accommodation, repair sheds, water towers and blockhouses for the troops. Finally, the completion of the line involved the preparation of the track-bed (ballast), and the laying of the rails and sleepers.

The construction was carried out by four divisions from the special railway battalions, each concentrating on a separate part of the operation. The first division went ahead, marking out the trace for the track to follow and preparing the earthworks. Behind it, a second division spread the required amount of ballast over the top of the embankment. The sleepers were then placed at right angles to the line of the track-bed by a third group. To complete the operation, the final division would lay the rails, attaching them to the sleepers by means of plates, bolts and screws. A goods train, pulled by a light locomotive and bringing up the rails and sleepers to the workers at the railhead, would pass slowly over the line as soon as the track was fixed in place. Further behind, smaller work parties would check the stability of the rails, filling in any cavities under the sleepers and shoring up the sides of the embankment where necessary.

BUILDING THE RAILWAY - I. THE MAIN LINE

Above:
Military conscripts building the roof of Muazzam Station.

Stations

As well as providing protection for both the railway and the telegraph, the stations acted as crossing points for the trains, with sidings provided to enable traffic travelling in opposite directions on the single track to pass. They were solidly constructed using local stone; colours varied according to the type of material available, from almost black, basalt rock around Madinah, to bright yellow sandstone in the area south of Zumurrud. Most of the station buildings had flat roofs, but where pitched ones were incorporated, they were

Left:
Carriage used by Meissner Pasha during the construction of the railway. The man at the window is Nedim Bey, Meissner's secretary.

THE HEJAZ RAILWAY

Above:
Smoke outlet in the engine shed at Medain Saleh Station.

covered with attractive red tiles. The only entrance was through an iron door, leading into a small courtyard onto which the windows of the downstairs rooms opened. Just inside the door, either a well (if water was naturally available), or more commonly a masonry cistern, was sunk into the floor. Provisions for 14 days were stored in one of the rooms.

In the south, where security was more of a problem, the stations were usually built with two storeys. Loopholes (slits for rifles) were set into the walls to enable the ten men generally posted to a station to withstand an attack by bedouin raiders. In some places a split-level panel was built half way up the front walls so that the men could fire from both the loopholes and the windows above them at the same time. The entrance to many of the stations in the northern Hejaz was covered with an arched portico. While decorative, this was clearly a strategic weak point and it was widely discarded south of Akhdar. Beyond Mashad, it was completely dispensed with. The flat roof gave a commanding view of the surrounding area and could be accessed by stairs in the two-storeyed stations, or by iron rings fixed in the walls in the single-storeyed buildings. In many places, particularly south of Tabuk where opposition to the railway was greatest, fortified blockhouses were built to lodge military garrisons.

Working Conditions

The building of the permanent way involved the largest concentration of workers, nearly all of whom were military conscripts. Their living and working conditions were extremely basic. They lived in small tents, which were constantly being moved forward to keep up with the progress of the work. Each company had a separate camp, and the food for both officers and men was prepared in a single large cauldron. As with the advance parties, there was very little variety in the diet, and although in places the land would have been suitable for cultivation, it included virtually no fresh fruit or vegetables. The meals consisted mainly of bread, biscuits or rice with only occasional additions of meat. Even when live sheep could be brought up to the railhead, the long journey caused them to deteriorate and lose much of their flesh. The bread was freshly baked in portable ovens, but only the poorest quality flour was sent from Damascus.

Another major cause of hardship was the severe climate, with its extremes of temperature between summer and winter, and even between day and night. In winter, the soldiers worked in their regular cloth uniforms but in summer, when the temperatures could rise into the 50s centigrade, they were allowed to wear white linen suits. As protection against the almost constant sun, they used the keffiyah, the traditional Arab head-dress.

The harsh living conditions, poor diet and extremes of temperature all contributed to a weakening of morale and an increased susceptibility to sickness and disease. Dysentery was rife owing to the heat, the general lack of hygiene and the poor water supply. The lack of fresh fruit and vegetables led to deficiencies in Vitamin C and a high incidence of scurvy. Even more serious was the threat of typhoid and cholera. Occasional outbreaks of the

BUILDING THE RAILWAY - I. THE MAIN LINE

latter, the greatly-feared killer disease of the age, could lead to widespread panic, with soldiers and contractors alike deserting their posts in droves and causing long delays in the work. The situation only improved after 1906, when medical staff attached to the 5th Army in Damascus were posted to the railway. There was also an attempt to provide facilities on the spot, with hospitals being set up in Ma'an, Tabuk and Al Ula.

Meissner made some effort to compensate the military workers for the harshness of the conditions by providing financial incentives. For the men employed at the railhead, these related to their particular area of work. On top of the regular army pay, the labourers preparing the earthworks would receive one piastre for digging out a cubic metre of earth, and three piastres for the same quantity of rock. Collecting a cubic metre of small rocks and stones from the ground alongside the railway would earn a worker two extra piastres. Those spreading the stones along the top of the embankment to form the track-bed made an additional piastre per cubic metre. One piastre was worth about two English pennies (2d.) and the rates were set so that a hard-working labourer could increase his salary by about three piastres a day. If a worker died while employed on the line, his family would receive a small payment as compensation. Extra wages were also available for the officers in charge of the construction teams, enabling them to double their standard army pay.

A further attempt to boost morale was the stipulation that after two years' duty on the railway, officers could transfer to alternative postings in the

Above:
Plaque on 11-arch bridge between Muazzam and Disa'ad acknowledging the name of the contractor who built it.

Below:
Stores piled up around the workers' camp at Medain Saleh during the building of the railway.

Above:
Wind-driven ('windmill') pump at Al Ula Station.

Right:
A short siding was built from Muazzam Station to the nearby pilgrimage fort in order to take advantage of its large birka.

empire with promotion. For the men, three years spent on the railway would count as four against the term of their compulsory military service. In practice however, many of the men were kept on 'under the flag' well beyond the official periods of duty. The authorities were able to do this by classifying their work on the railway as 'active service'. This category, usually reserved for times of war, carried with it an obligation to serve for six years.

Above:
The viaduct over Wadi Ithil was built high enough to cope with heavy flows of water in winter.

Technical Difficulties

As well as the extreme physical hardships, the railway workers had to overcome many technical difficulties. Perhaps the greatest of these was the scarcity of water, which was required in great quantities for the mixing of mortar for masonry work, as well as for the drinking and cooking purposes of thousands of workmen. Some of the water requirements could be provided from sources along the route of the railway itself; many of the old pilgrimage caravanserais had been built in places where the winter rain was collected in large cisterns or birkas (pools). These walled cisterns, some of which dated back to Roman times, could hold considerable quantities. The one at Qatrana for example, had a capacity of 36,000 cubic metres. The water however, was stored over a large surface area, and the lack of depth and the fact that the tanks were left uncovered, resulted in substantial losses through evaporation. In response, the railway authorities supplied a number of smaller metal cisterns, which were installed at various points along the line. By ensuring sufficient depth and by fitting proper covers, the water was protected not only from evaporation but also from harmful bacteria.

Due to the costs involved, cisterns were only provided where it was impossible to utilise natural sources. Old wells along the pilgrimage route were repaired, and where necessary, new ones dug. Water towers were built alongside many of the stations to store and distribute the water. Another common feature on the railway was the windmill pump, provided to maximise the supply of water from the natural wells. The almost constant winds, created by the great changes in temperature, meant that the auxiliary steam pumps, installed as back-ups, rarely had to be used. An early attempt to obtain water from artesian wells was abandoned after the machinery of a Belgian company boring into the rock near Zerqa was severely damaged. Later efforts were also unsuccessful, despite the bores being taken down to a depth of 110 metres.

Although for most of the year water was extremely scarce, ironically one of the main problems from an engineering point of view was the danger of flooding. In order to keep the track on even ground, the railway followed the

THE HEJAZ RAILWAY

Right:
Map 6 – Ma'an - Madinah

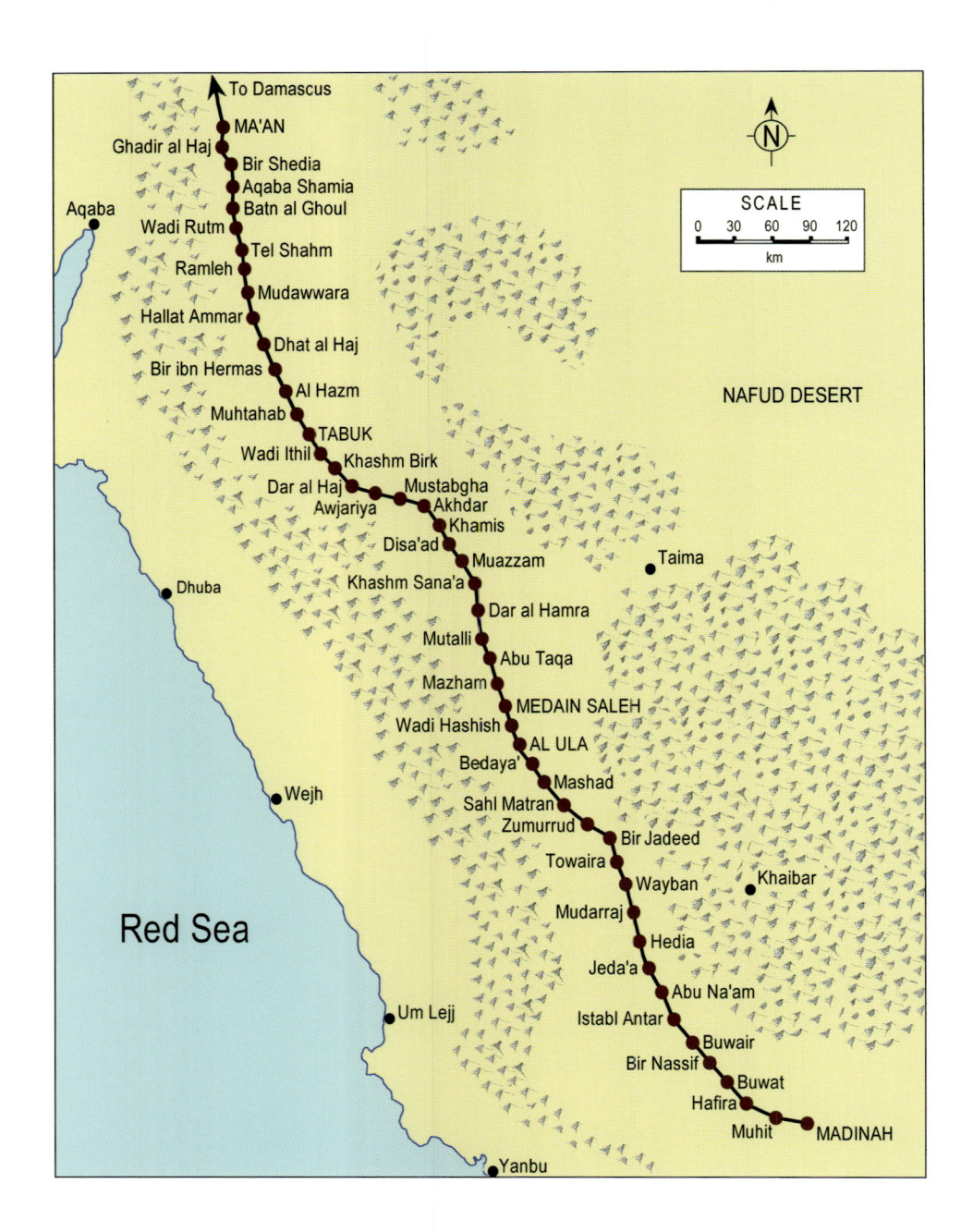

great wadis that cut through the mountainous terrain. During periods of heavy rain, the water quickly drained off the steep sides of the valleys, and violent rock-strewn torrents would surge across ground that had been dry for years. South of Tabuk a number of long bridges had to be built to traverse Wadi Ithil. Although the bed of this valley was usually dry and dusty, in the winter of 1906-07 the water beneath the new bridges quickly rose to a height of six feet.

Another problem faced by the construction teams was drift sand. On the northern half of the railway the ground consisted largely of hard limestone rock, which provided an excellent foundation for the track-bed. The only place where a significant stretch of sand lay across the intended route was between Batn al Ghoul and Wadi Rutm, and it was avoided by the simple expedient of a detour. Further south, areas of soft sand were more prevalent, and there were fewer trees and bushes to act as a natural foil against drifting. Good local supplies of clay and stone were therefore used to shore up the sandbanks, and this provided a stable bedding for the permanent way.

A more serious drawback for the railway was the almost complete lack of locally available fuel sources. Although coal could be obtained in small quantities from the Turkish mines at Heraklia on the Black Sea, it was found to produce too much smoke for use in the locomotives, quickly choking the tubes and requiring almost constant cleaning and maintenance. Coal from Cardiff was therefore purchased and mixed with the local supplies. The high cost of importing fuel however, was to remain a major problem for the railway throughout its short life. Auler Pasha, in his report of 1906, pointed out that the problem had been solved by the Russians in their construction of the Trans-Caspian Railway through the Karakum Desert by an early use of oil from deposits on the shores of the Caspian Sea. 'The naptha residuum obtained there not only provided excellent fuel for the locomotives, but was also successfully used in the lighting of the station buildings. The thought occurs that the large petroleum and naptha springs near Mosul might be used in a similar way for the Hedjaz Railway.'[9] In view of the fact that the Ottomans at that time also controlled the Eastern Province of what is now Saudi Arabia, they would have been surprised to discover just how easily all their fuel needs could have been met by what lay beneath the sands.

Ma'an - 'Gateway to Arabia'

By the beginning of September 1904 the main line had reached Ma'an. On 28 August, a large group of dignitaries arrived in Damascus by special train to attend the annual inauguration ceremony. As the direct representatives of the Sultan, they were greeted at the station by the officers of the garrison in full uniform, the senior civil functionaries, the police force, a military band and thousands of spectators. The road was lined with well-wishers all the way from the station to Government House. Two days later, together with the leading men of Damascus, they proceeded to Ma'an in four special trains. There, on 1 September, the official reception was conducted with befitting pomp and ceremony.

In 1904 Ma'an was already a place of some importance. The seat of a Kaimakam (a district governor), it consisted of about 500 flat-roofed mud houses a kilometre and a half north of the station, with another inhabited area of 200 dwellings just a kilometre further north again. It was one of the few places on the route with a plentiful water supply, which came from limestone springs close to the town. It was also still being considered as a possible junction for a strategic branch line to Aqaba at the head of the Red Sea. However, as the line continued to advance southwards, perhaps its greatest significance now lay in its new role as the railway's gateway to Arabia.

Beyond Ma'an the line ran through 60 kilometres of fairly level ground. South of Batn al Ghoul Station however, a steep wall of limestone rock, forming the edge of a south-facing escarpment, cut across the line of the track. Although Meissner searched along the edge of the plateau, he could find no easier route than the one followed by the old pilgrim road. This descended through an opening in the rock wall, a drop of nearly 300 feet into

Above:
One of two Hartmann 2-8-0s abandoned at Madinah Station after the line fell into disuse in 1925.

Below:
Lamp carried by guard or station master.

THE HEJAZ RAILWAY

Batn al Ghoul ('the Belly of the Monster'), over a distance of only five kilometres. The preparatory work, carried out by 400 soldiers over five months, entailed cutting away some 80,000 cubic metres of the cliff. The line was then laid parallel to the hillside, incorporating sharp curves of as little as 100 metres radius to cope with the overall 18/1,000 gradient. Although there were no bridges, a number of culverts were incorporated to ensure adequate protection from excess rain water.

In all, between Damascus and Mudawwara, there were 1,531 masonry works – 461 bridges, 271 aqueducts and 799 culverts. The importance of having so many drainage openings built into the rail embankment was well demonstrated during the heavy rains of 1904-1905. In one of the wadis south of Kassir Station a dyke with four bridges had been constructed to protect the line, but such was the quantity of rain that fell over the winter months that these precautions were found to be inadequate, and the bridges, together with 20 metres of the dyke, were swept away by flood water. Soon afterwards, with visibility impaired by pouring rain, a train going at 20 k.p.h. drove straight into the breach. The driver managed to stop in time to save five passenger carriages, but the locomotive and tender tumbled over the edge into the water. Fortunately no-one was killed in the incident, and even the Krauss engine was recovered and needed only minor repairs.

Railway Services

In his report of 1905, Lt Col. F. Maunsell, the British Military Attaché in Constantinople, described a journey from Damascus to Ma'an which he had made in the spring of that year. Except for two Germans, all the European

Below:
Building materials stored next to a siding during the construction of Tabuk Station.

Above:
Shakir Bey (on the track), commander of one of the battalions engaged in the construction, and Mokhtar Bey, the original surveyor of the railway and Meissner's right-hand man, standing on the line in front of the Mabrak al Naga escarpment north of Medain Saleh.

engine drivers had by that time been replaced by Turks, recruited from the naval dockyards at Constantinople. Their background and training had not prepared them for the operation and maintenance of the equipment under their control. Although later, in 1909, the upkeep and repair of the locomotives was enforced by the imposition of fines on irresponsible employees, in the early days much damage was caused through bad practice and inexperience. 'The naval sub-lieutenant who drove our train down to Ma'an was an excellent fellow, but perhaps he knew more of the sea than of engine driving, as, owing partly to his inexperience and partly to the tubes becoming choked by the inferior Turkish coal used, the steam gave out when we arrived in the desert, some 20 miles from Ma'an. It was impossible to get up sufficient pressure, and there we remained until rescued in the morning by another engine.'[10]

The overall traffic manager was a Pole, Mr Miclevich. However, most of the actual work of organising the day-to-day operations was carried out by the station-master at Deraa, an Armenian named Mr Topusian, who had received his training on the Anatolian Railway. The station-masters of the main depots so far constructed, Damascus, Deraa and Ma'an, were all Ottoman Christians who had previous experience of other railways within the empire. They were relied upon heavily for the efficient operation of services. Some of the more minor stations were entrusted to less experienced staff. One station-master Maunsell encountered on his journey was a 'professional gymnast, a native of Madinah, who has given fencing exhibitions in Constantinople, and who, while the train waited, showed me his skill in dumb-bell exercise.'[11]

THE HEJAZ RAILWAY

Above:
Sixty kilometres south of Tabuk, some heavy rock cutting and a 180-metre tunnel were required to clear a path through the mountainous terrain.

Tabuk Inauguration Ceremony 1906

On 1 September 1906 the Mudawwara to Tabuk section of the main line was opened amidst great public celebration. The usual collection of dignitaries, notables and religious leaders had been given a ceremonial send-off from Damascus, attended by large crowds and military bands. All along the line, at stations brightly decorated for the occasion, they were met by local officials and cheering schoolchildren. At Tabuk on 31 August a full reception committee of Ottoman dignitaries, tribal chiefs, railway representatives, merchants and religious figures was assembled at the station to greet them. The following day they all gathered at the newly-built Holy Mosque of Tabuk where the morning prayer was led by the Mufti of Damascus. The group then proceeded to a large, richly-decorated tent which had been erected beside a special commemorative arch. Enthusiastic speeches were made, and the Sultan's special envoy, His Excellency Rahmi Pasha, read out a telegram from the sovereign himself. The whole crowd prayed for the long life of the Sultan, after which the band played the Hamadiyah March.

At nine o'clock a large party, including Rahmi Pasha and the visiting Damascus Committee, travelled two kilometres out of Tabuk by train. There at the railhead, they took part in a special ceremony, in which they carried

BUILDING THE RAILWAY - I. THE MAIN LINE

some of the metal sleepers and placed them on the track. The troops then laid over a thousand metres of rail in one and a half hours so that their work could be admired. On the return to Tabuk another ceremony was conducted to lay the foundation stone of the town's new military hospital. Twenty-one cannons, sent by imperial order from Damascus, were fired and a military review was carried out of all the battalions and cavalry detachments. Even the assembled bedouin tribesmen joined in the parade on their camels. Following the inspection, numerous sheep were slaughtered and cooked, and served with coffee and other refreshments to all present. Finally, the soldiers who had completed their terms of service on the railway were drawn up in a long line, and with flags in hand received their medals and tezkeres, the commemorative certificate of the railway, as well as an extra month's wages.

The following day, on his return to Damascus, Rahmi Pasha reported enthusiastically to Izzat Pasha by telegram: 'Cannon fired five times during the glorious day of yesterday, were announcing each time the sacred character of the day, and all the Sheikhs and Bedouins who arrived in Tabuk, Imperial troops and other visitors were exclaiming prayers that the Lord may help our Sovereign. All day through, mutual congratulations were expressed... At night the whole city was splendidly illuminated with thousands of lanterns, artificial fires were burned, and the greatest enthusiasm lasted up to the morning.'[12]

Tabuk-Al Ula

Some 50 kilometres south of Tabuk the hills started to close in, requiring a large amount of rock-cutting to provide a suitable path through the difficult terrain. A 180-metre tunnel had to be built to negotiate a long limestone spur, and a steep path was cut through the Boghaz al Akhdar, a narrow rocky gorge. From this point, the line continued southwards through land that was

Above:
The old town of Al Ula, photographed in 1909.

Left:
The date groves and orchards of Al Ula made it an important oasis on the trade routes of the Hejaz.

41

uninhabited except for the local bedouin tribes. At Akhdar there was no settlement, but the qala'a (fort) had the reputation of possessing the best water on the pilgrimage road. It was available from a shallow well inside the fort, raised by means of a noria wheel (wooden water wheel) worked by mules, and stored in six cisterns. From this qala'a, the line followed the dried-out valley of Wadi Akhdar and its tributaries. It was a bleak waterless volcanic landscape but one which, from an engineering point of view, presented few obstacles. At Muazzam, another pilgrimage qala'a provided water from a large birka just outside the castle walls. The station and railway buildings were built close by, with a short spur line giving easy access to the supply.

Between Muazzam and Medain Saleh there was no more water, except for an unreliable supply at the Dar al Hamra qala'a. Here rain was collected in a birka set in the bed of a wadi, but even on the rare occasions that a supply was available, the contents tasted foul. Charles Doughty, the English explorer who had travelled with a Syrian pilgrimage some 30 years earlier in 1876, graphically described it in his classic, *Travels in Arabia Deserta*: 'There is also but a cistern at a freshet bed to be flushed by the uncertain winter rains; and if there runs in any water, within a while it will be vapoured to the dregs and teeming with worms.'[13]

Before this qala'a could be reached however, the line had to pass over harsh terrain, winding its way through steep sandstone ridges and dramatic rocky crags. In his unique, almost biblical style, Doughty perfectly captured the contrast between the utter desolation and the stark beauty of the country. 'This land lies abandoned to the weather, in an eternity, and nearly rainless; in all the desolate soil I have not perceived any freshet channel since our

Below:
Medain Saleh Fort before the building of the railway. The well was an important source of water for the construction workers on the line.

Above:
Dar al Hamra Station. "Ruddy is that earth.... high and terrible it showed in the twilight in this desolation of the world."
Doughty - Travels in Arabia Deserta

coming down from Akaba, the nomads may discern them, but not our eyes… The wady ground before us is strewn with volcanic drift for many miles; the Harra border, though hidden, lies not very far from the road. Further the sand is strewn with minute quartz grains, compared by the pilgrims to rice. East by the way, stacks are seen of fantastic black sandstone pinnacles, that resemble the towers of a ruinous city.'[14]

South of Muazzam the track climbed slowly from Khashm Sana'a Station to 1,200 metres above sea level, the highest point on the main line. It passed the abandoned and partly ruined qala'a of Dar al Hamra and then followed the Shuk al Ajouz, a narrow passage through a series of sandstone ridges. Beyond Mutalli was an open and relatively flat stretch of terrain. A few kilometres south of Abu Taqa, the line started to wind its way through tall sandstone outcrops until finally it swung to the left to avoid a wide belt of deep, shifting sand. From there it skirted the western face of a high sandstone escarpment, and continued on past Mabrak al Naga Station to Medain Saleh.

Medain Saleh and Al Ula

The station at Medain Saleh was a major depot, similar to those at Ma'an and Tabuk. It had 16 buildings including lodgings, repair workshops, barracks, a double water tower and a large engine shed. The complex was situated close to the old pilgrimage qala'a, which provided a good supply of water. Charles Doughty wrote a colourful account of his stay at this qala'a, where he was lodged for a number of weeks during the winter of 1876. In the courtyard, the Bir al Naga ('The Well of the She-Camel') reached a depth of eight metres. A birka just outside the qala'a was filled from the well, the water being drawn up by means of a noria wheel worked by two mules.

By 1 September 1907 the completed section to Al Ula was ready for its official opening. Al Ula was an important oasis and local trading centre

THE HEJAZ RAILWAY

consisting of a small walled town on the west side of a broad valley. As many as 2,000 inhabitants lived in about 400 houses, built of mud and stone plundered from the ancient Lihyanite city of Khuraiba. Life revolved around the rich swathe of date palms which stretched for over three kilometres along the wadi bed. A small network of canals irrigated the groves and a number of gardens where fruit, vegetables and even corn was cultivated, and livestock and poultry were kept. A track which cut through the mountains to the west connected Al Ula to the Red Sea at Wejh.

In view of its local significance, a major station complex was originally planned for the town. However, many of the construction workers came down with a malady which 'Agent G', who was investigating the route for the Cairo Intelligence Department in 1907, reported 'they compare with the well-known "Aleppo Button", but which in my belief is 'Madinah worm' – a disease prevalent in the Hedjaz and caused by swallowing the parasite in water.'[15] It was therefore decided that Medain Saleh, two stations up the line and easier to defend than Al Ula, should be the site for a full-scale depot. Al Ula still received larger than average facilities, and the inauguration ceremony was the usual festive affair, with plenty of speech-making and justifiable optimism about the progress of the line.

Opposition to the Railway

With the railhead rapidly approaching Madinah, local fears about the line were exacerbated by the belief that it would subsequently be extended to Makkah. The bedouin in particular, who relied on the revenue from hiring

Below:
Madinah Station after restoration.

camel caravans, saw the 'iron donkey' as a threat to their livelihood. Both the Amir of Makkah Sherif Ali Abdullah, and the Vali of the Hejaz Ahmed Ratib Pasha publicly supported the project, while making it known to the tribes that they were in fact opposed to it. Emboldened by this secret encouragement, and inflamed by the arrest of some of their leaders, the Al Harb, the paramount tribe in the Madinah region, rose up in revolt in January 1908.

Kazim Pasha, who had ordered the arrests, was attacked at Bir al Mashi on his way from Madinah to Rabigh. Although his escort of 1,000 cavalry protected him, the pilgrim route from Yanbu to Madinah was closed. The release of the imprisoned tribal chiefs improved matters slightly. However, following a bedouin attack on the Egyptian mahmal (the pilgrimage procession) and further arrests, the situation once again deteriorated. In May, taking advantage of the fact that most of the garrison were working on the railway, the bedouin launched a full-scale assault on Madinah. The local population preferred the Ottoman occupation to a bedouin free-for-all, and helped the remaining garrison of 200 to hold off the tribesmen. The fighting then moved to Hedia, a station 170 kilometres north of Madinah, where another bedouin attack was repulsed. The situation was only brought properly under control when eight battalions of troops from the 5th Army were transported down the line to the Hejaz.

As the line drew closer to Madinah, the political situation in Constantinople was also becoming increasingly volatile. The Young Turk movement, a reaction against the autocratic rule of the Sultan, was rapidly gathering momentum. Matters finally came to a head on 24 July 1908 when, following an insurrection of army officers in Salonica, Abdulhamid II announced the restoration of the Constitution. The abolition of the secret police, a general amnesty for political prisoners and other concessions quickly followed, and a wave of euphoria swept through the Ottoman territories; in Damascus the celebrations lasted several days. The revival of the Constitution caused a brief but marked resurgence in Abdulhamid's popularity, and the deeply suspicious Sultan ventured out of his palace and crossed the Golden Horn to pray at the Aya Sofia Mosque for the first time in 25 years. However, by the beginning of September 1908 when the railway's opening ceremony was due to be held in Madinah, it had become clear that the Sultan ruled in name alone. The always rather unlikely prospect of an imperial pilgrimage was now no longer even considered, and sadly the railway's greatest advocate and benefactor was no longer in a position to enjoy its inaugural celebrations.

Above:
Richard Hartmann of Chemnitz in Germany provided seven 2-6-0s and twenty-two 2-8-0s during the early years of the railway.

Al Ula - Madinah

The country between Al Ula and Madinah is generally mountainous and difficult. However, by following the great wadi beds that cut through the rocky terrain, the surveyors managed to overcome most of the worst obstacles and were able to avoid the need for tunnels or complicated bridges. Leaving Al Ula, the line at first ran through a wide, flat valley. Beyond Zumurrud, the country became more broken and the track had to twist its way through

THE HEJAZ RAILWAY

Opposite:
Guard of honour lined up for the inauguration ceremony at Madinah Station on 1st September 1908.

Overleaf:
Train decorated with flags on its way to Madinah to take part in the inauguration ceremonies.

numerous smaller wadis. By Mudarraj, it had dropped to its lowest point on the main line, just 345 metres above sea level. A large swathe of soft sand and a wide watercourse had to be negotiated just north of Hedia Station, but beyond this, the line followed the great Wadi Hamdh. About two kilometres north of Abu Na'am Station, a pair of adjacent bridges of 19 and 11 arches spanned the wadi, which was then separated from the line by a ridge of hills. Some 125 kilometres from Madinah, the distinctive twin-peaked Jebel Antar signalled that the traveller's long journey was nearly over.

The railway was completed with remarkable speed. The political requirement to finish by September meant that, in addition to an extra 2,000 workers drafted in from the Turkish 6th Army in Baghdad, 1,800 men from the garrison in Madinah were detailed to start construction from the southern end. The political pressure however, also had some negative consequences. Temporary detours, instead of bridges and culverts, were widely used to traverse the beds of watercourses. In the absence of Meissner, who as a Christian was unable to work south of Al Ula, basic procedures such as the fixing of rails and the laying of ballast were often carried out in a hurried and careless way. A.J. Wavell, who travelled to Madinah shortly after the completion of the construction work 'passed several wrecked engines that had run off the track owing to it not having been properly laid.'[16]

The line to Madinah was completed by 1 September, in time for the traditional inauguration ceremonies marking the anniversary of the Sultan's accession. The first through train reached the city on 22 August 1908. The official delegation was accompanied by a host of well-wishers and newspaper correspondents, paying either seven Turkish lira (third class) or 14 (first class) for the privilege. At the time it was still thought that the line would be continued on to Makkah. Perhaps because of this, or due to the recent unrest and the declining fortunes of the Sultan, the inauguration ceremonies weren't as spectacular as might have been expected. However, large numbers did turn out for the official reception, and more than 30,000 attended a subsequent ceremony to lay the cornerstone of the Hamidia Mosque (now the Al Anbaria Mosque).

The celebrations were overshadowed by the uncertainty of the future. Although the ceremonies were conducted in the Sultan's name, the principal speaker saw fit to declare that the Prophet had refused to let the railway reach Madinah before His Majesty had granted the people a Constitution. Whatever pleasure Abdulhamid took in the success of his greatest and most ambitious undertaking must have been thoroughly tempered by the knowledge that its primary objective, of glorifying his rule as Sultan and Caliph, was now of little significance. His final deposition the following year, together with the coming of the railway and the appointment of a new Amir of Makkah, Sherif Hussein ibn Ali, was to herald a new era in the history of the Hejaz. It would eventually bring world war to the region and an end to the established order. For the moment however, the Hejaz Railway was to enjoy eight years of normal operations.

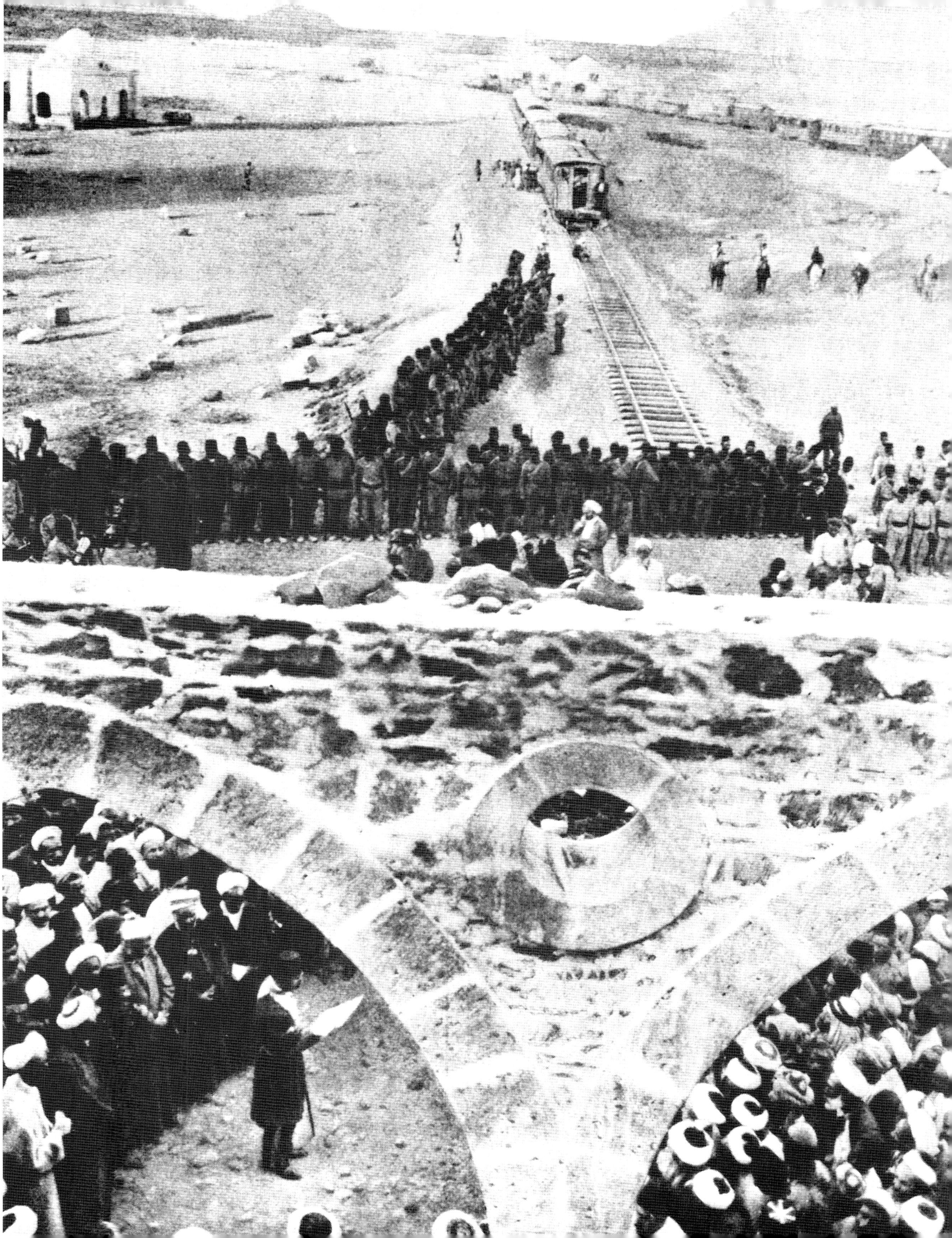

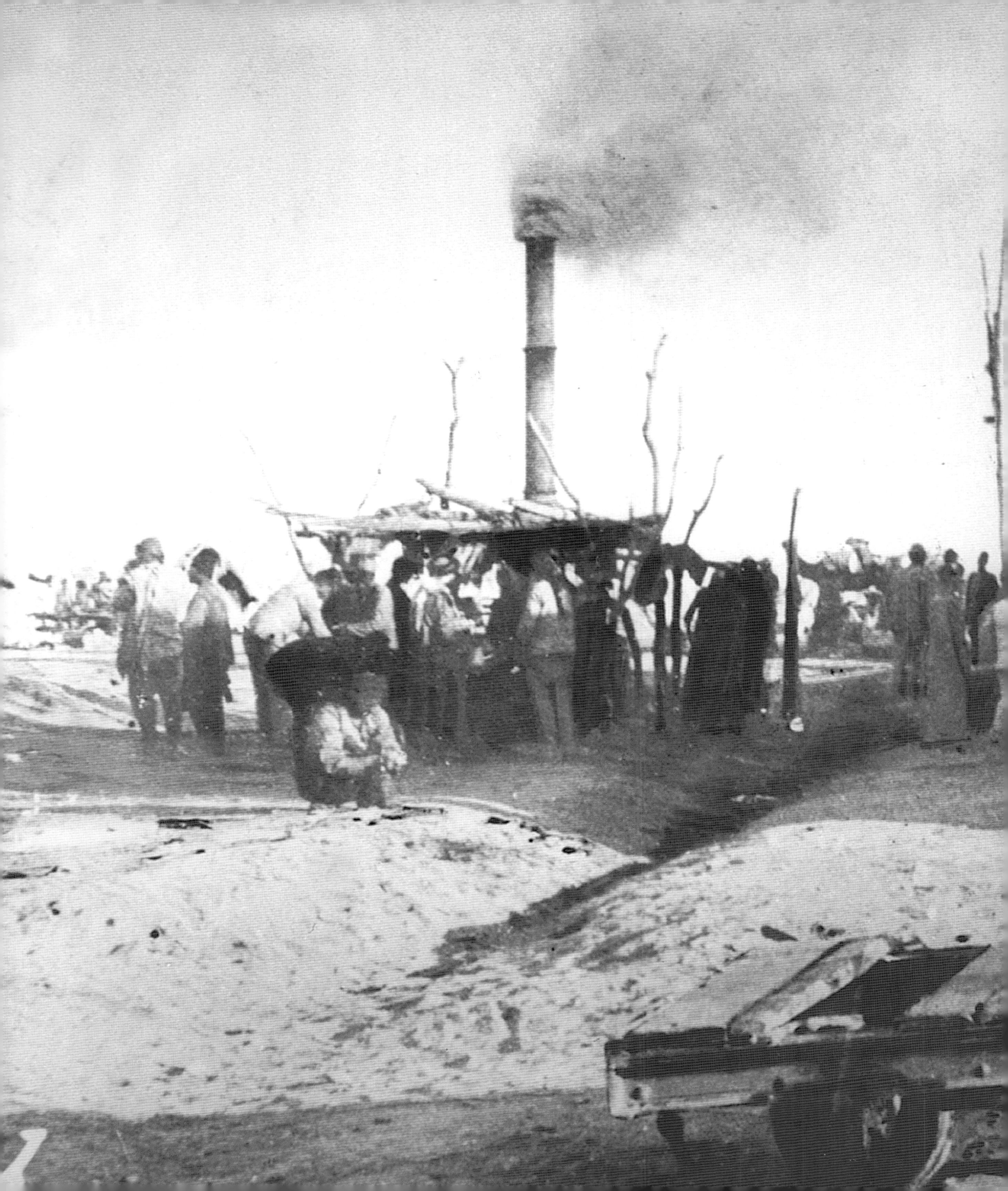

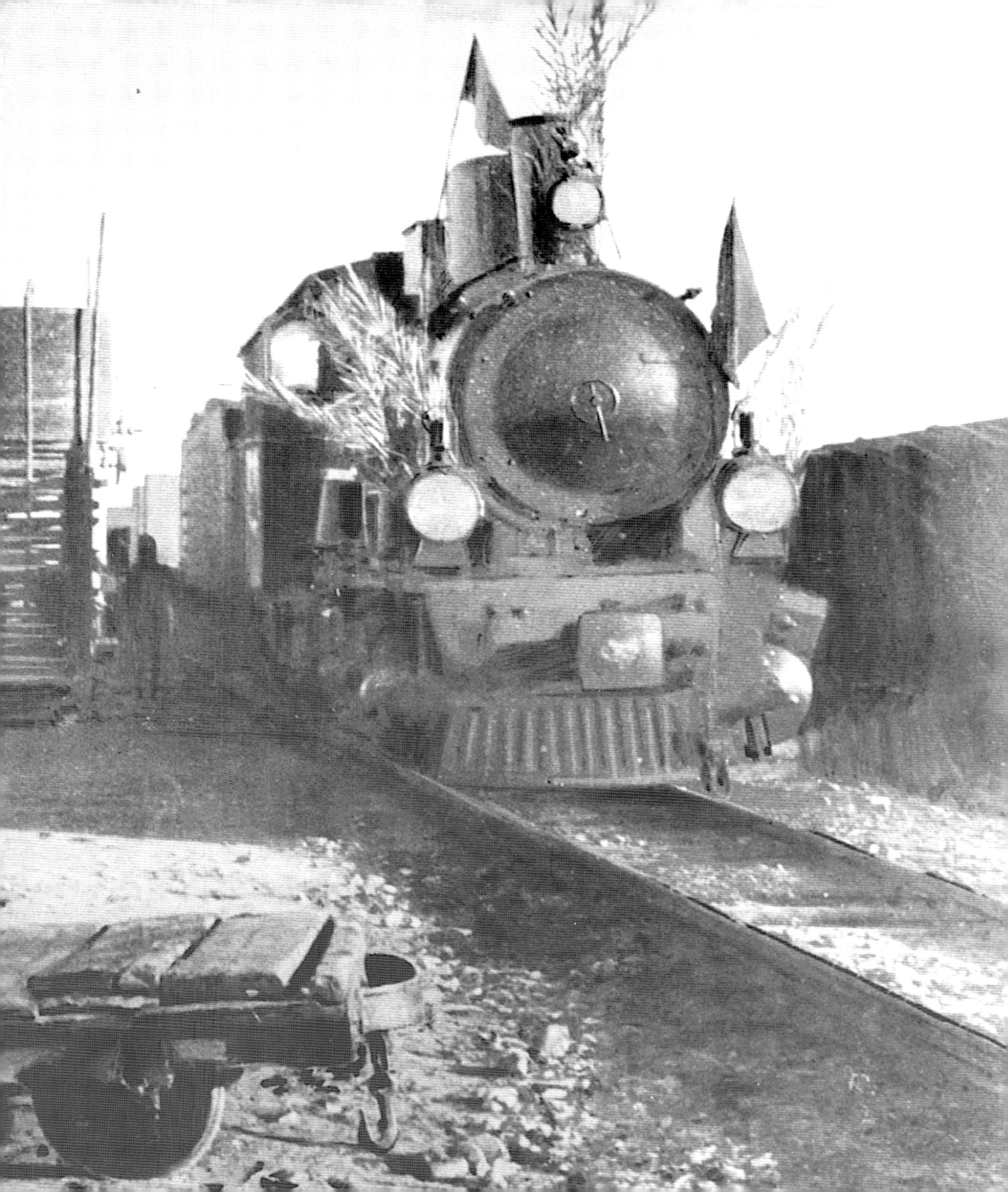

THE HEJAZ RAILWAY

3. Building the Railway

II - The Branch Lines

Haifa - Deraa Branch 1905

Construction of the Haifa-Deraa branch of the Hejaz Railway started eight years before work began on the main Damascus-Madinah line. As early as 1891 a concession had been granted to a British entrepreneur Robert Pilling, and his Lebanese partner Joseph Elias, to build a standard gauge railway between Haifa and Damascus. Work on the line commenced in 1892. Owing to financial difficulties, the concession was transferred after just eight uncompleted kilometres to a syndicate headed by Mr W. Hills of the Thames Ironworks Shipbuilding Engineering Co. Although construction was restarted in 1895, by 1902 the track had only been laid over the original eight kilometres, and some of the earthworks, rock-cutting and culvert building had been undertaken up to Beisan, almost 60 kilometres east of Haifa.

Once work had started on the main Damascus-Madinah line, imported materials were brought in on the D.H.P.'s Beirut-Damascus railway. A deal

Below:
Map 7 - The Hejaz Railway Haifa - Deraa Branch; Deraa - Bosra Branch; Ezra - Suweida Branch

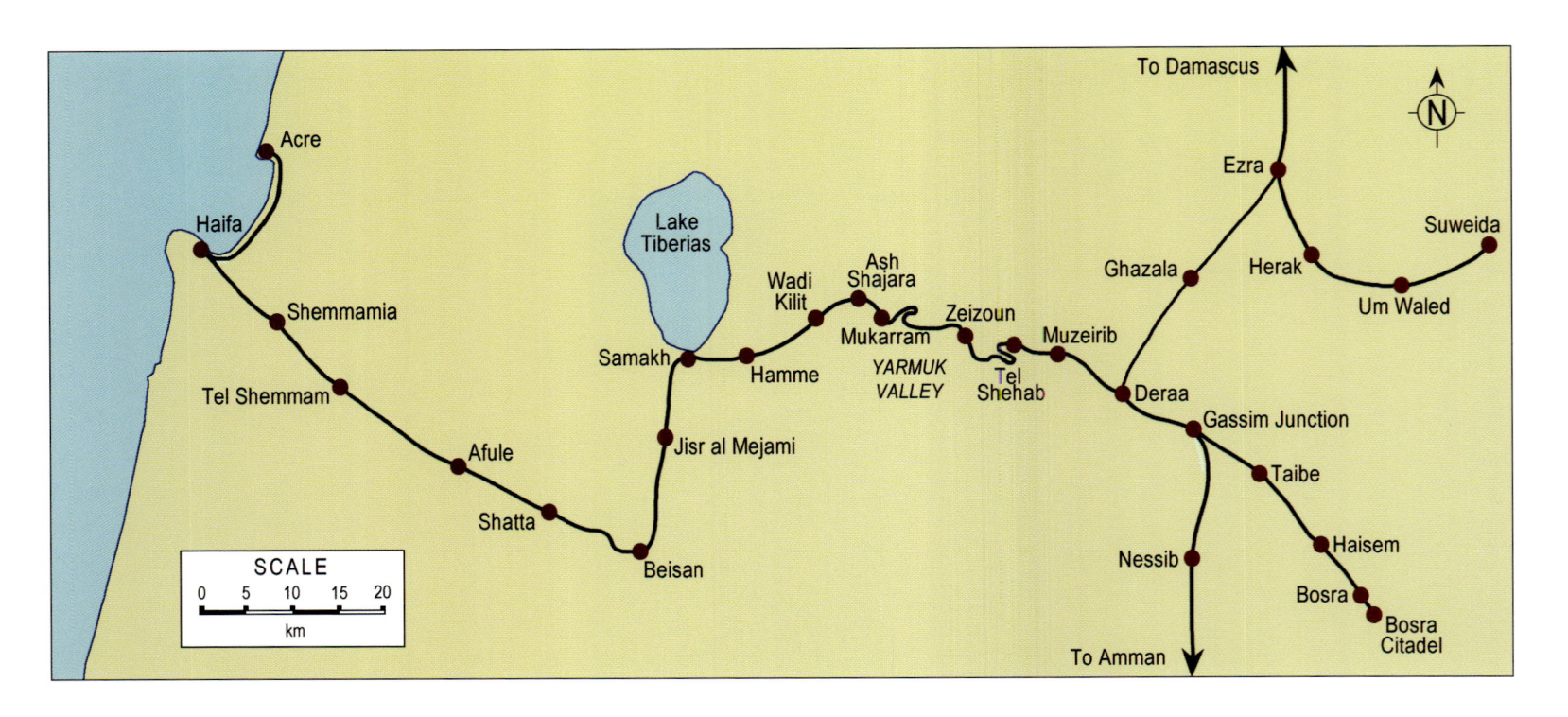

BUILDING THE RAILWAY - II. THE BRANCH LINES

Above:
Al Kuye Bridge, between Wadi Kilit and Ash Shajara, is the seventh bridge in the Yarmuk Valley. It was the first to be completed on the Haifa to Deraa branch, and on seeing a photograph of it, Sultan Abdulhamid II was moved to award Meissner Pasha with a gold medal.

with the French-owned D.H.P. in May 1900 resulted in rebates of 45 per cent being granted for the bulk shipment of these materials through Beirut. The enormous quantities involved, which had to be carried over the two mountain ranges between Beirut and Damascus, led to serious bottlenecks and delays. When the negotiations for the purchase of the D.H.P.'s Damascus-Muzeirib branch began to founder in 1902, the French company suddenly reneged on its agreement and cancelled the rebate. Faced with sharply escalating costs as well as a service over which they had no control, the Ottomans decided to buy back the concession for the Haifa branch.

In 1902 a price of £155,000 was agreed with Mr Hills, 'the tithe and the sheep tax being given as security.'[1] Payment was to be made in two instalments, with annual interest of 5 per cent accruing until the debt was settled in full. The British syndicate was also to be given first option on any contract if the Ottoman government decided to have the construction work carried out by a foreign company. In the end the Ottomans built the line themselves, but they only received the title deeds when, following British government pressure to honour their debts, they settled their account with Mr Hills in 1905.

Above:
Hartmann 2-8-2 crossing the River Ehrer on the 12th Yarmuk Valley bridge.

Meissner was sent to survey the proposed route in late 1902, and in April the following year work started from the Haifa end. It was decided to convert the track to the narrow 1.05 m. gauge to conform to the main Madinah line, and by August 1903 nearly 25 kilometres had been completed. Meissner was put in charge, with an additional monthly wage of 1,000 francs, and a local commission was set up in Beirut to oversee the work. Although it was answerable to the higher Istanbul Central Commission, particularly for financial matters, in practice it had considerable scope to make local decisions. Membership included the Vali of Beirut, the Kaimakam of Haifa and representatives of the engineering, parks and forests, religious endowments and accounting departments of the regional government.

The total length of the branch was 161 kilometres. However, the last 12 kilometres from Muzeirib to Deraa had been built in 1901 when the Ottomans were still optimistic about acquiring the D.H.P.'s Muzeirib-Damascus line. The first 60 kilometres east of Haifa traversed the fairly easy terrain of the Plain of Esdraelon. Upon reaching Beisan, the line dropped into the Jordan Valley and swung northwards to Lake Tiberias (the Sea of Galilee). Just beyond Jisr al Mejami, 257 metres below sea level - the lowest point on the whole Hejaz system - the line crossed the River Jordan on a solid five-arch bridge. Two kilometres on, a large 50-metre long, steel-span bridge carried the track over another river, the Yarmuk. From this point the line rose slowly to Samakh, where the railway station at the southern tip of Lake Tiberias was designed to serve as a landing stage for a boat connection.

The first, more straightforward half of the line, from Haifa to Samakh, was entrusted to Turkish engineers under Mokhtar Bey. From Lake Tiberias the branch entered the Yarmuk Valley, where the steep terrain and twisting river presented serious engineering difficulties. Initially, a military workforce was engaged, but it soon had to be withdrawn and the work put out to tender. In the end the section was awarded to private contractors, three Syrian, one Austrian, one Italian and two German. On one stretch near Tel Shehab where the work was retained by the military, the required rock-cutting took almost 18 months, delaying the completion of the rest of the line. The complicated nature of the construction work meant that the building costs on the Yarmuk Valley section rose in places to T.L. 12,000 per kilometre, over ten times the expenditure required for track on level ground.

In all, there were 15 major bridges along the River Yarmuk, some of them incorporating large metal sections. These were considered to be both better and more economical than masonry structures, due to the height of the gorge and the great distances to be spanned. The steep terrain meant that special attention also had to be given to drainage. This became particularly evident after severe flooding in the winter of 1904-1905 when, following heavy rains, a torrent of water four metres deep raced down the valley, tearing away all the temporary bridges and causing so much damage that the construction work was put back by four weeks. To cope with this, 246 aqueducts and culverts were incorporated on the Jordan to Muzeirib section alone. This compared with 56 culverts on the flatter stretch between Haifa and the Jordan Valley.

For the climb up the Yarmuk Valley, the maximum gradient was set at 1/50, with the minimum radius for curves restricted to 100 metres. In order to accomplish the ascent at the eastern end of the valley, the line had to make two loops into tributary valleys of the river seven kilometres above and six kilometres below Zeizoun Station. Beyond the second of these loops, the track finally emerged near Tel Shehab onto flat, agricultural land, and at the next station, Muzeirib, was connected to the already existing section to Deraa.

From an engineering point of view, the construction was extremely difficult. The general working conditions however, were much better than those on the main Hejaz line. There were plentiful wells along the route, and while in summer the River Yarmuk dried up, the River Jordan held water all year round. The temperatures were not as extreme as in the desert regions, and the fertile terrain provided a varied and healthy diet. The proximity to well-populated areas also reduced the feeling of isolation for the workers, and gave them access to adequate medical facilities. Many of the raw materials needed for the construction work were available locally, with excellent stone and sand for masonry being found in good quantities along the line.

Commercial traffic started in October 1903, when a grain shipment was transported on the 22-kilometre stretch of track between Tel Shammam and Haifa. As soon as the line reached Afule in November, a passenger train was put into operation to cover the 37 kilometres to the coast. These early services were only made possible by the relatively large populations living in the agriculturally-productive areas along the route. The line to Jisr al Mejami was opened in May 1904, and the inauguration ceremonies for the whole branch were held on 1 September 1905, despite some of the bridges being

Below:
Borsig 2-8-0 emerging from a tunnel west of Zeizoun in the Yarmuk Valley. In all, there were seven tunnels on the 58-kilometre section of the Haifa branch between Lake Tiberias and Tel Shehab.

THE HEJAZ RAILWAY

unfinished. Due to the outstanding work, regular services along the completed track could only be started in May 1906. Prior to the linking of the branch to the main Hejaz line, rolling stock consisting of six Krauss tank engines, eight passenger coaches and 62 wagons had been used. In 1905, four Hohenzollern (Dusseldorf) 0-6-0Ts were built for the Haifa branch, and in 1907 Henschel & Sohn of Cassell provided four 2-4-6-0 compound mallet engines for the difficult sections on the Hejaz Railway, with at least one of them being employed in the Yarmuk Valley.

Haifa possessed an excellent natural harbour, but owing to strong currents, deposits of sand had banked up, forcing ships to anchor offshore. A short siding from the station ran to a 350-metre pier, giving access to a depth of 15 feet of water. However, this only partially solved the problem, for in 1907 severe winter storms swept away 30 metres at its end, requiring further developments to harbour defences. Three cranes with a capacity of between 12 and 18 tons were positioned on the pier, and were able to unload heavy supplies, including engine parts for assembly in the local workshops. The station was solidly constructed out of stone, just outside the eastern wall of the old town. It incorporated an engine shed, a turntable, shunting facilities, repair yards, a water supply and a memorial column to commemorate the building of the branch.

Below:
Haifa, the railway's port link on the Mediterranean Sea, was provided with a large, prestigious station building.

Above:
Although a short spur ran beyond this point to the Roman Citadel, Bosra was the final station on the branch. The locomotive is a Borsig 2-8-0.

Deraa-Bosra Branch, 1912

In 1910 a revolt by the semi-autonomous Druze in the Hauran region was put down by Ottoman forces. Three battalions, under the command of Sami Bey al-Faruqi, were quickly transported to the area of the uprising via the Hejaz Railway. The success of this operation, and the ability to deploy troops swiftly by rail, resulted in a decision to extend the line 40 kilometres east of Deraa to Bosra (al Sham), close to the mountain stronghold of Jebel Druze. The branch was at the centre of a well-populated and agriculturally rich wheat-growing region, and generated a considerable amount of business for the railway's passenger and freight operations. By the end of 1910, engineers had already been sent out to survey the route. In 1912 the branch line, with three intermediate stops and a short extension beyond Bosra Station to the Roman citadel, was completed. Trains ran between Deraa and Bosra three times a week. A revolt by the Druze against the French occupation in 1925 also led to the building of a short branch line between Ezra and Suweida in the same area (see Chapter 10).

Haifa-Acre Branch, 1913

At the other end of the Deraa branch, the port of Acre, only 18 kilometres around the bay from Haifa, had initially been rejected as the terminus for the

THE HEJAZ RAILWAY

Above:
A monument was erected in Damascus to commemorate the construction of the Hejaz Railway and telegraph.

line owing to its inferior harbour. However, in 1911 it was decided that as the capital of the province, it should be incorporated into the system. Construction started on a short spur line from Balad al Sheikh, four and a half kilometres outside Haifa. Two rivers, the Qishon (Nahr al Mokatta) and the Na'amein had to be bridged, but there were no intermediate stations and the track ran along flat, easy terrain. The branch was ready by October 1913, and three trains a day connected the two port cities.

Extension: Damascus Qadem to Damascus Kanawat, 1911

On 31 December 1911, a three-kilometre extension was opened from Damascus Qadem Station to a new terminus in the centre of the city. Its convenient location would, it was hoped, attract new passenger and freight business. Damascus Kanawat Station was also built to provide a prestigious front for the railway's operations. Designed by the German architect Palmer, in typical Ottoman Damascene style, its imposing lines and impressive interior befitted its prominent position. The new extension ran alongside part of the French D.H.P.'s Muzeirib line, and in 1914 Kanawat Station was connected to the D.H.P.'s Baramke Station in west Damascus by a short spur line. In the same year, to facilitate the movement of military supplies southwards to Palestine, Baramke Station was also linked up to the main Hejaz depot at Qadem.

Afule-Nablus Branch, 1912-1915

In the years running up to the First World War tension mounted between the great powers, and with armed conflict looking increasingly likely, the Ottomans started to extend their rail network into Palestine. In 1912 a branch was started at Afule on the Haifa-Deraa line, with the intention of extending the Hejaz system as far as Jerusalem. By February 1913 the track had been laid up to Jenin. Nine kilometres beyond Sileh Station, the 250 metre-long Ramin Tunnel was constructed. The track to Massoudiah was completed in the autumn of 1914, and by the time the Ottomans entered the war in November, work had reached Sabastiya. Although the railway was continued on to Nablus in 1915 as part of the war effort, the intended extension to Jerusalem was never built. A whole network of strategic supply lines was constructed in Palestine during the war, and linked up to the Hejaz system at Afule (via Tel Keram and Massoudiah). Although these branches would be lumped together with the main Hejaz system and administered in the post-war years as 'Palestine Railways', they cannot really be considered a part of the original and integral Hejaz Railway.

First World War Branches / Extensions

The First World War tested the Hejaz Railway's strategic capacity to the full. While the network had been built with military considerations very much in mind, Madinah Station itself had been located outside the city walls. A short spur line was therefore constructed at the beginning of the war to extend the track into the security of the citadel. It was lifted in early 1918 to provide spare rails for the war-damaged sections of the main line. Another short branch was built to the oasis of Bir Ali, about 10 kilometres south-west of Madinah. It was also taken up in 1918.

One of the main problems the Ottomans faced after the outbreak of hostilities was a severe shortage of fuel for use in the locomotives. Coal could no longer be imported, and the railway was largely dependent on timber to maintain even a basic service. In 1915 a 40-kilometre branch line was constructed to run from Uneiza Station to the mountains above the great ruined crusader castle of Shobek, north of Petra. This gave access to the Hisheh Forest, which was badly damaged by the railway's huge timber requirements. A short branch line was also built to a woodcutting area six

Above:
The 250-metre long Ramin Tunnel was built 9 kilometres south of Sileh on the Afule to Nablus branch line.

THE HEJAZ RAILWAY

Above:
Hartmann 2-8-2 leaving Zeizoun Station on the north side of the Yarmuk Valley.

kilometres west of the railway between Mashad and Sahl Matran. At the very end of the war, another short stretch of track was laid at Buwat Station in order to collect wood from nearby sources. The armistice was signed before this line could be fully utilised.

Projected Branches / Extensions

Madinah-Makkah

The Hejaz Railway was originally intended to run from Damascus to Makkah, the holiest city of Islam. Madinah, the Muslim's second city, and the site of the Prophet's Mosque, was reached in 1908. It was hoped that the extension to Makkah would be completed by 1 September 1909, and two alternative routes were proposed to take into account the potential hostility of the local tribes. One of them followed a fairly direct route between the two cities, while the other headed westwards, touching at the Red Sea port of Rabigh before running inland again to Makkah. The growing opposition of the tribes, secretly supported and encouraged by a new Amir of Makkah named Sherif Hussein ibn Ali, ultimately prevented the line from ever being constructed. From early maps of the intended route, it is clear that the original plan was for the railway to continue south into Yemen, first to Sana'a and then to Hodeida on the Red Sea coast.

Jeddah-Makkah

With over 30,000 pilgrims arriving by sea at Jeddah, the idea of a branch line to connect the Red Sea port with Makkah had many advocates. According to a report by Mokhtar Bey, the original Turkish surveyor of the Hejaz line, the route between Jeddah and Makkah would present few engineering difficulties. The required gradients would not have to exceed 1/100, and the radius of the curves could be kept to a minimum of 300 metres. Due to the absence of sharp bends on the line, up to 480 pilgrims could be carried in one trainload of 12 full carriages. The journey of just over 75 kilometres would take about two hours, and it was estimated that three trains could make the journey four times a day. In this way, all the pilgrims arriving at Jeddah could theoretically be transported to the Holy City within a week.

The cost of constructing the branch, including rolling stock and the building of the stations, was assessed at 3.25 million French francs, as long as 1,000 military conscripts could be deployed to carry out the labouring work. The revenues from the pilgrimage, other religious visits and regular trade traffic would, it was calculated, quickly cover the cost of construction. As most pilgrims from the Indian sub-continent and North Africa chose to travel by sea, the building of the branch would also mean that many of the Muslims who had made voluntary contributions to the railway would accrue some benefit from it.

Otto von Kapp, a German expert reporting to the Central Commission, made the point that the branch would provide an extra outlet to the sea, increasing the railway's potential for trade revenues. The Sultan however, was unwilling to allow the line to touch, or even run close to, the coast. Fully

BUILDING THE RAILWAY - II. THE BRANCH LINES

aware that Britain had complete control of the seas, Abdulhamid was anxious to keep the line beyond the range of naval aggression. From the outset, the Ottomans had planned to build the Jeddah-Makkah branch only when they had completed the main Hejaz line, and they held to this decision. By the time Madinah had been reached in 1908 however, resistance to the railway had greatly increased, and as with the Madinah-Makkah extension, the opposition of the local tribes was eventually to cause the plan to be abandoned.

Amman-Salt

A 1905 survey of phosphate deposits in the area around Salt, some 30 kilometres north-west of Amman, led to proposals for a branch line to facilitate mining operations. Meissner himself estimated that there was up to a million cubic metres of phosphate. Concessions were granted, but work on the line was never started. The costs involved in mining, construction and transportation were considered too high to make the exploitation of the reserves economically viable, and the idea was abandoned. The building of other branches for the development of phosphate beds in the post-1960s, including the eventual construction of a line to Aqaba, is described in Chapter 10.

Ma'an-Aqaba (The Taba Incident, 1906)

In 1903 it became increasingly obvious that the Ottomans intended to build a branch from Ma'an to Aqaba at the head of the Red Sea. Mr Hills, the holder of the concession for the Haifa-Deraa route, wrote to the Foreign Office in alarm, pointing out the 'sinister political aims' behind the whole Hejaz Railway venture. He even went as far as to claim that 'the so-called Hejaz line is to be a strategical line to run only as far as Akabeh on the Red Sea… it is not laid out to Makkah at all in their plans, but takes from Ma'an a south westerly direction for Akabeh… I saw the plans myself.'[2]

Above:
Ottoman officials gathered around the commemorative monument for Haifa Station. Meissner Pasha (in the dark uniform) and Kazim Pasha (in the white jacket) are standing in front of the base.

Left:
A balcony extension with a flat roof has been added to the classic Ottoman construction of solid stone brickwork and a red-tiled pitched roof at Amman Station.

59

THE HEJAZ RAILWAY

Right:
Foreign Office file referring to the proposed branch from Ma'an to Aqaba.

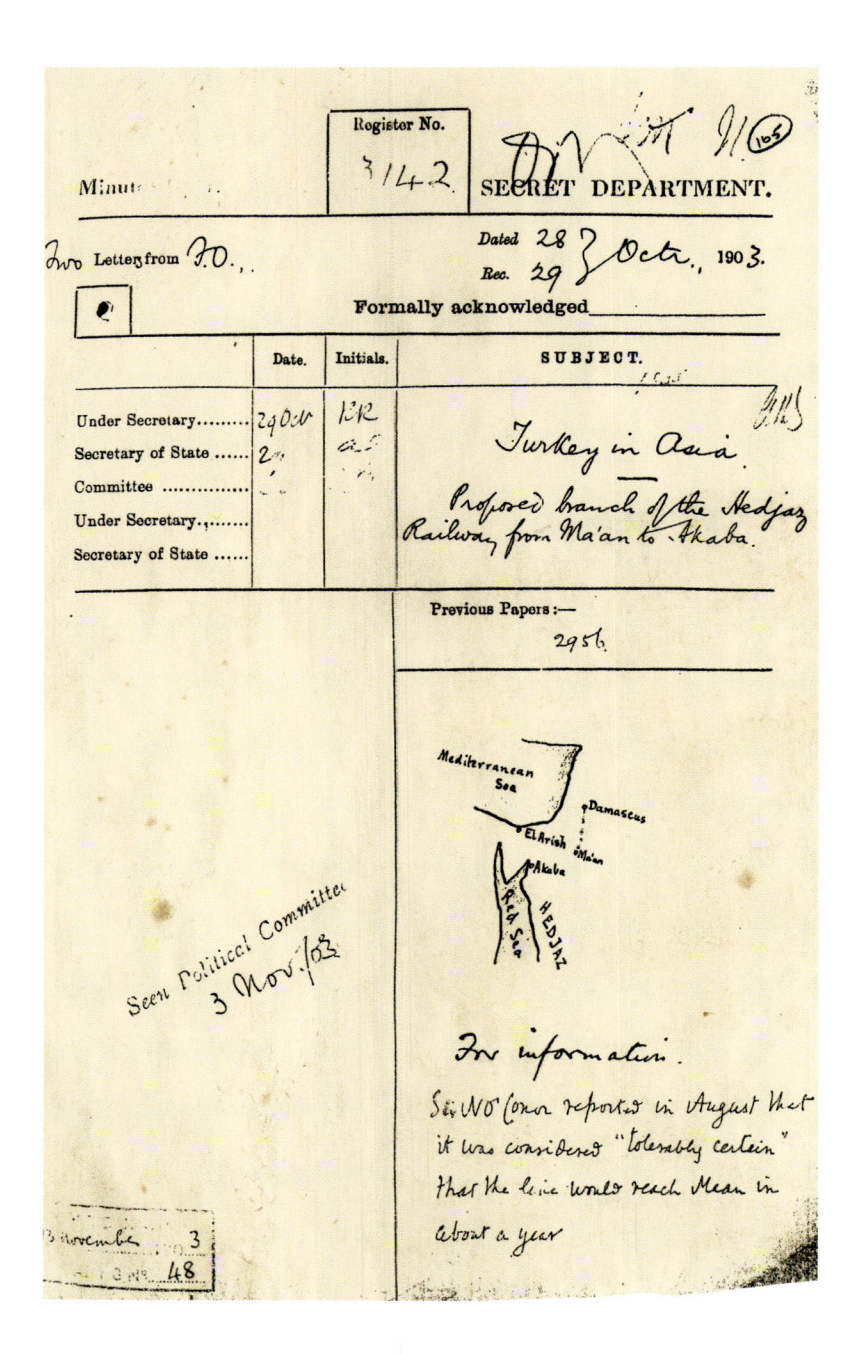

The British ambassador at Constantinople, while confirming to the Foreign Office the existence of the plan to build the Aqaba branch, rejected Hill's claim that it would take the place of the main Madinah line and downplayed its military significance. 'I am inclined to think that the supposed strategical value, both of the main line and of this branch, is a secondary consideration, and that the Sultan's real object is to mark his reign by affording his Moslem subjects greater facilities for their pilgrimage.'[3] The matter became more serious when the Ottoman surveyors realised that the harbour at Aqaba was unsuitable for heavy shipping. The subsequent attempt to move westwards along the coast into Sinai in order to find safe anchorage reopened the long-running dispute between the Turkish and (British-controlled) Egyptian governments over the exact boundary between their territories.

In February 1906, Ottoman troops moved into Taba on the Egyptian side

BUILDING THE RAILWAY - II. THE BRANCH LINES

of the previously-agreed border, and attempted to occupy Firaun Island to gain access to its deep-water anchorage. The British objected and on 2 May 1906 the ambassador in Constantinople handed the Ottoman Prime Minister a ten-day ultimatum to withdraw his forces. At the same time, the British Mediterranean fleet moved up towards Piraeus, within striking distance of the Ottoman capital. Sir Ronald Storrs in Cairo noted, 'England was trebly committed to calling this bluff. She could not yield to threats, she could not hand over the territory of an Egypt she had undertaken to protect, and she could not forget that, from the 15th century B.C., history had shown that the Power, whether from the East or West, holding the Sinai held Egypt also.'[4] Having received no support from any of the other major foreign powers, the Sultan had no option but to back down, and the ultimatum was grudgingly accepted one hour before its expiry. Without access to adequate anchorage facilities, the plan to build the Ma'an-Aqaba branch was abandoned.

Below:
In 1905, the Turks attempted to occupy Firaun Island in order to obtain a deep water anchorage for the proposed branch to Aqaba. British military intervention prevented their use of the island, and therefore the building of the branch.

61

4. Paying for the Railway

The Campaign for Donations

When the Sultan announced the decision to build the Hejaz Railway in 1900, there was considerable scepticism among Western diplomats as to whether sufficient capital funds could be raised to finance the project. Public borrowing requirements and heavy indemnities from successive disastrous wars had brought the Ottoman Empire to the verge of bankruptcy. The Sultan's declaration that the railway was going to be paid for by donations from Muslims around the world did little to convince the sceptics. Sir Maurice de Bunsen, Her Majesty's Chargé d'Affaires in Constantinople, expressed the prevailing view when he wrote: 'No competent railway

Below:
Large military blockhouses were built alongside stations to protect the railway from attack, adding to the overall construction costs. This one at Muhit Station is 12 kilometres north-west of Madinah.

authority believes that a sufficient fund can be raised by so-called voluntary subscriptions to build a railway of 1,600 kilometres.'[1] In the end, the Ottoman government did have to look for alternative sources of income, but the fact that nearly a third of the cost of such a vast public project could be met by contributions was in itself a remarkable achievement.

One of the most important effects of the campaign to collect donations was that it strengthened the religious nature of the railway. Muslims from all parts of the world were able to feel that they were participating in a great pan-Islamic enterprise. They saw their subscription as a charitable deed, aimed at helping fellow-pilgrims to reach Makkah. The railway was considered a religious endowment, held in trust by the Ottoman Sultan, but owned by the Muslim community as a whole. By contributing, the citizens of various different nations, many of them outside the Ottoman Empire, were tacitly acknowledging the Sultan's position as Caliph, the leader of all the Muslims. This suited Abdulhamid's wider aim of creating a pan-Islamic movement to strengthen his hold over his Arab territories and gain prestige and influence with the European powers.

Ottoman Donations

In 1900 the Central Committee for the Collection of Donations was established in Constantinople. Directly responsible to the Treasury, it coordinated the work of the large number of local committees, informal bodies and individuals engaged in collecting donations throughout the empire. In 1905 its work was taken over by the Administration of the Financial Affairs of the Hejaz Railway, created to control all aspects of the railway's finances. Six large volumes in the Prime Minister's Archive in Istanbul attest to the success of the donations campaign, with more than 20,000 names recorded as having subscribed to the project.

The Sultan himself started the ball rolling, pledging T.L. 50,000 to the fund. His ministers dutifully followed suit, donating sums befitting their position in the ruling hierarchy. The employees of all the various ministries also felt obliged to contribute, and the process quickly gathered momentum. Some departments organised joint collections, while others pledged a month's salary per employee. Many private companies, especially those holding contracts with the government, either gave money or payment in kind. The coal mines in Heraklia, for example, donated 458 tons of coal, which was desperately needed by the railway. In the provinces, the collections followed a similar pattern, with members of the local government making contributions according to their rank and standing. The Vali of Beirut for example, as the government's highest representative, donated T.L. 100, while the deputy governor and the treasurer gave T.L. 25 each.

The donations weren't limited to government officials: people from all walks of life contributed generously to the fund. Some of them were concerned to gain official approval, but many were genuinely inspired by the religious nature of the enterprise. Committees were set up throughout the empire's territories to publicise the campaign and coordinate the collections.

Above:
An ornate chandelier serves as a centrepiece for the beautifully wood-panelled main hall at Damascus Kanawat Station.

THE HEJAZ RAILWAY

The Hejaz Railway Medal

The Imperial Ottoman Mint produced gold, silver and cupro-nickel medals to acknowledge contributors to the Hejaz Railway fund. The different classes were awarded according to the size of the donation.

There were three separate issues. The first was brought out in 1900 at the commencement of the construction project, when the drive for donations was at its highest. In 1904 a second set of medals was produced to coincide with the inauguration of the railway as far as Ma'an. The final issue was provided in 1908 to commemorate the completion of the line to Madinah.

The medal shown has a locomotive (the commonly-used 2-6-0 configuration) within a laurel wreath. Above the locomotive is the Tughra (the decorative representation of the Sultan's name) of Abdulhamid II. The Hejira (Islamic) date 1318 corresponds to 1900.

On the reverse side, a Turkish inscription in Arabic script describes the award as 'The Hamidiah Hejaz Railway for Enthusiastic Service'. The medals were originally presented with a red or green ribbon.

Below:
Letter from the British ambassador in Constantinople informing the Foreign Office that Indian contributors to the railway fund are to be awarded medals.

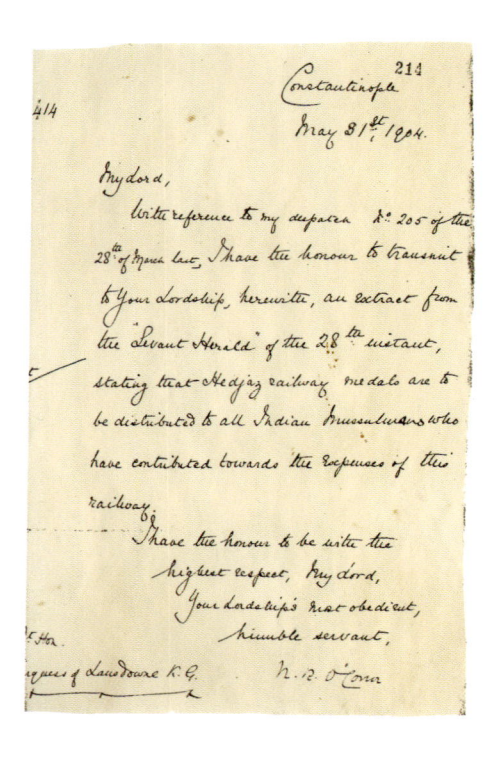

Medals and certificates were produced to provide contributors with an official recognition of their gifts. The certificates could be issued for quite small amounts, allowing even the poorest of donors to display them as symbols of their piety. At the other end of the scale, the wealthy Beirut merchants Abbud and Halbuni received individual decorations from the Sultan for their donation of T.L. 2,000, which was to be paid out in instalments on completion of the various sections of the railway.

Despite the good response to the donations campaign, it soon became apparent that the amounts collected would be insufficient to cover even part of the enormous expenditure required for the project. An imperial order was therefore issued to compel all employees in the government's service to 'donate' one month's salary to the fund. In parts of the empire, the pressure exerted on some individuals and communities amounted to open coercion. Particularly in rural areas, set contributions were imposed on whole districts or villages, and the collection was backed up by the use of local militias. In the towns and cities physical force was less common, but official and moral pressure was still exerted to persuade the citizens to 'contribute'.

Foreign Donations

In the regions outside the empire's territories, the fund had to rely wholly on voluntary donations, often collected by local mosques, and passed on through the nearest Ottoman diplomatic representative. The best source of contributions was India, which was governed by Britain and still incorporated the areas covered by the modern Islamic states of Pakistan and Bangladesh. A number of prominent Muslims including Mohammed Insha Allah, who claimed to be the instigator of the Hejaz Railway project, publicised the campaign through the press and by delivering sermons and speeches. Abd al Haq, the Imam of the Manarat Mosque in Bombay, stressed the religious nature of the railway, and appealed to the faithful to give freely, for 'to present gifts for the realisation of the Hejaz Railway is to demonstrate the love of God and his Prophet.'[2]

After India, the next most fertile area for donations was Egypt. With the support of the Khedive, Abbas II, a number of semi-official committees were set up to organise the collections. The campaign was well-publicised in the local media, and Egyptians were exhorted to subscribe to a project that was compared to the Suez Canal in its significance for the Muslim world. Some nationalist newspapers set up their own extremely successful collections, and the payments were seen as symbolising resistance to the British occupation. Donations were also received from a large number of other places, including Singapore, Sri Lanka, Burma, Iran, Bukhara, Russia, China, the Netherlands, South Africa, America and North Africa. The ruler of Kuwait, Sheikh Mubarak al Sabah, contributed T.L. 500.

Other Sources of Revenue

The campaign for donations was partially successful, but it could not meet the enormous cost of the railway's construction alone, and the Ottoman government had to look for alternative sources of revenue. As a result, a number of additional taxes were levied on an already tightly-stretched population. Every Muslim head of a family was obliged to pay a flat-rate poll tax of five piastres, which generated at least T.L. 100,000 per annum for the fund. Other administrative taxes were introduced, including stamps of different values required for a whole range of official documents and petitions. Anyone buying, selling or renting property was subject to the payment of new charges, and even the receipt of government wages was dependent on the affixing of a special Hejaz Railway stamp.

Several other methods of obtaining revenue were also introduced. The skins of animals sacrificed at Eid al Adha (the traditional feast at the end of the Pilgrimage) were sold as mementos. The fares of steamers plying the Bosphorus were increased and the additional income donated to the railway. Honorific distinctions were conferred on worthy recipients only after the payment of a special charge. In areas of the empire where foreign coins were in use, the revenue generated by the exchange of money was channelled into the construction fund. Pilgrims arriving by sea at Jeddah were compelled to pay a special landing fee, and were not allowed to proceed inland until it had been received. Several commodities, including cigarette cases, books, maps and forest products, were sold to raise money for the railway. Funds were borrowed from the Ottoman Agricultural Bank, and concessions sold along the route of the line helped to make up any shortfall. Finally, as the

Above and below:
Stamps issued in Jordan to mark the opening of the railway museum at Amman Station in 1999.

THE HEJAZ RAILWAY

Right:
Extract of letter from the British Consul in Damascus, W. Richards, to the ambassador in Constantinople, listing sources of revenue obtained for the Hejaz Railway.

> 9. The proceeds of the sale of the skins of all animals killed on the occasion of the Courban Bairam.
>
> 10. Proceeds of the sale of fancy cigarette cases made of gelatine and sold by the Tobacco Régie agents for 20 paras each, in addition to the cost of cigarettes which they contain.

construction work proceeded, increasing revenues were obtained from both passenger and freight services on the sections of track already open for business.

The Absence of Corruption

One interesting feature of the railway's finances, and the donations campaign in particular, was the almost complete absence of corruption. Following the Young Turk Revolution and the deposition of the Sultan in 1909, the new government investigated a number of allegations concerning the misuse and misappropriation of railway funds. Izzat Pasha's property was confiscated pending the results of an official audit, but he fled Constantinople and went into exile before any charges could be levelled. Although it was never followed up, questions were even asked as to whether the Sultan's pledge of T.L. 50,000 had actually been received. These and other accusations can be seen largely in the light of the new government's desire for a political witch hunt. The Young Turks had a vested interest in discrediting the old regime and Izzat Pasha, as an Arab, was an obvious target for their attacks.

Although inevitably there were a few instances of financial malpractice, the overwhelming lack of corruption was certainly remarkable, if not unique. Whether this was due to the religious nature of the enterprise, or the personal involvement of the Sultan and some of his high-ranking ministers, it undoubtedly illustrates the high public regard in which the project was held. Even Lt Col. Maunsell, Military Attaché at Constantinople, and no admirer of the Ottoman administration, was able to report: 'A curious point in connection with this railway construction is the absence of any peculation among the higher officials of the Commission; all the money collected or subscribed appears to be devoted to its proper purpose, and the members apparently look on the construction as an important religious duty.'[3]

Below:
This clock used on the Hejaz Railway is now an exhibit in the museum at Damascus Qadem Station.

Overall Income and Expenditure

The proportion of the railway's total income derived from donations declined during the years of construction between 1900 and 1908. The accounts for 1903 show revenues of T.L. 651,184 received from contributions, making up about 63 per cent of the total income of T.L. 1,033,465. In 1904 the proportion of income from donations dropped to 56 per cent, in 1905 to 36 per cent, in 1906 to 35 per cent, in 1907 to 32 per cent and in 1908 to 28 per cent. The total cost of construction, including all the branch lines built up to 1912, was T.L. 3.25 million. With the expenditure on rolling stock, this figure rises to just over T.L. 4.25 million, averaging out at almost T.L. 3,000 per kilometre.

Although the donations, both voluntary and forced, made up only about a third of the total income of the railway, they played a vital role in reinforcing its religious character. By contributing to the project, Muslims from all around the world were able to feel that they were taking part in a great philanthropic work on behalf of the Islamic community. The fact that their donations were made to the Ottoman government helped to endorse the Sultan in his position as Caliph and strengthen the Pan-Islamic movement Abdulhamid was so eager to establish. As Ochsenwald has written: 'All of the emotions and attachments associated with Pan-Islam became attached to the Hijaz Railroad. It was the only embodiment of the movement.'[4]

Overleaf:
Windmill water pump silhouetted against the evening sky.

Below:
Hartmann 2-8-0 (No. 37 – later No. 90). Constructed in 1907, this is the same model of locomotive as the one currently standing derelict at Buwair Station, 90 kilometres north of Madinah.

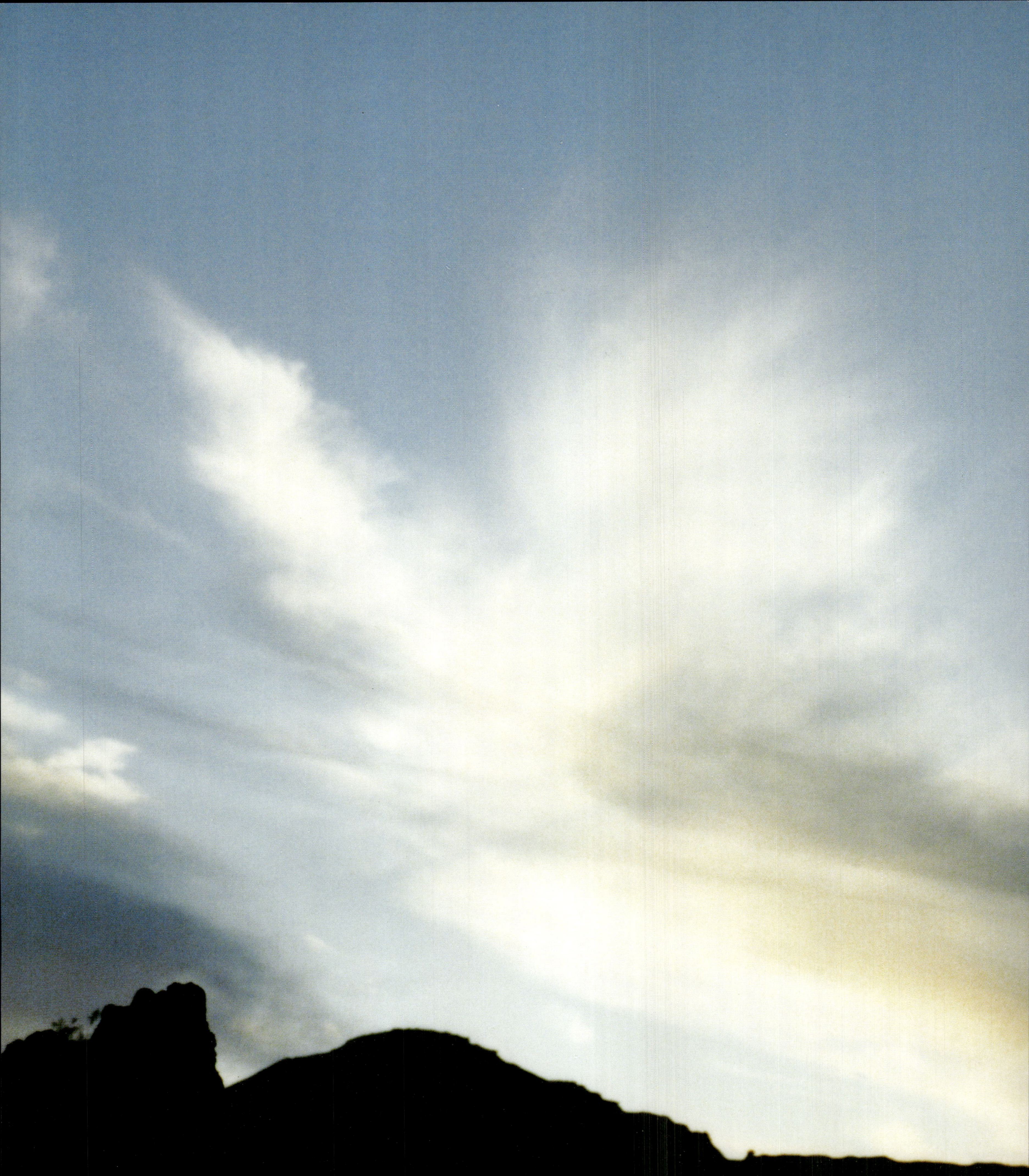

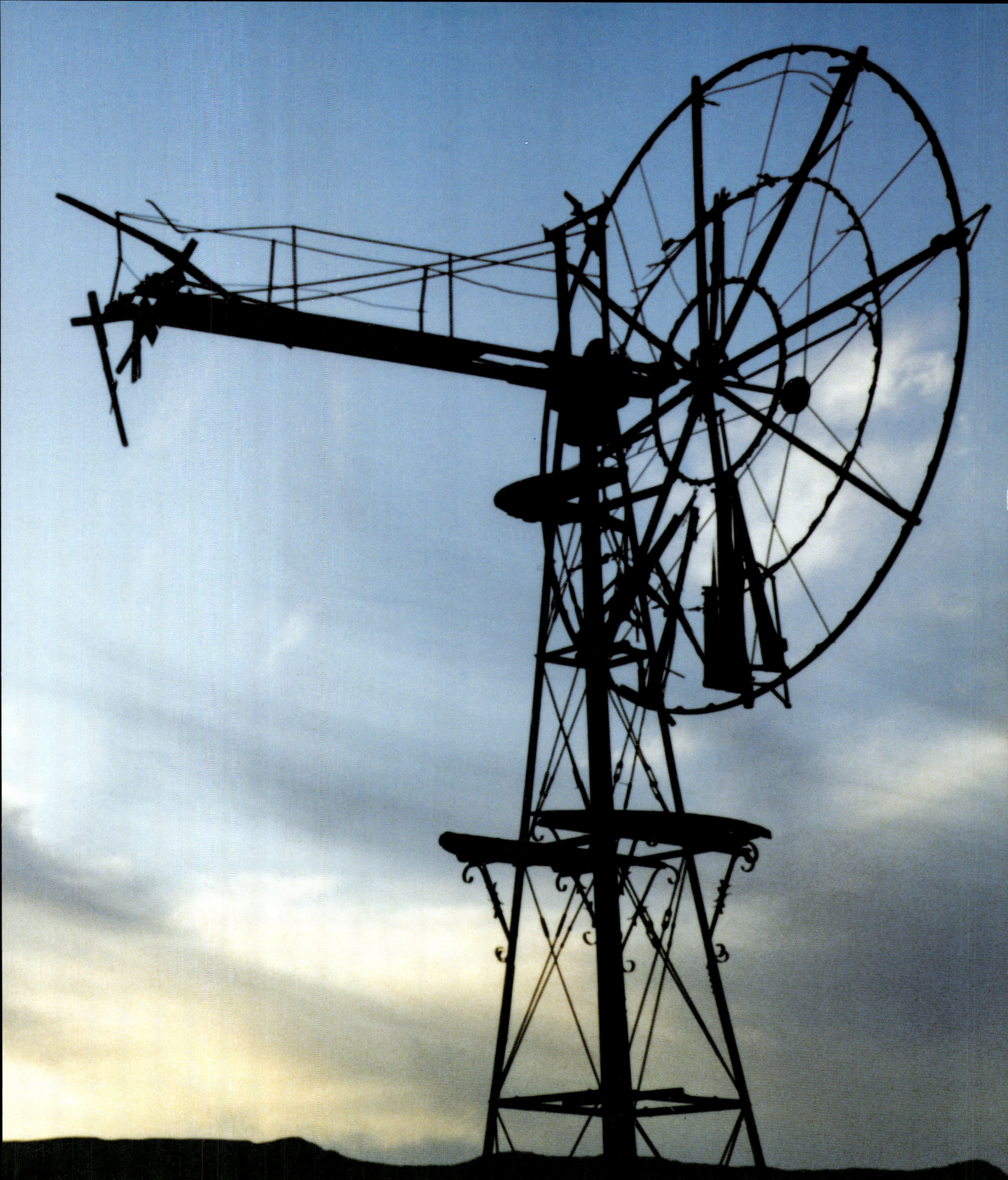

5. Running the Railway

Sherif Hussein and the Young Turks

Below:
Appointed as the Amir of Makkah in 1908, Sherif Hussein ibn Ali was strongly opposed to the extension of the railway from Madinah to Makkah. During the First World War, aware of the Young Turks' intention to depose him, he threw his hand in with the British and proclaimed the Arab Revolt in June 1916.

Between 1908 and the outbreak of the First World War in 1914, railway operations were carried out against a background of increasing hostility between the local Arabs and their Ottoman overlords. In 1908 Kazim Pasha, the Chief of Construction, was decorated with the Ottoman Order of Merit, and promoted to the position of Vali of the Hejaz and commander of the provincial armed forces. He had been brought in to implement the reform programme of the Young Turks, and was also determined to carry out their policy of extending the railway to Makkah. Unfortunately, his appointment coincided with the arrival of a new Sherif of Makkah, Hussein ibn Ali, who was vehemently opposed to both these measures.

Sherif Hussein knew that the Young Turks were planning to bring the Hejaz under complete Ottoman control at the first possible opportunity, and he realised that the extension of the railway to his power base in Makkah would enable them to achieve this. He therefore immediately set about undermining the authority of the Vali and encouraging the local tribes to make the running of the railway as difficult as possible. Abdulhamid II's final deposition and exile in 1909 considerably weakened Hussein's position, depriving him of the support of an autocratic leader who had a vested interest in preserving allegiance to traditional forms of rule. Although a new sultan, Mohammed Rashid V, was chosen by the Young Turks to replace him, he was 64 years old at the time of his accession, 'and a gentler, more self-effacing and ineffectual old man was never girded with the sword of Othman.'[1]

The increasingly powerful Young Turks, with their ideas of constitutional government and equality under the law, were viewed by Hussein as little better than heretics. Their policy of Pan Turanianism (Turkish nationalism), and the crushing of Arab hopes of self-rule, quickly created an opposition movement with a number of secret nationalist societies throughout the Arab provinces. At the same time, British concerns were growing over the increasingly close relationship between the Young Turks and Germany, causing them to reassess their traditional policy of safeguarding the Ottoman Empire. For the first time, possible alternatives to Turkish rule over the Arab

RUNNING THE RAILWAY

territories were being considered. It was becoming increasingly clear that open confrontation with the new order in Constantinople was inevitable. This was to have important consequences, both for the region and for the railway during the First World War.

Security Measures

Sherif Hussein had no difficulty in inciting the tribes of the Hejaz to sabotage the railway. As well as the wider political implications of increased Turkish control, such as taxation and conscription, the bedouin considered the railway a direct threat to their livelihood. When the first train arrived from Damascus and they saw it disgorging hundreds of men and tons of baggage, they began to realise that something new had come into their very conservative country and to resent it.'[2] With the camel trade essential to their economic survival the tribes needed little encouragement from Hussein to begin raiding the stations and disrupting operations on the line.

The fighting of 1908, which had started as the railway approached Madinah, continued after the official opening of the line. Attacks were commonplace; in January 1909 services to the north of the city were severely disrupted for almost a month. To counter the threat from the bedouin, additional measures were taken to bolster the railway's defences. South of Medain Saleh, the stations were fortified with trenches and barbed wire. Closer to Madinah, A.J. Wavell, the first European to make the complete through journey in 1908, noticed that, 'the stations were now protected by considerable earthworks and had garrisons of a company or more.'[3] In addition, the traditional subsidies given to the tribes for protecting the roads and pilgrimage caravans were quickly reintroduced as grants for guarding the railway. To finance these payments, a special surcharge was imposed on travel between Medain Saleh and Madinah. In 1911 the charge was extended to any journey south of Deraa.

Above:
Ticket machine with first class ticket from Deraa to Amman.

Passenger Services

Passenger operations accounted for about half the total revenue generated by the Hejaz Railway. Most people travelled third class, with only about five per cent of passengers able to afford first class. In the early years before 1913, there were no second class compartments available. Although the railway was justifiably famous for the service to Madinah, there was actually a greater amount of passenger traffic on the more heavily populated Haifa-Damascus line. A daily service was operated on this route, which took about 12 hours. Passengers requiring connections to the south would change at Deraa. In 1908 a third-class ticket from Damascus (or Haifa) to Madinah cost T.L. 3.10, about the same as the slower journey by ship from Beirut. The train from Damascus to Madinah ran three times a week and was scheduled to take two and a half days. In practice however, the official times were rarely achieved, with the journey generally taking three or four days. There was

Below:
Tickets for express train. The period of validity is fifteen days.

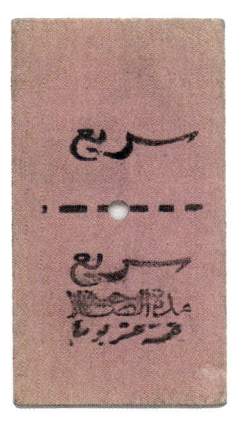

71

THE HEJAZ RAILWAY

little sense of urgency to run services according to the published timetable. Replacement drivers would sometimes fail to turn up, and passengers would be left waiting at a station while the original driver rested. Mark Sykes, travelling along the track north of Ma'an by camel in 1909 '…. met a train from Damascus, which stopped for a chat, the engine driver salaaming just as he would have done had he been riding a donkey.'[4]

Conditions in third class were extremely basic. Wavell complained that his carriage 'consisted of plain wooden benches with a passage down the middle. These were in pairs facing one another with just room for two to sit on… There was no room for anything, and we were jammed up together with our belongings, in a most uncomfortable way.'[5] During the pilgrimage, when services were at full stretch, many of the passengers made the journey on open flat-bed trucks. This left them exposed to the dust and the elements. However, if space permitted, they were allowed to erect their tents. In 1913, some of the first- and new second-class carriages were equipped with proper sleeping facilities. A mosque carriage, complete with its own miniature minaret, was also available for services to the Hejaz.

The lack of experience of the maintenance staff resulted in excessive wear and tear and the premature ageing of the rolling stock. Lt Col. Maunsell reported that the third-class coaches were in an extremely neglected state. There were hardly any windows in the carriages, and in bad weather rain would pour through the empty holes, as well as from the roof. However, as Maunsell discovered, the railway staff could occasionally be persuaded to undertake temporary repairs: 'For my journey a friendly engineer went round and unscrewed any windows he could find in other carriages, and by this means a sheltered corner at one end of the carriage was obtained.'[6]

In addition to the discomfort, passengers also had to contend with the danger of attack from the tribes along the railway. Before boarding his train at Damascus, Wavell was given the rather disconcerting advice that 'If you are attacked in the train… by overwhelming numbers, do not try to fight, give up your things quietly, and no harm will befall you.'[7] When he arrived in Madinah, the sound of gunfire could be heard from the other side of the city, and he learned that the station itself had been attacked earlier on the same day.

Another early passenger on the railway, who was later to play a major role in its wartime destruction, was a young archaeologist named T.E. Lawrence. In 1911 he travelled from Haifa to Damascus with his Oxford mentor and subsequent Arab Bureau Intelligence chief, David Hogarth. As the train twisted its way over the great bridges of the Yarmuk Valley, he admired the splendid views, little knowing that just seven years later he would return on camel to try to destroy one of them. At Deraa, where they changed trains, 'all was sunny, and we had a French déjeuner in the Buffet.'[8] His experience on the main Hejaz line in February 1914 was not so agreeable. Returning from a pre-war expedition under Capt. S. Newcombe (who would also play an important part in the war on the railway) to carry out a military survey in northern Sinai, he found himself stranded at Ma'an. The train from Madinah was delayed and he wrote home: 'The Turks on the Hedjaz line, thinking their own genius sufficient unto the working thereof, sacked all their foreign

Below:
Name plate on rolling stock at Medain Saleh Station. The Arabic word simply says 'Hejaz'.

Above:
Pilgrims on the long journey south would sometimes stop to pray by the side of the line.

mechanics: and now at times engines are scrapped, at times they blow themselves up, and at times they come in punctual. Mine was of the class that come late: it was 13 hrs. behind time on a 28 hrs. journey: and I got very sick of waiting for her.

Pilgrims

One of Sultan Abdulhamid II's primary objectives in building the Hejaz Railway had been to provide pilgrims from Syria with a cheaper and easier way to undertake the long journey to the holy cities, and in the years before the war, the number of pilgrims travelling to Madinah by train was more than double that of the old caravan route. Thousands of pilgrims from Turkey, Russia, Central Asia, North Africa, Persia and Mesopotamia converged on Damascus to take advantage of the new line. In 1909 quarantine facilities for the railway were established at Tabuk. The centre was capable of processing up to 4,000 pilgrims at a time, and was financed by a special tax on tickets. After some dispute, the British in Egypt accepted the measures taken as adequate. The relative convenience and cheapness of the quarantine station in Tabuk, compared to the British facility at Tur in Sinai, contributed to making the railway a more attractive proposition than the sea route.

The large number of pilgrims using the railway during the Haj season put services under considerable strain. The carriages were even more cramped

THE HEJAZ RAILWAY

Above:
Pilgrims waiting by the track at Madinah Station. The Suqia Mosque is on the right of the picture, and to the far left some pillars of the main station building are just visible. The station master's residence is in the middle (with unfinished pitched roof), and to its left are the toilet facilities.

Opposite:
Hajjis, with samovar for tea, making the pilgrimage to Makkah on the new Hejaz Railway.

than usual, and long delays were frequent. In 1912, 4,000 pilgrims decided to take the sea route from Yanbu, after waiting in vain at Madinah to find room on the packed trains. The conditions on the railway were extremely hard, and Sykes, witnessing a medical inspection of pilgrims at Deraa Station, wrote that they 'were bundled out on to the sloping embankment - a full thousand of them - and were beaten, cuffed and kicked in the process. They were helpless, piteous, hungry, and cold; for three nights had they been in open trucks, exposed to rain and frost.'[10] However, despite these privations, the railway still represented a vast improvement on the old 40-day overland journey.

Troop Movements

The building of the Hejaz Railway was intended to facilitate troop movements to the more remote areas of the Ottoman Empire in times of crisis. During its construction, it was used to transport soldiers at least part of the way south to suppress rebellions in the Hejaz (1904) and Yemen (1905-06). In 1909, 8,480 out of 119,033 passengers on the railway were military. In 1910 this figure jumped to 77,661, owing primarily to revolts in the Hauran and Kerak regions. The uprising by the Druze in the Hauran was

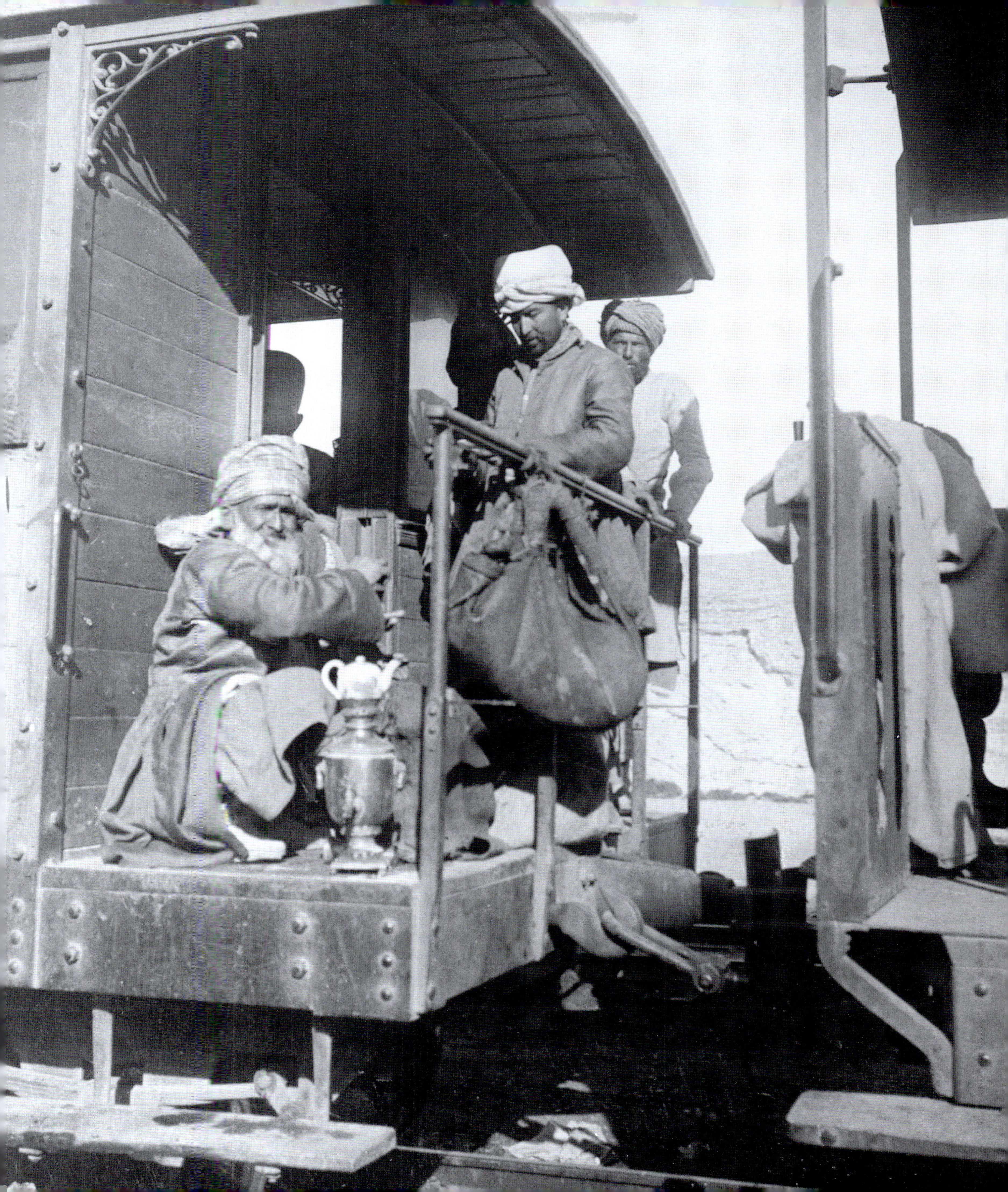

THE HEJAZ RAILWAY

Right:
Map 8 – Early Ottoman map of the railway showing the intended route to Makkah.

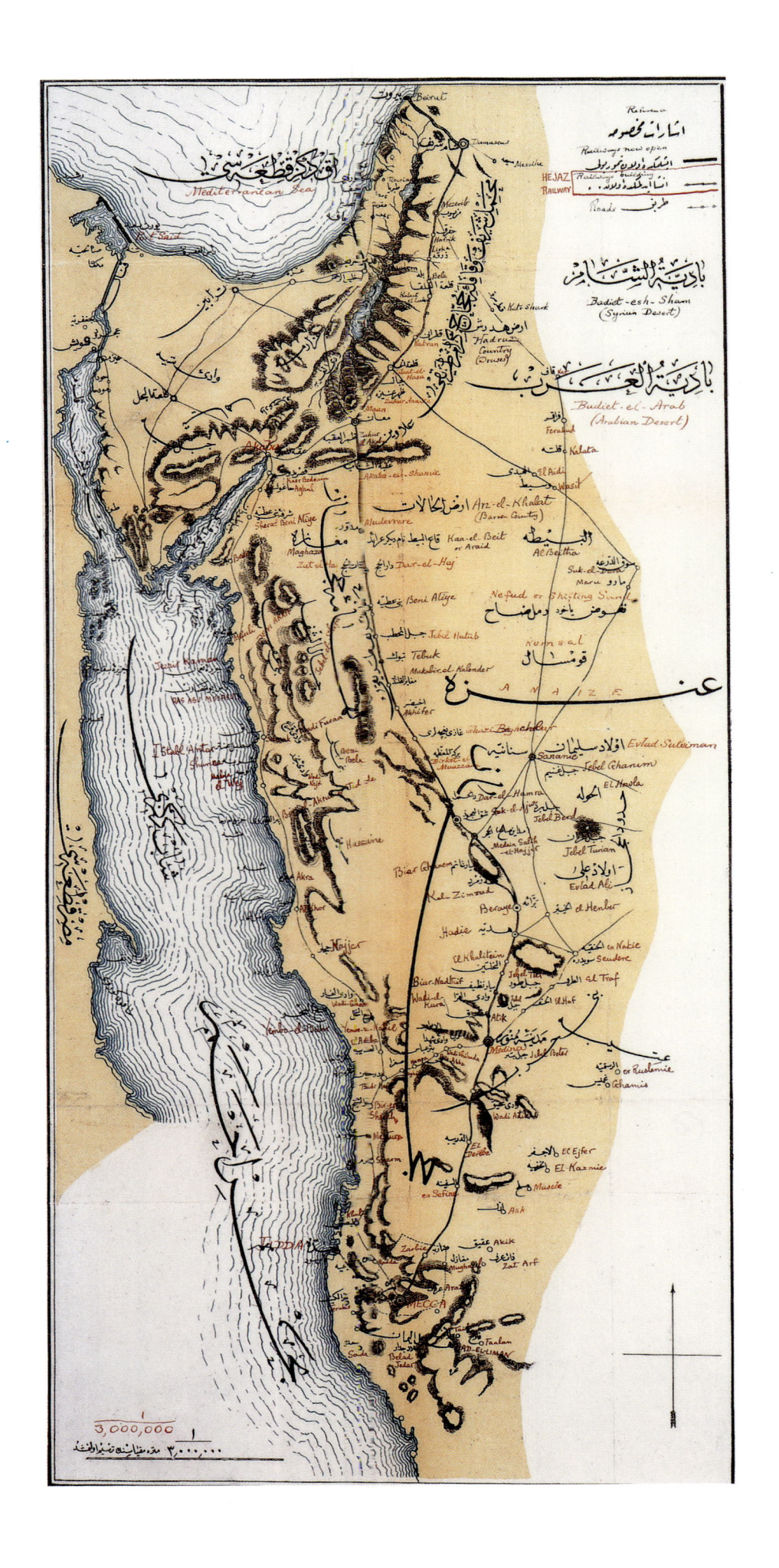

successfully put down by 31 Ottoman battalions, which had been rapidly brought in and well provisioned by the railway.

Following completion of the line, the Young Turks attempted to impose stronger central control over the area around the town of Kerak, 15 kilometres west of Qatrana Station. In 1910 the threat of land registration, conscription and the confiscation of arms provoked the previously autonomous Kerakis to revolt. They were quickly joined by the principal tribes of the region, the Beni Sakhr and the Beni Atiyya. Angered by the failure of the Turks to pay their subsidy to protect the line, the Beni Sakhr ambushed a train, killing a number of railway employees. Qatrana Station was also attacked, more workers were murdered and considerable damage was caused to the station, rolling stock and track. The Beni Atiyya carried out similar raids on the railway around Ma'an, but once repairs had been made to the line, the military quickly transported in large numbers of troops from Damascus and brutally suppressed the uprising.

Above:
Hartmann 2-8-0 at Buwair Station, with its tender and wagons.

Freight

Freight operations provided the railway with an important source of revenue. In 1910 the movement of goods generated T.L. 62,224, compared with T.L. 139,802 received from passenger (excluding military) services. Following the appointment of Peter Dieckmann as Director of the Hejaz Railway in 1910, the freight side of the business was accorded greater priority. From 1912 a new set of fees, including special rebates and incentives for shippers, enabled the railway to offer cheaper rates than those of the French D.H.P. Damascus to Beirut line. Within four years, the volume of freight being transported almost doubled, from 65,757 tons in 1910 to 112,007 tons in 1913.

The main commodity transported on the Hejaz Railway was grain. In 1912 it constituted over half the freight carried on the line: 52,320 tons out of total of 91,626 tons. The thriving Hauran wheat trade was primarily responsible for the large quantities of grain being transported, much of it for export via Haifa. There was also a significant amount of wheat sent to the Hejaz, both to feed the cities, and to provide subsidies to deter the bedouin tribes from attacking the railway. The next most important individual item was flour. The volume of fruit and vegetables increased rapidly from 3,186 tons in 1910 to 11,357 tons in 1914, reflecting the growing confidence of the shippers in the railway's ability to transport fresh produce. Other significant items were wood, salt, rice, petrol, coal, metal, liquorice, sacking and tobacco. Items brought in to the Hejaz included flour, wood, petrol, coffee, sugar, rice and carpets, and in return, the Hejaz exported dates, dairy products and sheepskins.

Rolling Stock

By 1918 a total of 129 locomotives had been acquired for use on the Hejaz Railway. The majority of these were supplied by Germany. Major

THE HEJAZ RAILWAY

Above:
Details of wheels on Jung 2-6-0. The numerical specification of locomotives refers to their wheels. A 2-6-0 would therefore have 2 leading wheels, 6 coupled driving wheels and no trailing wheels.

contributors were Hartmann with forty-one (seven 2-6-0s; twenty-two 2-8-0s; twelve 2-8-2s), Krauss with twenty (twelve 0-6-0Ts; eight 2-8-0s) and Jung with nineteen (seven 2-6-0s; twelve 2-8-0s). The other suppliers were Henschel with ten (four 2-4-6-0s; six 0-6-6-0Ts), La Meuse with ten (one 0-4-0T; three 0-6-0Ts; three 2-6-2Ts; three 0-10-0Ts), S.L.M. (Swiss Locomotive and Machine Works) with ten 2-8-0s, Hohenzollern with eight 0-6-0Ts, Borsig with five 2-8-0s, Hanomag with four 2-8-0s and St Leonard with two 0-6-0Ts.

On 25 August 1918 the coaching stock comprised 116 coaches and 35 baggage vans. Seventy six of the coaches were third-class, with only two being allocated purely for first-class and four for second-class. The others were either mixed first-class and second-class (13), or mixed second-class and third-class (16). There was also a mosque car, a saloon and three service cars. Some of the baggage wagons were used by the military, or as kitchen vans, hospital wagons and accounting offices. The freight side of the business had 1,034 wagons at its disposal, including six animal wagons, 404 vans, 562 open wagons, 61 tank wagons and a steam crane. By 25 August 1918 as many as 350 of these had either been captured or damaged by the Allies, or put out of service due to general wear and tear.

78

Maintenance

Major repair facilities were established in Damascus (Qadem), Deraa, Ma'an, Tabuk, Medain Saleh, Madinah and Haifa. The overall works manager was based in Damascus, where the largest repair yards were located. The Qadem facility had workshops covering an area of over 40,000 sq. metres, and was able to carry out major repair work to locomotives and coaching stock. A 50-ton traverser for locomotives was driven by electricity from Damascus' new power station at Ain al Fije. Most of the equipment in the workshops had been imported from the Belgian firm, Baume et Marpent.

In the Hejaz, the general upkeep and maintenance of the line was left largely to the military garrisons of the stations. The extra security measures taken in 1909 helped to reduce the incidence of attack on the railway. However, many of the tribesmen - especially those not benefitting from the special Turkish subsidies - still considered it fair game. The Austrian explorer, Alois Musil, travelling through the Hejaz in 1910, reported that despite being heavily fortified the stations continued to be subjected to bedouin raids and even sieges. The soldiers 'go to their work in gangs of 20 to 50 men, all carrying guns, place sentries in the most commanding positions, and hurry back to the station on the trolley as soon as the Bedouins are sighted from the look-outs. No Bedouin may come within range of the station without permission. Yet the soldiers are often outwitted, plundered and even massacred.'[11]

The harsh conditions and the lack of experience of the engineering staff in the early years of operations had a detrimental effect on the condition of the rolling stock. 'The continual wind on the highlands soon causes the machinery to be clogged with dust and sand.'[12] Without the regular cleaning the tubes required, the engines quickly became defective. Mark Sykes noticed 13 locomotives out of service at Ma'an Station in 1909. He was particularly scathing in his criticism of the permanent staff of the railway, calling them 'a loathsome crew.' He continued, 'Alas! When the East takes to the mechanical arts it grows far fouler than the West… And I cannot weep or wonder at the fact that the Bedawin pull up the rails and wreck the trains by instinct.'[13]

Left:
Tanks mounted on flat-bed trucks were used to transport water from areas with natural supplies to the isolated garrisons of the Hejaz.

THE HEJAZ RAILWAY

Administration and Personnel

Between 1903 and 1919, overall control of the railway was held by several different government departments: 1903-1909 Ministry of Commerce and Public Works; 1909-1912 Prime Minister's Office; 1912 Ministry of War; 1912-1914 Prime Minister's Office; 1914-1916 Ministry of Awqaf (Religious Foundations); 1916-1919 Ministry of War. These moves reflected both the shifting priorities of the government and the particular significance that the railway held for the Ottoman leadership at various times. However, as well as depriving it of continuity of management, the changes resulted in the line being administered by officials who had little or no experience in the transport field.

The day-to-day running of the railway was left largely in the hands of the local officials in Damascus. Following the fall from power of Abdulhamid II and Izzat Pasha, the role of the Central Commission was reduced. In 1914 it accounted for only 2.7 per cent of total administrative expenditure. Although the general management of the line was based in Damascus, the responsibility for various operational areas was delegated to other stations. Traffic was directed from the important junction town of Deraa, while freight

Below:
Railway workers revolving a Nippon 4-6-2 (No. 82) on the turntable at Amman Station in 1979.

operations were run from Haifa. Between 1910 and 1917 the post of director-general was held by two Germans; Zehringer for the first two years and Peter Dieckmann from 1912. A Frenchman, Paul Gaudin, was appointed as commercial director in 1905. He was replaced three years later by a Turk, Mokhtar Bey, the original surveyor of the railway and Meissner's assistant during its construction.

In the early years of the railway, the top and middle-level management posts were almost exclusively filled by Europeans, the majority of them German. The lower ranks, on the other hand, were nearly all Ottoman. Despite attempts to replace the European staff with local personnel, the only area in which the latter were guaranteed employment was south of Medain Saleh, where Christians were prohibited from working. In 1913, 3,799 workers were employed by the railway. Of these, 685 received annual salaries, 460 were paid on a monthly basis and 2,654 were labourers, taken on by the day. The majority of the staff on annual salaries (477) were employed in the Traffic Department. General and Operations Administration accounted for 121, while 48 were engaged in overseeing further construction and maintenance. For the day labourers, building and repair work was the main area of employment, and around 65 per cent of their number were engaged in this sector.

Economic Development

The bedouin trade in camels may have been threatened by the coming of the railway, but there were economic advantages for the settled population of the region. Haifa became an important centre of trade, benefitting from its connections to Damascus and the Hauran. Although the section of line between Haifa and Damascus represented less than a fifth of the total network, it accounted for more than three-quarters of the overall passenger and freight traffic. This included a small but lucrative tourist trade, with the majority of the railway's first-class travel originating in Haifa. As a result of the increase in economic activity, the town underwent rapid expansion. A large number of Arab labourers from Palestine, Syria and Egypt were attracted to Um al Amal ('the Mother of Work'), the area at the eastern end of the town where the repair yards were located. A sizeable German community was established and new schools, banks, post offices and other facilities were opened to support it.

Ma an, 'the Gateway to Arabia', also experienced a development boom as a result of the railway. Following an increase in population, the town was provided with a proper water supply and a hospital. A hotel, 'a substantial building'[14], was built to serve tourists visiting the Nabataean site of Petra nearby, and passengers breaking their journey on their way to the Hejaz. Further south, Tabuk was undergoing an even more dramatic period of growth. In 1884, an attack by the powerful Rashidi tribe from Hail, and subsequent raids by the Beni Atiyya, had forced most of the settled population to abandon the village. When the construction parties arrived in 1906, they found only seven out of the 60 houses inhabited. The coming of

Above top:
Metal wagon (K 1093) standing at Damascus Qadem Station.

Above below:
Wooden wagon with sliding door, out of service at Damascus Qadem Station.

THE HEJAZ RAILWAY

Right:
The building of a hospital at Tabuk in 1907 led to the establishment of the railway's quarantine centre in the town.

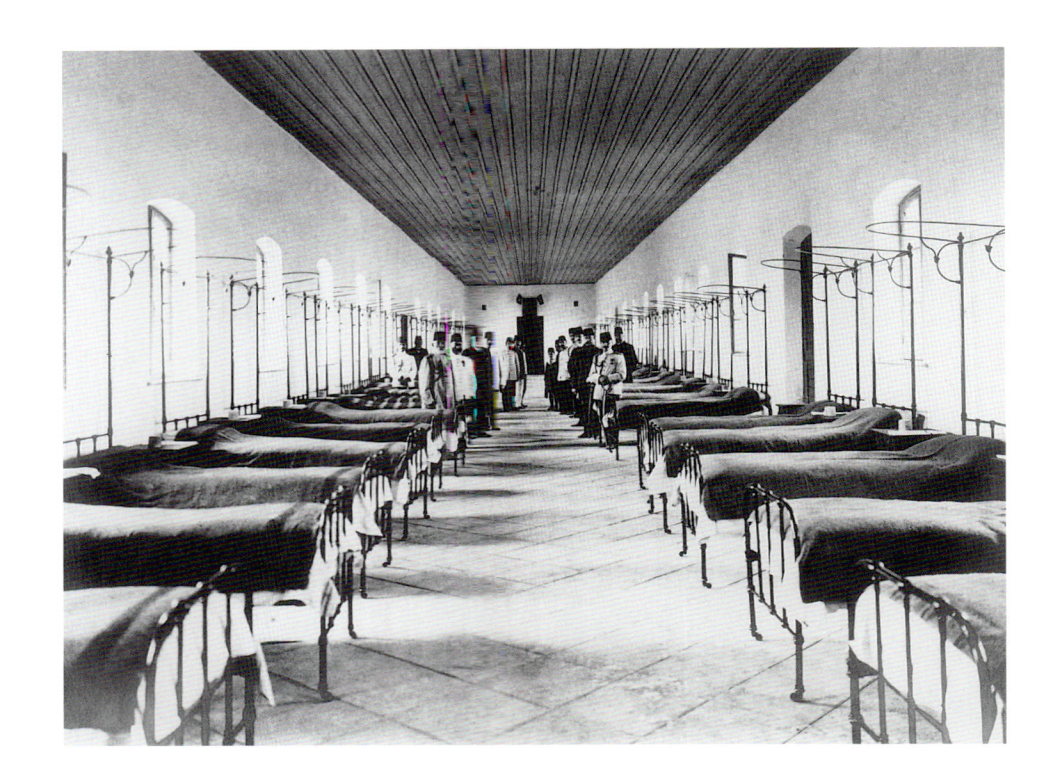

the railway however, brought greater security, and with the return of the villagers, the area began to develop rapidly. The station depot included a repair shop, stores, a guard-house, dwellings for the workers, over a kilometre of sidings, a water tower (equipped with both a steam and wind-driven pump) and engine sheds. A well, 22 metres deep, could provide 90,000 gallons of water a day. As the depot expanded, three new wells were dug in the area to ensure an adequate supply of water.

A large hospital was built 1.5 kilometres south of the station in 1907. It was constructed around one long, well-ventilated room and contained 50 beds. There was also a smaller, separate building with ten beds for patients with contagious diseases. The hospital provided the medical facilities necessary for the subsequent opening of the railway's quarantine centre. Agriculture and trade were also revived and a new market place was established near the local fort. Kazim Pasha, the Chief of Construction, had a mosque and a small school built at his own expense, on ground where the Prophet was said to have prayed during his expedition to the town in 630. The growing prosperity even persuaded the chief of the Beni Atiyya tribe, Sheikh Harb ibn Mohammed to build a house close to the garrison post, 'thus giving a guarantee of future good conduct which the Turks are delighted to have obtained.'[15]

The economic success of the railway, and in particular the development of Haifa as a competitor to Beirut as the leading regional trading centre, represented a threat to the French-owned D.H.P. operations in Syria. The D.H.P.'s Damascus to Beirut line had to traverse two mountain ranges and was hampered by steep gradients and snowfalls in winter. This gave the Hejaz Haifa-Deraa branch a clear advantage. It was able to offer cheaper rates for freight transport, and quickly took over much of the D.H.P.'s grain exporting business. The section between Deraa and Damascus on the main Hejaz line, being built parallel to the D.H.P's Muzeirib to Damascus branch, also deprived the French company of valuable revenue. However, while the religious aspect of the Hejaz Railway encouraged many Muslim travellers to use it in preference to the French D.H.P. line, this was partially offset by the poor condition of the rolling stock on the Hejaz line, which actually led some passengers to 'leave at Deraa, cross over to Mezerib, and continue their way to Damascus by the French line'.[16] Although compensation of T.L.150,000 was provided by the Ottomans in 1905, fears of further losses of the market share prompted the D.H.P. to try and gain control of the Hejaz system.

Ottoman military reverses in North Africa and the Balkans provided the French with the opportunity they needed to attempt the takeover. Close to bankruptcy, and with Constantinople under direct threat of invasion from the Balkans, the Ottomans were willing to accept any terms in order to raise funds on the Paris Bourse. An agreement in September 1913 imposed a French director on the Hejaz Railway for a period of ten years. In addition, its rates were regulated so as to undermine its economic advantage over the D.H.P. This agreement was never ratified. While the French prepared new terms ensuring them even greater control, the Ottoman government was inundated with objections, both from its own citizens and from Muslims outside the Empire. Concerns that the French proposals would include a demand for a concession to run the Hejaz Railway resulted in it quickly being registered as a religious trust foundation (waqf) under the Ministry of Awqaf. As a religious institution, it could not be taken over by non-Muslims, and the new agreement of April 1914 therefore stopped short of granting the French a concession. In practice, its operations were placed under effective D.H.P. control, but a final development was to deprive the French of their objective. With the outbreak of war, the agreement was never implemented, and

Below:
Sherif Hussein (with the white beard) riding in state, with a cortège of city notables and a bodyguard of slaves.

Above:
Twin water tank at Muazzam Station.

ironically, the reverse took place. In November 1914 the D.H.P. lines were seized as enemy property, and their administration was handed over to the Hejaz Railway.

The Hejaz Railway on the Eve of the First World War

As the Young Turks tightened their grip on the Arab provinces, opposition to their rule steadily increased. A number of societies, both public and secret, were set up in Damascus and Beirut to promote Arab unity and campaign for a degree of local autonomy. In 1913 however, the Young Turks introduced the new Law of Vilayets, extending Turkish bureaucratic reforms into the provinces and strengthening the power of the regional governors. In order to ensure the effective implementation of the reforms in the Hejaz, a new Vali named Vehib Bey was appointed, and given the backing of seven extra battalions of infantry and one of artillery. In addition to imposing the Law of Vilayets, the aggressive Vehib Bey was charged with extending the Hejaz Railway from Madinah to Makkah.

His appointment was not welcomed in the Hejaz. Encouraged by Sherif Hussein, the local population held public meetings of protest. Even Vehib Bey was unprepared for the ferocity of the opposition. In the country around Makkah and Madinah the bedouin took control of the roads, cutting off all communications between the two cities. Trade was stifled and the routes between the coast and the interior were blocked. The prospect of famine loomed. The military outposts on the road between Jeddah and Makkah were besieged and the Vali's Commander of the Gendarmerie, Said Bey, was taken prisoner by tribal forces. In the main cities, the streets were full of protestors demonstrating against the Turkish proposals. Hussein informed the Vali that he would have to leave the province, as he could no longer be responsible for the actions of his people. The Turks were powerless to defeat the bedouin on their own terrain, and the matter finally had to be resolved diplomatically. A cable from the Turkish Prime Minister was read out in the Grand Mosque, stating that the special rights of the Hejaz would be maintained and that the extension of the railway to Makkah would not be pursued.

Having failed to achieve the extension by force, the Young Turk leadership now turned to power diplomacy to accomplish its aims. The Sherif's second son, Prince Abdullah, was invited to Constantinople and was issued an ultimatum by the Minister of the Interior Talaat Pasha. 'We do not care, Amir Abdullah, if we have to change the Vali every month, but we are determined about the construction of the railway from Madinah to Makkah, from Jedda to Makkah and from Yanbu to Madinah. If your father will see that this is done we will support him, but if he refuses he will have to go.'[17] Talaat then presented the conditions of the deal. As long as Hussein was prepared to support the extension of the railway, he would receive a third of the revenues generated, a quarter of a million pounds to distribute among the tribes in compensation, control over the forces involved in the construction and guaranteed hereditary succession for his family.

On his return to the Hejaz, Prince Abdullah conveyed the Turkish government's proposal to his father. Hussein was not impressed, commenting, 'This is bribery. Man indeed looks at others through his own eyes.'[18] The Amir was in no position to deliver a blank refusal to the powerful Turks, and sent back a vague, non-committal telegram, assuring them that Abdullah would be returned to the capital at the first opportunity to discuss how the planned extension could be carried out 'without prejudice to the livelihood of the tribes and the inhabitants of the Muslim Holy Land.'[19] He then dispatched his son on a minor military expedition into the heart of Arabia. By the time the young prince finally arrived back in Constantinople on 29th June 1914, Hussein's delaying tactics had paid off, for just a day earlier the Archduke Franz Ferdinand had been assassinated in Sarajevo, providing the spark that would ignite the Balkan tinder-box and start the First World War. At a meeting with the Minister of War, Enver Pasha, it was confirmed to Abdullah that the scheme to extend the railway had been shelved.

Below:
Ceremony held on the open ground between Madinah Station and Al Anbaria Mosque.

6. Outbreak of the First World War

The Ottoman Empire Enters the War

When the European nations plunged into the First World War, it was by no means inevitable that the Ottoman Empire would enter on the side of the Central Powers. As late as November 1913, the appointment of a German general named Liman von Sanders as commander of the First Army in Constantinople had been balanced by the choice of a British mission under Rear Admiral Sir Arthur Limpus to reorganise the Ottoman navy. Cabinet opinion over Turkey's best interests at the start of the war was divided, and it was not until November 1914 that the strongly pro-German Minister of War, Enver Pasha, engineered the empire's entry as allies of the Central Powers. The Germans, with their own expansionist designs in the Balkans, persuaded the Turks to advance eastwards against the Russians in the Caucasus and southwards against the British in Egypt.

The war started disastrously for the Ottomans, with heavy defeats against Russia in north-eastern Turkey. Morale was somewhat restored by the successful defence of Gallipoli and the capture of the British army at Kut in Mesopotamia. In Syria, Jemal Pasha was appointed governor, with the task of leading an expeditionary force to break through the Allied defences on the Suez Canal and drive the British out of Egypt. However, despite attempts under both Turkish and German leadership, the numerically superior British were able to hold the line of defence. By the end of 1916, with the appointment of Sir Archibald Murray as Commander-in-Chief, the Allied forces were ready to mount their own offensive in southern Palestine.

Sherif Hussein and the British

Declaring war on the Allied powers in November 1918, the Sultan in his role of Caliph had also proclaimed a jihad (holy war), calling on the Muslims of the world to join the fight against the infidel. Conveniently ignoring the fact that their own European allies were no less 'infidels' than the enemy, the Ottomans conducted a vigorous propaganda campaign against the British and French. The declaration of holy war, however, stimulated only a very

Below:
Cartoon showing Mark Sykes in discussion with Sherif Hussein.

limited response. This was largely due to the fact that the secularist policies of the Young Turks had seriously undermined the Sultan's role as a religious leader. The Sherif of Makkah's backing was therefore considered crucial, but despite being urged on all sides by the Turkish leadership to declare himself openly in support of the proclamation, the recent opening of communications with the British had for the first time provided him with an alternative to continued Ottoman rule. He decided to stall for time.

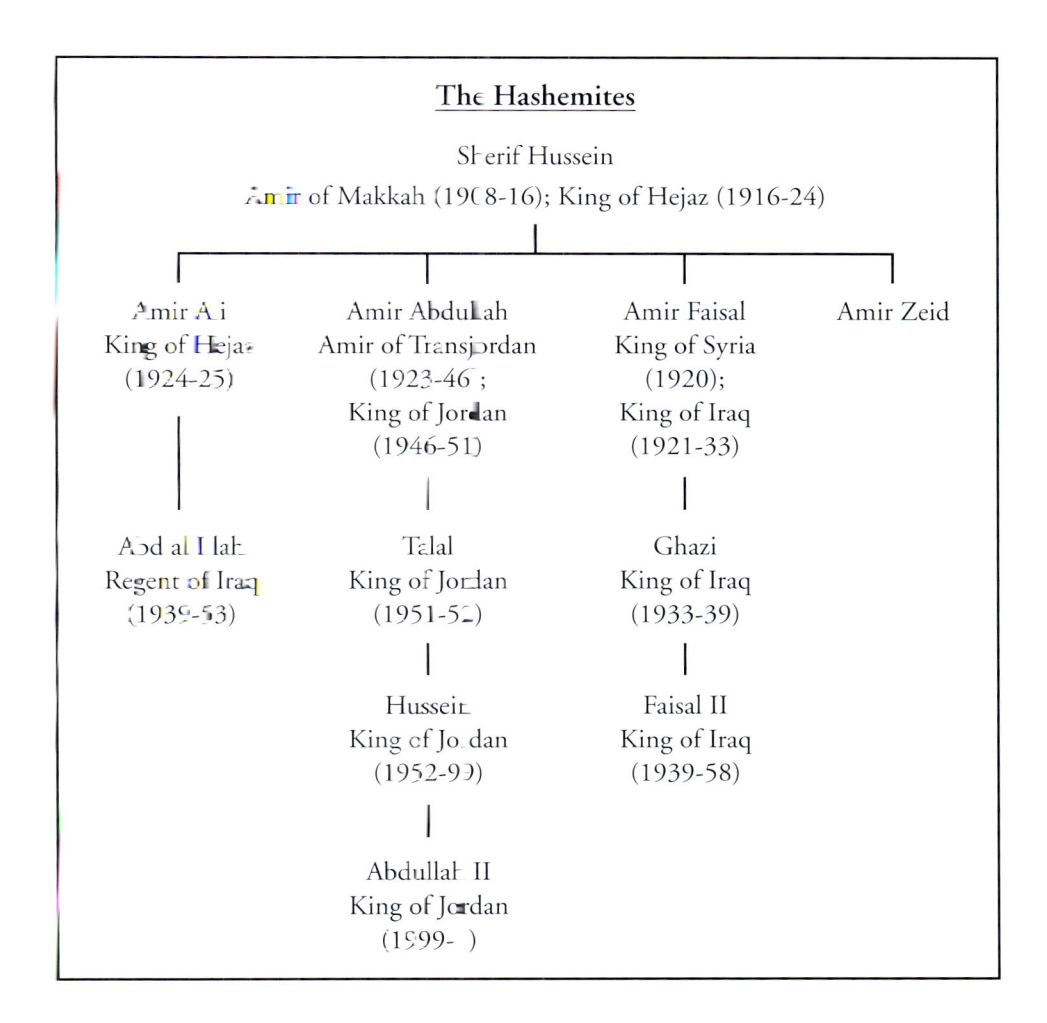

```
                         The Hashemites
                         Sherif Hussein
              Amir of Makkah (1908-16); King of Hejaz (1916-24)
    ┌────────────────┬────────────────┬────────────────┐
  Amir Ali      Amir Abdullah      Amir Faisal       Amir Zeid
 King of Hejaz  Amir of Transjordan King of Syria
  (1924-25)      (1923-46);          (1920);
                 King of Jordan      King of Iraq
                 (1946-51)           (1921-33)
     │                │                 │
 Abd al Ilah        Talal             Ghazi
 Regent of Iraq   King of Jordan    King of Iraq
  (1939-53)       (1951-52)         (1933-39)
                    │                  │
                  Hussein            Faisal II
               King of Jordan      King of Iraq
                 (1952-99)          (1939-58)
                    │
                 Abdullah II
               King of Jordan
                  (1999- )
```

From the outset of hostilities, the British had been aware of the potential of inciting the Arab tribes to revolt. 'I was talking to Crewe the other day at the Turf Club,' wrote Lord Cromer to his former Oriental Secretary, Harry Boyle, in October 1914, 'and he agreed with me that a few officers who could speak Arabic, if sent into Arabia, could raise the whole country against the Turks.' Lord Kitchener, the British Agent and Consul-General in Egypt, had no doubt entertained similar thoughts when Prince Abdullah, Sherif Hussein's second son, had stopped to meet him in Cairo in February on the way to Constantinople. Abdullah, describing the increasingly strained relations between his father and the Turks, had enquired in carefully guarded diplomatic language where Britain would stand in the event of an open conflict. Kitchener, as the senior British representative in Egypt, had no alternative but to respond with the official line, pointing out that Turkey was

THE HEJAZ RAILWAY

Above:
Local bedouin guard line up for inspection at Al Ula Station.

a friendly nation and that Britain would therefore be unlikely to intervene.

Two days later, and again on his return from Constantinople in April, Abdullah met with the Oriental Secretary, Ronald Storrs. While delivering the same discouraging official message, a close personal friendship was struck up between the two men, enabling the urbane and erudite Arab-speaking diplomat to hint that the British rejection might not be 'as final or irrevocable as it, at first sight, seemed to be.'[2] Although nothing concrete was achieved by Abdullah's approach, personal contacts were established which at a later date would prove to be of great significance.

The whole situation was dramatically altered by the outbreak of war. In September 1914, with the Ottoman entry on the German side looking increasingly likely, Kitchener, now Minister for War in London, instructed Storrs to send a secret messenger to the Hejaz to find out where Hussein's allegiance lay. The ensuing exchange of messages and letters culminated, after lengthy negotiations, in the McMahon Letter (actually a series of four separate notes), providing the Sherif with both the motivation and the confidence to raise the banner of revolt against the Turks. At the same time, the British were making a number of other commitments - including the famous Sykes-Picot Agreement - which were incompatible with the undertakings given to the Arabs. The resulting discrepancies and misunderstandings have been held responsible for many of the problems still afflicting the Middle East today.

While Hussein was attempting to obtain guarantees of British support, his relations with Turkey were becoming increasingly precarious. Aware that preparations were underway in Constantinople to depose him, he took the opportunity of sounding out the Arab nationalists in Syria and Iraq. Before committing himself to the Allied side, he wanted to be sure that he had genuine support among the populations, which one day, so he hoped, his agreements with the British would enable him to rule. In 1915 the Sherif's third son, Prince Faisal, was sent to Damascus as the guest of the new Turkish governor, Jemal Pasha. While in the city, he made secret contacts with members of the Arab nationalist societies, in order to assess the conditions under which they would be prepared to support a revolt led by the Hashemites. He returned to Syria in January 1916 with the aim of encouraging an uprising, but found that the situation had radically changed. Humiliated by his failure to defeat the British at Suez, Jemal Pasha had started to move against the nationalists. Ottoman battalions made up of Arab troops had been transferred to remote fronts of the war, and large numbers of prominent citizens had been deported to Anatolia. At the same time, Jemal had ordered the arrest of several Arab notables on charges of treason. In May, 21 of them were publicly hanged in Beirut and Damascus. The executions sent a shock wave through the Arab world, and when a force of 3,500 reinforcements under Khairi Bey was dispatched to the Hejaz, Hussein decided to recall Faisal and declare the Arab Revolt without further delay.

The Stotzingen Mission

On 4 May 1916 a train from Damascus pulled in at Al Ula Station and a small group of Europeans disembarked. The head of the party was a German army major named Baron Freiharrr von Stotzingen. He had letters of introduction from Prince Faisal, including one to his father, Sherif Hussein. Also concealed in the men's kitbags were instructions of a more sinister nature. The mission was to proceed down through the Hejaz to Hodeida on the coast of Yemen and there to set up a German propaganda wireless post. An Arabic newspaper would be started in Madinah to undermine Arab support for the British, and at the same time radio contact would be established with German East Africa. It was believed that with a bit of

Below:
Photograph of the waterfront at Yanbu, taken in 1917.

THE HEJAZ RAILWAY

Above:
This wonderful vantage point overlooking Al Ula Station provided the perfect site for a fortified outpost.

Below Right:
View of Al Ula Station from the fortified position in the above picture.

encouragement, revolt could be incited among the local populations in Sudan, Abyssinia and Somaliland.

The mission set out from Berlin on 15 March and crossed eastern Europe on the new 'Balkan Train'. Stotzingen, an Arabic speaker and widely travelled, presented himself to the Turkish Minister of War, Enver Bey, in Constantinople with a rather ambivalent recommendation from Countess Schlieffen: 'He does not obtrude his personality and has not those characteristics which often make the Germans disliked in foreign parts.'[3]

After some delay, Enver Bey allowed him to proceed. In Damascus the party joined up with Khairi Bey, who was leading the expedition of 3,500 men to reinforce the Turkish presence in the Hejaz and Yemen. They journeyed south on the railway together, but the German party had to leave the train at Al Ula, the furthest point to which Christians were allowed. While their heavy baggage and wireless installation continued on to Madinah by rail, Stotzingen and his group had to make their way by camel to the Red Sea coast at Wejh, and from there by boat and track to Yanbu. They were to get no further. Sherif Hussein, alarmed by the arrival of Khairi Bey's troops in Madinah, and suspecting that they were intended to strengthen the garrison at Makkah, rather than the Turkish presence in Yemen, decided to raise the banner of the Arab Revolt before it was too late.

Cut off from Khairi Bey's column, Stotzingen's mission received the alarming news that a German naval officer named Captain von Moller and his party of six had been attacked on the road between Jeddah and Yanbu. By 8 June, it was clear that the Arab Revolt was more than a local disturbance. Dumping most of their equipment into the sea, the Germans burned their secret codes and fled for their lives. Three of them disappeared, but despite an unreliable escort and a hostile local population, the others made it back to Al Ula and from there by rail to the security of Damascus.

The Arab Revolt: First Attacks on the Railway

The scarlet banner of the Hashemites was first unfurled beneath the walls of Madinah at dawn on 5 June 1916. The main assaults on cities started five days later, when simultaneous attacks were carried out at Makkah, Madinah, Jeddah, Taif and a number of small ports along the Red Sea coast. After some initial heavy fighting, Makkah was taken within a month, thus providing Hussein with a base free from Turkish interference. Jeddah was captured even more rapidly, falling on 16 June to a force from the Al Harb tribe, after two British warships had bombarded the city from the sea. Taif, being surrounded by a strong, well-defended wall, took longer to capitulate, and held out against Prince Abdullah until September. Following the capture of Jeddah, the ports on the Red Sea fell in quick succession; in July, Rabigh and Yanbu, and in August, Al Lith, Al Qunfudah and Um Lejj.

Madinah itself would prove to be a far more difficult proposition. Its massive walls and strong fortifications were defended by 14,000 well-equipped and experienced regular Turkish troops, led by a resolute commander, Fakhri Pasha. The garrison had at its disposal 16 mountain guns and two heavy-duty field pieces, and unlike the other main cities of the province, it was connected to the outside world by the Hejaz Railway. This enabled it to be properly provisioned with supplies of food and water, as well as military equipment and troop reinforcements.

With such formidable defences, and with the railway track providing the city's lifeline to the main Turkish command centres in the north, it is perhaps not surprising that the first military actions of the Revolt were carried out against the Hejaz Railway itself. Having raised the Sherif's flag on 5 June and

Below top:
Muhit Station was constructed using locally available black basalt stone. Note the loose pieces scattered around the building.

Below:
The pockmarked name plaque above the entrance to Muhit Station showing evidence of the heavy fighting in the area.

called upon the tribes to support the uprising, Ali and Faisal (Hussein's eldest and third sons) initially took their bedouin forces northwards from the city and attempted to cut the railway by 'tearing off lengths of the metals with their bare hands and throwing them down the bank.'[4] Without proper equipment or explosives however, the work was of limited value, for the Turks had efficient repair teams and large reserves of track and were able to avoid any real disruption to services.

The force was then divided into three groups. One remained close to Madinah, while the others moved north towards Muhit and Hafira. On 8 June the second of these groups launched a surprise attack on the railway. The closest station to Madinah, Muhit, was heavily garrisoned. As well as the station buildings, there was a large blockhouse for over 200 men and a fortification on a nearby ridge. The bedouin force opened the fighting with a heavy barrage of fire from their positions in the surrounding hills. At the same time, another group advanced towards the station across open ground. The Turks however, safe behind their strong defences and armed with machine-guns, had little difficulty in repulsing the attack. When a force of infantry under Fakhri Pasha arrived from Madinah, the bedouin had no alternative but to disperse and retire into the safety of the hills.

The third group under Prince Faisal advanced to Hafira, the next station along the line. The aim was to capture it and then continue up the railway to

Below:
Arab forces on the march in December 1916, led by Prince Faisal, Prince Zeid, Sherif Sharraf and an Ageyl bodyguard.

attack Buwat. Faisal was eventually forced to abandon this plan, as his troops were unable to confront the armoured trains employed by the Turks. Instead, he returned to Madinah and an attempt was made to overrun the city's defences with a full-frontal charge. This engagement was to give Prince Faisal his first real insight into the futility of attacking entrenched and well-armed Turkish regulars with bedouin forces. Unaccustomed to the noise of heavy guns, an artillery bombardment threw the tribesmen into disarray and they were cut down by machine-gun fire. Despite Faisal's best attempts to rally them, they fell back to their watering holes. The Turkish forces immediately left the city to pursue them, fortifying the outlying posts as they drove them towards the sea. By mid-June, the Arabs had been forced to split into two groups, with Ali retreating fifty kilometres to the southwest, and Faisal to Yanbu al Nakhl on the Madinah to Yanbu road.

The Turks now consolidated their position in Madinah with large quantities of supplies brought in on the railway. Arab damage was limited to removing individual rails and piling rocks to block the line. In August, Turkish prisoners reported that an average of between one and two trains per day were running through to Madinah. Although Hussein was still in control of Makkah, a new Amir, Sherif Haidar, was officially appointed by the Turks to take his place. Arriving in Madinah on 1 August, he moved quickly back up the line to the area around Abu Na'am Station in an attempt to stir up the Arabs of the Hejaz against the Revolt. Hussein immediately responded by proclaiming himself 'King of the Arab Lands', although the Allies only agreed to recognise him as 'King of the Hejaz'.

The Turks strengthened their system of defence in order to prevent further raids being carried out against the railway. A chain of small blockhouses was built on some of the more vulnerable stretches of track, and to cover strategically important features, such as large bridges. The interval between any two outposts was no more than three kilometres, so reinforcements could be brought up quickly in the event of an attack. As well as patrols by troops on camels and mules, there were inspections of the track carried out each morning by trolley parties of up to 20 men. The Turks also provided the bedouin tribes with T.L. 30 and ten loads of corn a month to 'guard' the line. However, Lt Col. S. Newcombe reported that if more generous offers were forthcoming, the chiefs were always 'open to argument from the other side, and generally got paid twice over.'[5]

Having bolstered their defensive position at Madinah, the Turkish offensive forces pushed the Arabs steadily back towards the coast. Although they were reinforced by a small section of Egyptian artillery, the tribesmen were no match for the well-disciplined Turkish troops. By October, Faisal and his bedouin army, poorly equipped and running low on ammunition, had retreated to Wadi Safra. Despite the potentially adverse effect on the tribes (as well as the Muslim world as a whole), Hussein and his sons for the first time suggested allowing a limited British force to enter the Hejaz in order to shore up the defence of Rabigh. In Cairo, military opinion was divided over the issue, but in the end, British High Command decided that the Revolt was no more than an ill-conceived 'sideshow' of little value to the overall war effort, and rejected intervention.

Above:
When T.E. Lawrence met Prince Faisal for the first time at Hamra in October 1916, he felt "…. at first glance that this was the man I had come to Arabia to seek - the leader who would bring the Arab Revolt to full glory." Seven Pillars of Wisdom

THE HEJAZ RAILWAY

Right:
Jemal Pasha, commander of the Turkish forces, with Sherif Ali Haidar, the intended replacement for Sherif Hussein as Amir of Makkah, at Damascus Kanawat Station in April 1917.

With the weather cooling, it was increasingly evident that the Turks were planning a major offensive to recapture Makkah. If Hussein's capital fell, the Arab Revolt would be over. Rabigh, the main water stop on the Darb Sultani, the road to Makkah, was unlikely to be able to withstand a full-scale Turkish assault. By October, Faisal's demoralised and rapidly-dwindling force in the Wadi Safra was the last line of real defence. It looked as if the Arab Revolt, which had opened with such spectacular success only four months earlier, was about to collapse.

The Arrival of the British

On 16 October 1916 a young British captain disembarked from a small converted liner, the *Lama*, and stepped onto the Arabian Peninsula for the first time. He carried no orders and had no official mission. In fact he had only been able to get away from his desk job in Cairo by applying for leave. Two years later he would had written himself into the history of England. At the time of his arrival however, the Arab Revolt was on the brink of disaster, and if the Turks had pushed through to Rabigh and retaken Makkah, as they threatened to do, T.E. Lawrence, or 'Lawrence of Arabia' as he subsequently became known, would never have become a household name.

Lawrence came ashore at Jeddah with Ronald Storrs, the Oriental Secretary in Cairo. They were joined by Lt Col. Cyril Wilson, the British representative in the Hejaz, and meetings were held with Prince Abdullah. During the discussions, the prince complained that the British had failed to cut the railway in the north around Ma'an to prevent men and supplies being sent down to reinforce Madinah. It was pointed out that dynamite sent to the Arabs to carry out their own demolitions had been returned by Hussein as 'too dangerous'. Nevertheless, Storrs realised the importance of severing the rail link to Madinah, and a sapper from the Royal Engineers, Bimbashi (Major in the Egyptian army) Herbert Garland was posted to Yanbu to train

T.E. Lawrence

Thomas Edward Lawrence was born in Wales on 15 May 1888, the illegitimate son of Thomas Chapman, a wealthy Anglo-Irish landowner, and Sarah Lawrence, the governess of his four daughters. Having been refused a divorce by his wife, Chapman eloped with Sarah, relinquishing his family lands and inheritance in order to avoid the stigma imposed by late Victorian puritanical morality. Moving from place to place the couple finally settled in Oxford, where their dark secret lay hidden behind the respectable facade of a normal, church-going, middle-class family life.

Lawrence studied history at Oxford University, and it was his interest in medieval architecture that first took him to the Middle East in 1909 to research Crusader castles. Impressed by his work, David Hogarth, the Keeper of the Ashmolean Museum, arranged for Lawrence to join him on an archaeological dig at the ancient city of Carchemish, north-east of Aleppo. In March 1911, the two men made their way up to the site together, Lawrence travelling for the first time on the Hejaz Railway between Haifa and Damascus. When the First World War broke out in 1914, his knowledge of Arabic, together with his experience of the Ottoman Middle East, made the young archaeologist an obvious choice for a post with British military intelligence in Cairo.

In 1916, at his own request, Captain Lawrence received the mission that took him to the Hejaz. His meeting, and subsequent close relationship with Prince Faisal, provided him with the opportunity to play a significant role in the Arab Revolt, and ultimately to achieve world fame. In the years following the war, his deeds became elevated to the status of legend. In an attempt to avoid the full glare of the ensuing publicity, Lawrence changed his name and disappeared into the ranks of the armed forces as an ordinary serving man. He was killed in a motorcycle accident in Dorset in 1935, shortly after his discharge from the R.A.F.

In the 1950s and 1960s, following the release of new information, his reputation suffered a backlash, with writers queuing up to debunk the Lawrence myth. Recently, a more balanced picture has emerged, with both the strengths and weaknesses of this extraordinary and complex character acknowledged. Countless biographers and historians have picked over his every word and deed, and controversy still surrounds many of the incidents of his life. His exploits on the Hejaz Railway however, remain beyond dispute. A deeply resourceful military leader, with exceptional powers of physical endurance, his ability to understand and identify with the Arab tribes enabled him to influence the course of events in one small corner of the war to the advantage of the Allies. Still capable of inspiring the interest and fascination of a wide and diverse audience, in the final analysis it was perhaps his skill with the pen, and in particular his classic account of the war in the desert, *Seven Pillars of Wisdom*, which has assured him a permanent place in the annals of British military history.

THE HEJAZ RAILWAY

Above:
Lt Col. C. Wilson, the British Representative in the Hejaz (wearing the cap), was the main liaison between Allied military headquarters in Cairo and Sherif Hussein in Makkah. On the left is the Medical Officer, Major W. McConaghy.

the bedouin in the use of explosives and lead demolition raids. Garland's arrival signalled the real start of the war on the railway.

One further outcome of the meeting, which was to have a major influence on subsequent events, was the decision to allow Lawrence to ride inland to meet Prince Faisal. Although he had come to the Hejaz without an official mission, Lawrence's visit to the region had received the firm backing of the Chief of Intelligence in Cairo, General Gilbert Clayton, who was desperate for first-hand information about the military situation on the ground. At his meeting with Faisal at Hamra in Wadi Safra, Lawrence quickly established a close relationship with the prince, claiming later that he had 'felt at first glance that this was the man I had come to Arabia to seek - the leader who would bring the Arab Revolt to full glory.'[6]

Realising the potential of the Revolt, Lawrence returned to Cairo, calling for supplies of machine guns, artillery, money and technical assistance for the Arabs. By the time he rejoined Faisal's army as liaison officer in December 1916, Fakhri Pasha had ordered the expected offensive. Lawrence arrived at the height of the crisis, for the Turkish forces had already broken through the Arab defences and were threatening Yanbu. Only the presence of British naval vessels caused the advancing Turks to lose their nerve. Having 'assessed their chances of storming the town surrounded by the Red Sea on three sides and protected by naval guns, barbed wire, searchlights and machine guns,'[7]

OUTBREAK OF THE FIRST WORLD WAR

the Turks decided instead to move southwards to threaten Rabigh. It was a decision which Lawrence believed ultimately cost them the war.

By this time, Rabigh was equally well defended by the guns of the British Red Sea Patrol. A flight of aircraft under Major A. Ross had also recently been deployed to the town and began to harry the attackers. With their supply lines now severely overstretched, the Turkish offensive ground to a halt. Behind them in Madinah, an outbreak of cholera was claiming up to 20 men a day. To add to their difficulties, Prince Abdullah's force had moved up to the west of the railway and was carrying out raids against the track and the telegraph line. On 18 January Fakhri Pasha decided to recall his men to Madinah. Five days later, an Arab force was landed from British ships and seized the port town of Wejh. The Turks could now no longer threaten Makkah for fear of an outflanking attack from the north. They were pinned down to Madinah and the garrison posts of the railway, and would remain there for the rest of the war. For the Allies, the possibility of attacking the Hejaz Railway was now open, and with Wejh providing a well-positioned strategic base from which to launch raids, a new phase of the war began.

Overleaf:
During the war, a look-out post was established on the summit of Jebel Antar, 110 kilometres north of Madinah. The railway ran along the east (right) side of the valley.

Below:
Photograph of Wejh taken by Lawrence. With the capture of the Hejaz Red Sea port in January 1917, British and French forces, together with Arab regulars, were able to participate in the campaign on the railway.

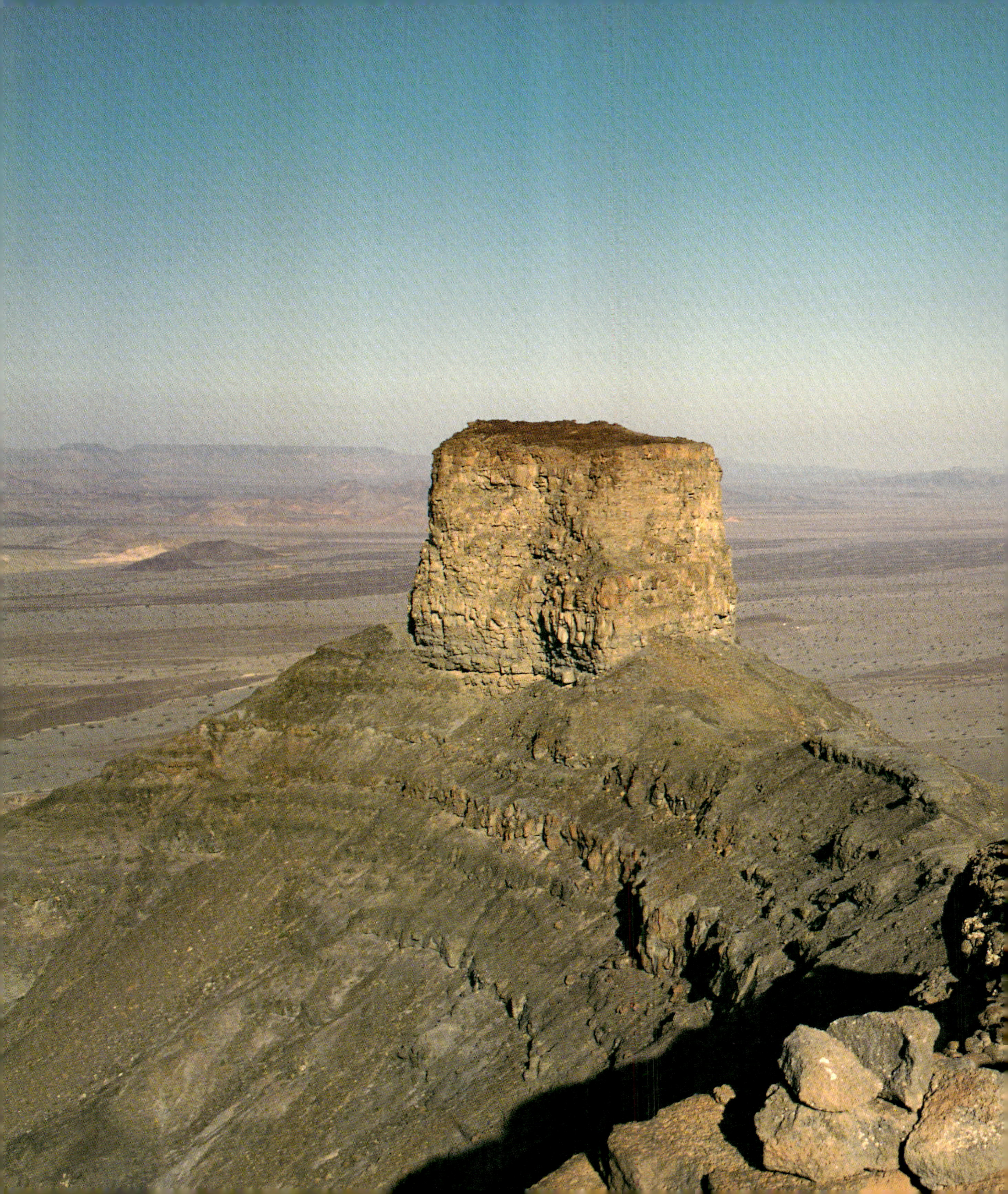

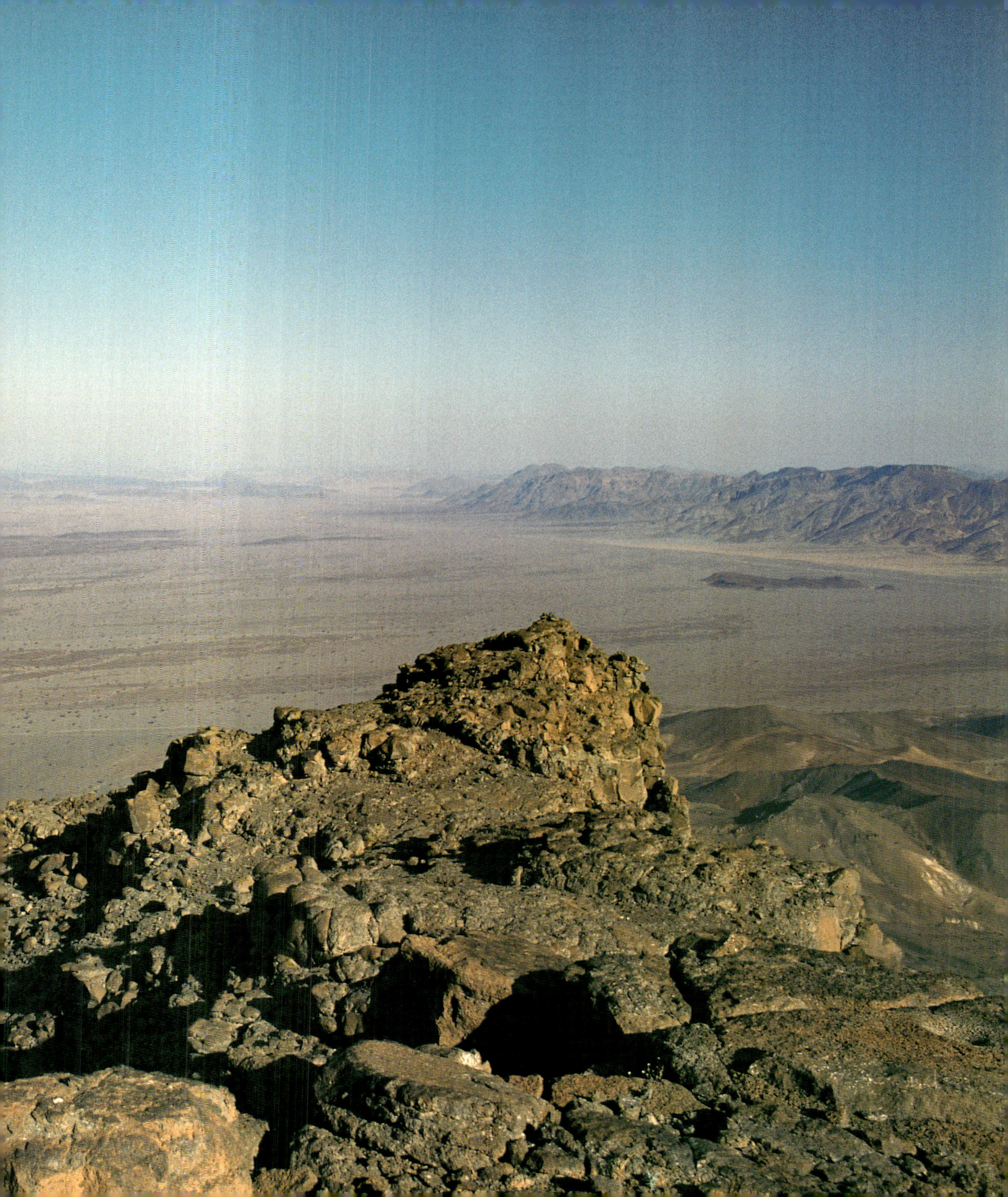

THE HEJAZ RAILWAY

7. The War along the Railway

I - The Hejaz

The Significance of Wejh

The seizure of Wejh in January 1917 removed the threat to Makkah, and by pushing the Turks back to cover Madinah, changed the psychological balance

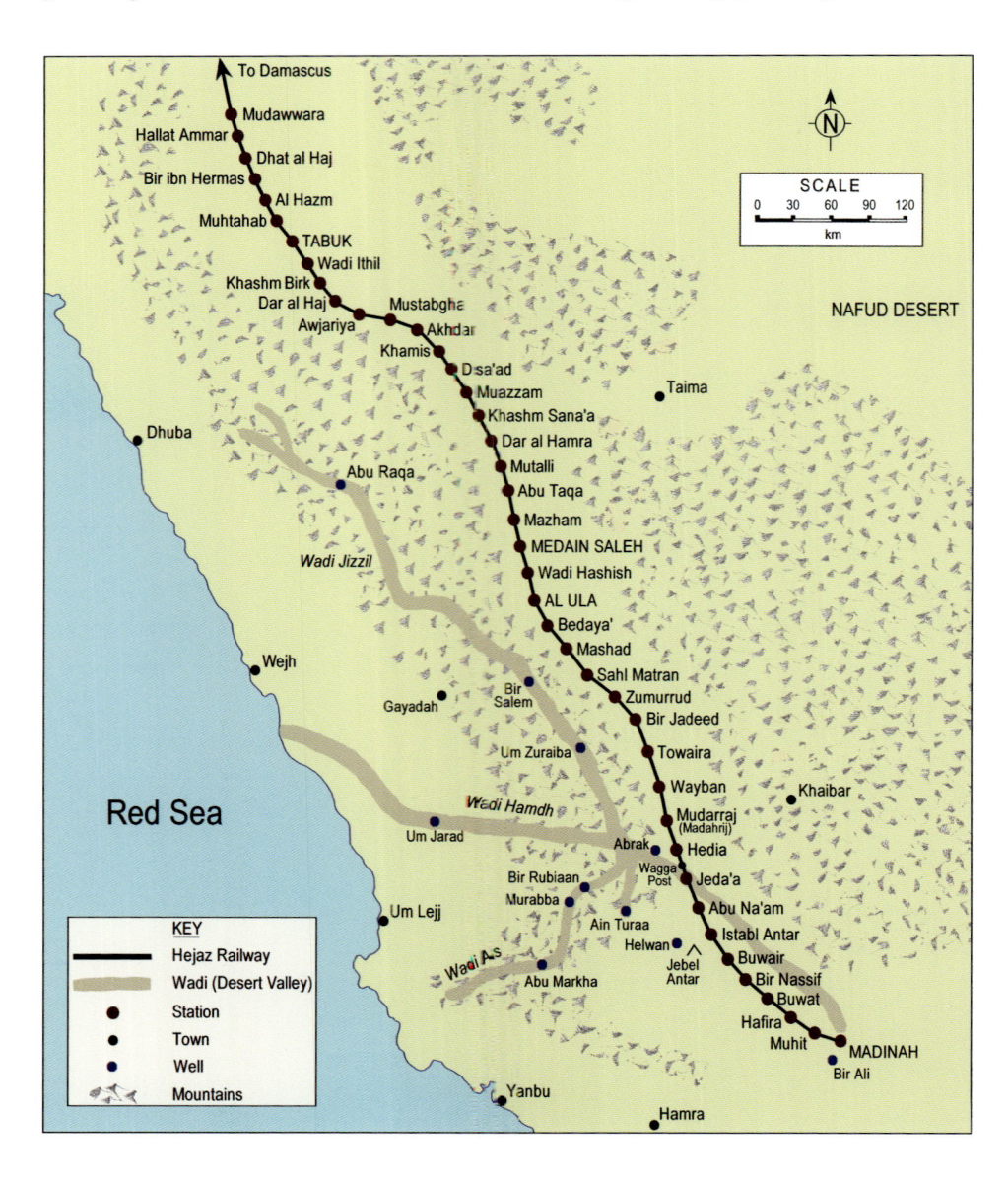

Right:
Map 9 – The Northern Hejaz

of the conflict. From now on the Arabs, together with their British and French allies, were on the offensive, while the Turks were effectively pinned down to their garrisons, 'strung like beads on the long thread of the Hejaz Railway.'[1] The establishment of a secure coastal base also gave easier access to the Hejaz from the British supply depots in Egypt. With the arrival of greater numbers of British and French military personnel came large quantities of munitions and a great deal of technical know-how. This meant that trains as well as rails and the telegraph could now be considered viable targets for attack.

T.E. Lawrence, although not the first to arrive in the Hejaz, would certainly become the most famous. His role in the war has also created the most controversy, with countless historians and biographers disputing his significance. Although he has sometimes been accused of overstating his own part in the Revolt, he always acknowledged that his was one effort among many, Arab as well as British and French, by ordinary serving men as well as by officers. But for the accident of 'a fluent pen, a free speech and a certain adroitness of brain'[2] their stories might be as widely known as Lawrence's own. As it is, the record of their achievement can be found in reports filed long ago in the heat of battle, but still preserved in the archives of the Great War.

Above:
Lawrence in Arab dress, standing on a ridge overlooking a military camp near Wejh.

Bimbashi H. Garland: First Train Derailed - Towaira, February 1917

The British did not take long after the capture of Wejh to move against the railway. On 12 February 1917 Bimbashi (Major) Herbert Garland (Egyptian Army) set out with a party of 52 Juhanni and Ageyl tribesmen. After a hard journey through the mountains, a forward camp was set up at Gayadah, about 60 kilometres west of Al Ula, and a night-time advance was made from there to the railway. Believing themselves to be somewhere midway between Towaira and Wayban, they began to lay charges along the rails. A small, solidly-built two-span bridge was located and Garland instructed some of the Ageyl how to prepare and position the necessary charges. He then moved down the track to lay a heavy mine with the intention of blowing up a train. After only five minutes of digging, one of the Ageyl ran over and told him that a train was approaching. 'It being contrary to all our intelligence that the Turks ran trains in the dark, and hearing nothing personally, I paid no attention to the matter and proceeded arranging the mine. A few minutes later however, another man came up and said that certainly a train was coming. We listened, and much to our astonishment heard a train leaving a station, blowing off steam, and also an engine-whistle. The guides had taken us to within 500 yards of the rather important blockhouse of Toweira!'[3]

Garland's preparations were only half completed, and he had to make a snap decision. He could either let the train pass and then lay a full mine at his leisure, or go ahead with a smaller than intended charge and inflict only partial damage. Considering it of paramount importance to find out whether

101

THE HEJAZ RAILWAY

this type of mine would function properly against a locomotive, he decided to go ahead with a reduced charge. With no time for further digging, he quickly filled the hole with about 15 lbs of explosives. He had just finished when he heard the train approaching. He turned and ran, but having taken off his boots to avoid leaving footprints close to the rails, his retreat was slow and painful, 'and I had only gone 50 yards when I turned round and had the good fortune to see the mine explode, being much closer to it than was desirable. I saw the engine rock with the force of the explosion, leave the rails, turn over, and fall with a crash down a small embankment. Soon after, military commands were heard as well as the cries of the injured. We formed the idea that it was a troop train, and reports from Arabs who have since passed the scene confirm this.'[4]

Lt Col. S. Newcombe: Raids to the North of Medain Saleh, Spring 1917

Before Garland's raiding party returned to Wejh, another expedition accompanied by Lt Col. Newcombe (Royal Engineers) had set out for the section of railway north of Medain Saleh. Leaving on 21 February 1917, the force included Sherif Nassir of Madinah and about 160 Ageyl tribesmen.

Above:
Herbert Garland was the first British officer to derail a train in the Hejaz.

Right:
Sherif Nassir played a major role in the campaign on the railway as commander of the bedouin forces. His importance was well described by Lawrence: "He was the opener of roads, the fore-runner of Feisal's movement, the man who had fired his first shot in Medina, and who was to fire our last shot at Muslimieh beyond Aleppo on the day that Turkey asked for an armistice, and from beginning to end all that could be told of him was good."
('Seven Pillars of Wisdom')

Left:
Lt Col. Stewart Newcombe carried out a number of successful raids on the railway. He was eventually captured, operating behind enemy lines near Hebron in Palestine.

They took eight days to cover the 160 kilometres to Abu Raqa (about 85 kilometres north-west of Medain Saleh), where they set up their base camp. The force then split into three parties. Sherif Nassir was detailed to attack Dar al Hamra to engage the Turkish garrison, while parties under Shawish Aziz and Newcombe moved to the north and south of the station to cut the line. Nassir's first shots were heard at 7 a.m. and the demolition works started immediately. About 100 rails were destroyed by the southern party, and a trolley patrol was run down by the Ageyl with eight prisoners taken. The northern party blew up about 150 rails and 15 telegraph poles. Although at one stage the Turkish force at Dar al Hamra Station seemed on the point of surrender, ultimately the attack by Sherif Nassir came to nothing. The bombs laid to the north and south of the station however 'proved effective, two

THE HEJAZ RAILWAY

Above:
Looking north from his vantage point at Abu Na'am, Lawrence could see the railway twisting away into the barren mountains of the Hejaz.

Below:
Bullets from the 7.92 mm Mauser Modell 1898 found at Abu Na'am Station. The epitome of bolt-action rifles, the Mauser 1898 was sold and copied around the world. It was widely used by the Turkish troops in the First World War.

engines at least being blown up with several trucks.'[5]

The group returned to the base camp to pick up further supplies of gelignite. Rearmed, they moved northwards back onto the line between Khashm Sana'a Station and Muazzam Fort, where an electric mine was laid and about 80 rails were destroyed. The following day the mine was detonated by a train. The force then headed back to Abu Raqa, but although they were anxious to remain in the area until a fresh consignment of explosives could be brought up, a shortage of supplies meant that they eventually returned to Wejh.

On 14 April Prince Faisal sent a detachment of 1,000 Arabs, accompanied by Newcombe and Garland, to the sector north of Medain Saleh. The party cut the track in five places between Dar al Hamra and Khamis. Although four of the five breaks were patched up within 24 hours, the fifth one, which had been made by Garland himself, took longer to repair. The force then moved north to Muazzam and attacked the qala'a (fort) and the station buildings. 'The Muadhdham fort is the old stonebuilt pilgrim qalah; but the Turks had constructed also out of rocks a pyramidal gun-emplacement of considerable strength. They numbered about 200 and except for a small guard left in the fort, all took up positions at once in prepared trenches.'[6] The Arabs were unable to overrun the Turkish positions and, pinned down by machine gun fire and running low on water, decided to withdraw. Newcombe took advantage of the attack to move northwards and demolish the track and telegraph in a number of places on both sides of Disa'ad Station.

T.E. Lawrence: First Raid on the Railway - Abu Na'am, March 1917

Soon after the capture of Wejh, Lawrence was shown a copy of an intercepted telegram from the Turkish commander Jemal Pasha, to Fakhri Pasha in Madinah. It contained orders originating from Enver Pasha, the Turkish Minister of War, for an immediate evacuation of the Holy City, in order to bring its garrison north to reinforce the Turkish front in Palestine. Although the capture of Madinah had always been a major objective of the Arab Revolt, the British commander Sir Archibald Murray, did not want to acquire it at the expense of strengthening the force facing the main British army in the north. It is at this point in *Seven Pillars of Wisdom* that Lawrence describes how he devised his strategy to pin down as many Turkish troops as possible in Madinah and the stations and blockhouses along the railway. Realising that a continued occupation of the city would be more of a liability than an asset to the overall Turkish war effort, he concluded that it would be far better if their forces could be coerced into remaining in the city. To achieve this, he proposed a series of pin-prick attacks along the length of the railway. 'Our ideal was to keep his railway just working, but only just, with the maximum of loss and discomfort… The surest way to limit the line without killing it was by attacking trains.'[7]

Lawrence recognised that the only way this could be achieved using local

Above:
Prince Abdullah's camp at Abu Markha in Wadi Ais served as a base for Lawrence's early raids on the railway in the spring of 1917.

bedouin forces was by avoiding conventional pitched battles. Arab strength lay in mobility, in the age-old tradition of raiding - the ability to attack swiftly and decisively and to disappear just as quickly into the secure reaches of the desert. Tribal custom would not tolerate the level of casualties sustained under regular military conditions, so entrenched fighting had to be avoided at all costs. Lawrence's vision of hit-and-run tactics was an early prototype of guerilla warfare, and the British historian Sir Basil Liddell Hart later lauded him as one of Britain's greatest military thinkers.

Lawrence's first attempt to put his theories into practice was in March 1917. Setting out from Prince Abdullah's camp at Abu Markha in Wadi Ais on the 26th, his party included Captain Raho, an Algerian in the French army, Mohammed al Khadhi, Sherif Fauzan al Harthi and about 25 Otaibi and Juhanni tribesmen. Despite having been stung on the hand by a scorpion, Lawrence continued on through a series of valleys towards the imposing landmark of Jebel Antar. A camp was made in the low hills at the edge of the wadi through which the railway ran. At sunset some of the party climbed a steep hill about two kilometres from Abu Na'am Station. From the top, the station buildings, bell-tents, huts and trenches, as well as a sizeable garrison, were all clearly visible. Two men were sent to fire off a few shots into the darkness near the station. 'The enemy, thinking it a prelude to attack, stood-to in their trenches all night, while we were comfortably sleeping.'[8]

In the morning they were woken early by a cold wind blowing across the valley. Climbing back to their observation point at the top of the hill in the warming sunshine, they had a perfect view of the early morning proceedings. 'We lay like lizards in the long grass round the stones of the foremost cairn upon the hill-top and saw the garrison parade. Three hundred and ninety-

105

THE HEJAZ RAILWAY

Above:
Lawrence's first raid on the railway took place at Abu Na'am in March 1917. During the attack, the station buildings were bombarded and a locomotive mined and damaged.

Below:
Mohammed al Khadhi returning from the attack on Abu Na'am Station in March 1917. (Photograph by Lawrence)

nine infantry, little toy men, ran about when the bugle sounded, and formed up in stiff lines below the black building till there was more bugling: then they scattered, and after a few minutes the smoke of cooking fires went up. A herd of sheep and goats in charge of a little ragged boy issued out towards us. Before he reached the foot of the hills there came a loud whistling down the valley from the north, and a tiny, picture-book train rolled slowly into view across the hollow sounding bridge and halted just outside the station, panting out white puffs of steam.'[9]

The shepherd boy was taken captive in case he sounded the alarm, and the group settled down to wait for the arranged reinforcements. Sherif Shakir (a cousin of Abdullah and Faisal) arrived that evening, but with only 300 men instead of an expected 900, ruling out the possibility of a full assault on the station. Instead, prior to an artillery attack at dawn, two groups moved out in opposite directions along the railway to cut the line. The first party headed to the north of Abu Na'am and demolished some rails and a length of the telegraph. Mohammed Khadhi guided the second group to a deserted stretch of track south of the station, and there in the darkness, Lawrence laid a trigger action mine, using 20 lbs of blasting gelignite. Leaving some machine gunners in a little bush-screened watercourse nearby, the group then moved further down the line to cut the telegraph. The station was therefore isolated from both sides, and it was hoped that this would encourage the Turks to send their train out for reinforcements when the attack began.

Lawrence arrived just as the guns opened fire. The two main buildings were hit, as were the pump room and the water tank. 'The well house… was demolished and the tents and the wood pile burned and a hit was obtained on the first wagon of the train in the station. This set it on fire and the flames spread to the remaining six wagons, which must have contained inflammable stores since they burned furiously.'[10] The locomotive quickly uncoupled and headed southwards out of the station. Lawrence and his men 'watched her hungrily as she approached our mine, and when she was on it, there came a soft cloud of dust and a report and she stood still. The damage was to the front part, as she was reversed and the charge had exploded late but, while the drivers got out, and jacked up the front wheels and tinkered at them, we waited and waited in vain for the machine-gun to open fire. Later we learned that our gunners, afraid of their loneliness, had packed up and marched to join us when we began shooting. Half an hour after, the repaired engine went away towards Jebel Antar, going at a foot pace and clanking loudly; but going none the less.'[11]

The artillery attack was followed by an Arab advance on the station which destroyed one enemy outpost and captured another. The Turks quickly withdrew to their main entrenched position. The lack of men and the reduced visibility because of thick smoke caused the Arabs to break off the action. Two parties were left in the area to carry out further damage to the railway and telegraph. In April, Lawrence reported that the Turkish garrisons on the Mudarraj to Buwair section of the line had 'entirely abandoned night patrol as a result of sustained sniping of the stations.'[12] Lawrence and the rest of the raiding party returned to Abdullah's camp at Abu Markha in good spirits. 'We had taken 30 prisoners... and had killed and wounded 70 of the garrison, at a cost to ourselves of one man slightly hurt. Traffic was held up for three days of repair and investigation. So we did not wholly fail.'[13]

Below:
Photograph taken by Lawrence of the force returning from the raid on Abu Na'am. Sherif Shakir (in the middle on the black camel) is leading the party, and the man in uniform riding beside him is the French Algerian, Captain Raho.

THE HEJAZ RAILWAY

T.E. Lawrence: Mining of a Train at Km. 1121, April 1917

On his return to the camp at Abu Markha, Lawrence quickly put together another party for a second raid on the railway. Accompanied by Otaibi and Juhanni chiefs, about 40 Juhanni tribesmen and a machine gun crew of 13, he set off along Wadi Ais in hot early April sunshine. The party headed into the great Wadi Hamdh, but as the afternoon passed the light grew dimmer and the heat heavier and more oppressive. Finally the weather broke and they were caught in a short but violent sand storm. After the sand came heavy rain and a strong cold wind. One of the men slipped on the wet rocks and had to be buried where he fell. Approaching the railway through a misty valley, they could hear the food-call of Turkish bugles at Mudarraj (Lawrence calls it Madahrij) Station, below which they intended to operate. 'So we steered on the hateful noise, hateful because it spoke of supper and of tents, whereas we were shelterless, and on such a night could not hope to make ourselves a fire and bake bread from the flour and water in our saddle-bags, and consequently must go hungry.'[14]

They reached the railway at 10 p.m. on 5 April. In the intense cold and darkness Lawrence started to dig out a hole for a mine in the wet sand at kilometre 1121, about five kilometres south of Mudarraj Station. It took him four hours to lay it to his satisfaction, but by dawn the party was secluded at a safe distance from the line on some low mounds. An early morning patrol on a trolley passed over the mine harmlessly to Lawrence's relief 'for we had not laid a beautiful compound charge for just four men and a sergeant.'[15] A force of about 60 Turks then emerged from Mudarraj Station, but only to repair telegraph poles blown down by the previous day's storm. At 7.30 a.m. another patrol of 11 men came down the tracks inspecting the rails. Seeing all the footprints in the sand where the mine was buried, they stopped and 'concentrated there upon the permanent way, stared at it, stamped, wandered up and down, scratched the ballast; and thought exhaustively. The time of their search passed slowly for us: but the mine was well hidden, so that eventually they wandered on contentedly towards the south.'[16]

Shortly afterwards a train heading northwards from Hedia Station, full of refugee women and children from Madinah, passed over the mine without detonating it. 'As artist I was furious; as commander deeply relieved: women and children were not proper spoil.'[17] Expecting it to have exploded, a number of Lawrence's men had rushed out into the open and their hill-top lookout 'became suddenly and visibly populous.'[18] From Mudarraj there now came a heavy barrage of rifle fire, harmless because of the excessive range. Hedia was also alerted by telegraph, and this was more serious, for there were 1,100 men at the station, well-positioned to block their retreat down Wadi Hamdh. In order to make the party more mobile, Lawrence sent the machine-gun crew on mules, plus 15 Juhanni tribesmen, back to Wadi Ais.

They returned to the line and in darkness tried to retrieve the defective mine. The Juhanni tribesmen joined the search, but this only added to Lawrence's concern. 'Laying a Garland mine was shaky work, but scrabbling

Below:
Mohammed Khadhi, an eighteen year old of the Juhanna tribe, accompanied Lawrence on his first two raids on the railway - at Abu Na'am in March 1917 and between Mudarraj (Madahrij) and Hedia in April 1917.

in pitch darkness up and down a hundred yards of railway, feeling for a hair-trigger buried in the ballast, seemed, at the time, an almost uninsurable occupation.'[19] It took him an hour to locate it, and having remedied the fault he eased it back into position. The group then blew up a small four-arch bridge, destroyed about 200 rails and pulled down a stretch of the telegraph. Worried that the Turks would cut off their retreat, they quickly rode out to safety through Wadi Hamdh. The following morning as they sat at Bir Rubiaan, the first well in Wadi Ais, they felt the distant shock of a great explosion, and a day later the two scouts they had left at the railway caught up with their party. They reported that while the Turks had been repairing the damage to the bridge, a train carrying a labour gang and spare rails had come up from Hedia, setting off the mine. 'This was everything we had hoped, and we rode back to Abdulla's camp on a morning of perfect springtime, in a singing company.'[20]

Above:
Lawrence took this photograph of Bir Rubiaan in Wadi Ais on the way back from the attack between Mudarraj and Hedia Stations. As he rested with his raiding party at the water hole, he felt the distant thud of an explosion, set off by a train passing over the charge he had laid at Km.1121.

'Lawrence's Trains'?

There are four locomotives currently left abandoned on the long-deserted Saudi stretch of the railway:
- A German-made Hartmann 2-8-0 at Buwair Station
- A German-made Krauss 0-6-0T at Hedia Station
- An S.L.M. (Swiss Locomotive and Machine Works) 2-8-0 between Mudarraj and Wayban Stations
- A Hartmann 2-8-0 just south of Hallat Ammar Station, close to the Saudi-Jordanian border *(picture inset left)*

(There is also a restored 1906 German-made Jung 2-6-0 at Medain Saleh Station, and 6 locomotives at Madinah Station - see Appendix I)

These derelict engines are not uncommonly referred to by local expatriate off-roaders (as well as occasionally by more serious researchers) as the trains that Lawrence blew up. In fact however, the only one derailed in a sector in which Lawrence was operating, is the damaged engine standing some three kilometres south of Wayban (between Mudarraj and Wayban Stations). In his essay 'Lawrence's Kilometre 1121 Train: Still Out There?' J. Lockman considered the possibility that the Wayban wreck could have been the one mined by Lawrence in April 1917 at Km 1121, between Mudarraj (Lawrence calls it Mudahrij) and Hedia. This was based on his discovery that the intelligence manual (the 1917 Arab Bureau's 'Handbook of Hejaz') and maps available to Lawrence at the time contained no reference to Wayban Station. This omission, together with conflicting evidence relating to the exact location of Km. 1121 (measured from Damascus), seemed to suggest that the popularly held view of the train's origin could in fact be the correct one. However, having examined the relevant archives, and compared the terrain at Wayban with Lawrence's descriptions of the attack, Lockman eventually ruled out such a possibility, coming to the "regretful but firm conclusion"[1] that the Wayban train could not have been a relic of Lawrence's handiwork.

A confirmation of this conclusion came with his discovery of a message from Major Garland, which included the information that: "On 19th November [1918] Sherif Abdulla received a report from Farhan El Aida that the Arabs had attacked a train about 8 days previously, derailing and capturing it, and afterwards wrecking Wayban station, capturing 154 prisoners, including 7 officers, and one Mountain Gun and one Machine Gun. Sherif Abdulla stated that this had taken place before the official news of the armistice had reached Farhan El Aida."[2]

As Lockman pointed out, both the timing (i.e. right at the end of the war) and the location of this incident make it highly probable that it is the origin of the Wayban locomotive. His assessment was confirmed by a report that I found in the Public Records Office (FO 882/6), in which Lawrence stated: "April 6th [1917] - Locomotive mined and put out of action *temporarily*"[3] (my italics). It also tallies with the fact that during the war, any damaged locomotives were quickly repaired and put back into service. As the hostilities drew to a close however, the station garrisons with their recovery teams and experienced engineers had either been taken prisoner or fled northwards.

By a similar process of reasoning, the locomotive lying on its side just south of Hallat Ammar Station can almost certainly be attributed to an attack by an Arab force on 28 June 1918. The Arab Bureau Bulletin of 9 July reported that a party of Beni Atiyya attacked the station, and "… sixty prisoners, including four officers, and also a machine gun, were captured. A locomotive and the station tank were wrecked, and permanent way and culverts were demolished…"[4] There were no further reports of attacks on trains in this area. While the incident took place earlier than the one at Wayban, it is highly unlikely that the damaged engine would have been recovered, as the line north of Hallat Ammar had by this time been completely dislocated in the devastating series of raids carried out in April 1918.

Royal Flying Corps: The 'Arabian Detatchment' No. 14 Squadron

One of the lesser-known British contributions to the early fighting in the Hejaz was made by the 'Arabian Detachment', C Flight, No.14 Squadron, of the Royal Flying Corps. Arriving at Rabigh as early as 16 November 1916, more than two months before the capture of Wejh, their initial impact was as much psychological as military. The Turks were at this point advancing on Rabigh. Had they captured it, this would have thrown open the road to Makkah and signalled the collapse of the Revolt. Early operations by the airmen involved harrying the Turkish advance and reconnoitring the mountain wadis to monitor troop movements.

With the capture of Wejh in January 1917, the Turks withdrew to Madirah and the strategy changed. Gaining a new base for their planes at Wejh brought with it a new objective. 'We now arrived at the Hejaz Railway, the enemy's sole line of communication, along which he was very busy bringing in supplies of food and ammunition and at the same time evacuating the civil population.'[21] The first task was to find forward landing grounds, as the railway could not be reached directly from the coast without

Above:
The capture of Wejh allowed large quantities of supplies to be brought in on British ships from Egypt.

THE HEJAZ RAILWAY

a stop for refueling. Major A. Ross, the commander of C Flight, located a favourable area at Um Jarad in Wadi Hamdh, about 160 kilometres from Al Ula. In April a number of reconnaissance missions were carried out and valuable information was passed to the raiding parties out on the line.

Large, well-garrisoned stations like Al Ula and Medain Saleh, while difficult to attack by land, were susceptible to raids from the air. On 15 May 1917, two aircraft carried out a sortie against Al Ula in which 12 bombs were dropped on the camp and station buildings. One of the planes was forced to land with cylinder damage, but was later repaired and brought back to safety. The main difficulty facing the airmen throughout the summer months was the heat, with the cracking of cylinders proving to be a persistent cause of trouble. As early as April the machines were 'beginning to show signs of deterioration. The fabric was soggy from the sun and the wood dry and inclined to crack.'[22]

Eventually it was decided that there should be a major land assault on Al Ula, with an attempt to hold the station for at least 30 days. During this period, the railway and telegraph southwards to Madinah would be demolished 'in such manner as to ensure the complete and permanent interruption of railway or telegraphic communication for the remainder of the operations in the Hedjaz.'[23] In preparation for the supporting air attack, a forward base was established at Gayadah, where a plentiful supply of water had been found. On 14 June, a tender with a working party was sent out from Wejh to clear a suitable road to the new base.

The great heat and difficult terrain made conditions extremely hazardous. 'A certain R.F.C. officer in charge of this tender and working party very nearly lost his life. He and his driver having run short of water owing to

Above:
Among the sorties carried out by Major A. Ross of No. 14 Squadron was one over Madinah, during which he managed to photograph the railway depot. A train is waiting at the main station building, and a number of wagons can be seen on one of the sidings next to the L-shaped main storehouse on the left of the picture.

Right:
The establishment of a forward landing ground at Gayadah opened up the possibility of air attacks on Al Ula Station.

Above:
The old town of Al Ula, constructed out of mud bricks and stone from the nearby ancient ruins of Khuraiba, is now completely deserted.

losing their way among the mountains were forced to subsist on their own urine to quench their thirsts for two days. They were eventually brought in by Bedouins who found them just in time. Having drunk all the available water, they had succeeded in running the tender using a mixture of grease and petrol in the radiator for engine cooling.'[24]

In the end, it was clear that there were insufficient water sources close to the line, and that a full-scale attack on Al Ula could not be undertaken. Instead, various smaller stations between Al Ula and Hedia were to be raided and the railway cut in as many places as possible. Nevertheless, 14th Squadron was ordered to go ahead with its part in the plan as originally intended; the bombing of Al Ula. On 11 July, three machines at Gayadah were detailed to carry out a sortie on the station. One of the aircraft crashed on take-off, hitting a bush just as it left the ground. The other two machines continued on to the target area where 14 bombs were dropped, causing considerable damage to the military camp and station buildings. On the following day another mission was carried out, with two aircraft dropping eight 20 lb bombs each on the station. The Turks responded with four high-angle guns firing shrapnel, but the aircraft were flying at a height of 2,500 feet and they were unable to bring them down.

By now the extreme weather conditions were causing severe problems, such as deterioration of the surfaces and working parts of the aircraft. Damage was also being caused by strong winds. As the heat of the day intensified, the air temperature rose rapidly and 'at about noon daily we were attacked by "sand devils" - a whirlwind of sand and small stones - which very

THE HEJAZ RAILWAY

Above:
'Sand devil' approaching British aircraft at Gayadah. The damage caused by these whirlwinds eventually resulted in the withdrawal of the Arabian Detachment of No. 14 Squadron from the Hejaz.

often carried the machines bodily about 50 feet. Luckily they gave one warning as the large whirling tower of sand would appear somewhere down the wadi bearing down on the camp and machines. Everyone would stand to and hang on to the machines. The tents went down every time. Sometimes they went up. Afterwards all was chaos and the noise of the sandstorms was only equalled by the expressions of discontent by the R.F.C. personnel and the wailings of the Arabs.'[25]

A fourth and final raid was carried out against Al Ula on 16 July. Three aircraft inflicted considerable damage to the station buildings, including the water tower. The following day, a powerful sandstorm struck the camp and the aircraft were severely battered. As a result, on 19 July the machines were flown back to Wejh, where they were inspected and pronounced unfit for further service. They were then dismantled, packed in cases and shipped back to Egypt, ending No. 14 Squadron's brief but colourful tour of duty in the Hejaz.

Co-ordinated Offensive on the Railway: Lt Col. S. Newcombe and Lt Col. P. Joyce, July-Aug 1917

In July 1917, Prince Abdullah and Prince Faisal decided that a coordinated offensive should be carried out by all the various groups engaged in demolition work on the railway. To pull off an operation of this scale in the heat of summer, it was imperative to have adequate supplies of water. Seven wells were therefore dug by Egyptian troops along Wadi Jizzil to the west of Zumurrud. On 26 July Newcombe, accompanied by 30 Egyptians with four machine-guns, and 15 Indians, advanced to Zumurrud Fort. Although there was evidence that the Turks had been in the area, the qala'a was deserted. They found an excellent well within the walls and another one just outside. As there was no other water in the vicinity, they decided to occupy and hold the fort. The day before the attack, reconnoitring parties moved out onto the

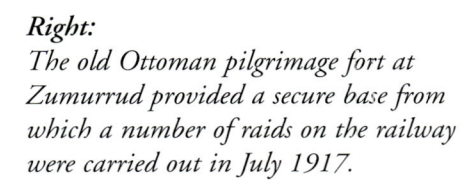

Right:
The old Ottoman pilgrimage fort at Zumurrud provided a secure base from which a number of raids on the railway were carried out in July 1917.

Left:
A railway raiding party, including Lt Col. Newcombe in Arab dress on the left, and Lt Hornby in army uniform on the right.

railway. Major Davenport (West Yorkshire Regiment, attached to the Egyptian Army) scouted the area to the north of Zumurrud, while Newcombe and M. La Motte (from a French force operating in the same sector) followed the line to the south. The Turks spotted the two groups and quickly dispatched a small force of their own. On their return to Zumurrud, the Allied scouting parties discovered that the Turks had occupied a large hill overlooking the fort. From this vantage point, snipers were well placed to subject the returning men to a heavy barrage of fire.

Newcombe was concerned that this situation would disrupt the main aim of cutting the railway, and set out before dawn on 31 July to find Ja'afar Pasha, the commander of the Arab regular troops. Reaching his sector at 5.30 a.m., he discovered that Ja'afar's men had already begun operations on the railway and were unable to provide cover around the fort until midday. In the afternoon a relief force was sent, and Newcombe quickly prepared his men for an attack on the railway. Before they could set off however, the news came through that Sherif Sharraf had captured Sahl Matran Station to the north and was requesting urgent assistance.

Assured by the messenger that there was an ample supply of water at the station, Newcombe's party moved out immediately. After a journey of more than three hours, they found that the information concerning the water was false. For two and a half hours the desperately thirsty troops carried out as much demolition work as possible. The points at the station were destroyed, along with 100 spare rails found in a store. A water-tank truck and a number of telegraph poles were also set on fire. On the line they detonated 800 charges, totally destroying 600 rails and damaging 200 others. Having completed the demolitions, they headed back to Zumurrud Fort to relieve Ja'afar's force. On arrival, they were greeted with water and with the good news that the Turks had been driven off their hill by a mule company under Maulud Mukhis. The following morning, a mountain gun was brought up and the Allied positions in and around the fort were bombarded. This continued until a direct hit from Ja'afar's own artillery piece put the Turkish gun out of action.

THE HEJAZ RAILWAY

Above:
The wide section of line in front of Mudarraj Station clearly showing where a double track was provided to allow trains travelling in opposite directions to cross. During the First World War, Lawrence carried out an attack on the line just south of this station (which he called Madahrij).

Other attacks were carried out as part of the overall plan to cut the railway, and met with considerable success. To the south of Zumurrud, a force of 500 Juhanni tribesmen under Sherif Mastur attacked and cut off Bir Jadeed Station. Newcombe sent a French team to assist with the demolitions, and 80 rails were destroyed. Newcombe himself remained in the area for another two days, but after a skirmish with the Turks near Zumurrud Station, a lack of fighting men and good camels forced him to withdraw to Gayadah.

As part of the same joint offensive, on 23 July Lt Col. P. Joyce (Connaught Rangers) had advanced to Murabba, 40 kilometres west of Hedia. Having informed Prince Abdullah that he was short of rations and without forage for his animals, he was permitted to proceed to the line prior to the other groups taking part in the operation. The prince also sent Sherif Fauzan al Harthi (of the al Harith), who had been with Lawrence at Abu Na'am in March, and Dakhil Allah al Qadi who had been with him at Mudarraj in April. On 26 July they moved up to the Abrak wells, about nine kilometres west of Hedia Station. From there they advanced on the line in darkness, and at dawn laid about 700 charges of gun-cotton between Mudarraj and Hedia Stations. There was heavy rifle fire from both stations, and a mountain gun pounded them with about 20 rounds of shrapnel, but their force of 300 Arabs with two machine-guns provided effective cover while they placed the charges. Interestingly, Joyce noted in his report that there were signs of a previous demolition having been carried out on this portion of the line, and that 'some of the rails replacing those broken were very old and rusty, and the fish plates were fastened with two bolts only.'[26] This damage was almost certainly the result of Lawrence's earlier demolitions in April, when he blew up the train at Km. 1121.

On his return to Murabba, Joyce quickly put together a second raiding party. He again took Sherif Fauzan and Sheikh Dakhil Allah al Qadi with him, and accompanied by about 500 Arabs, a French contingent and some Syrian officers, he advanced to the Um Zuraiba wells. Here, a base camp was established about fifty kilometres west of Towaira. The next day, 2 August, the party moved up to the railway before dawn and laid about 1,450 slabs of gun-cotton over a distance of six kilometres. This work continued until the two extremities of the group came under direct fire from Towaira and Wayban Stations. After detonating the charges, the party returned to check the line and additional explosives were placed on any unbroken rails. Seven culverts were demolished and a long stretch of the telegraph line was destroyed.

All of these raids, carried out simultaneously by the various different groups during the last days of July and the beginning of August, met with considerable success. Although the Turks were extremely skilled at repairing sections of broken track, the scale of the attacks put enormous pressure on their already stretched resources. In August, Davenport reported that a Harbi tribesman, who had recently escaped from Madinah, informed Prince Abdullah that there were no more spare rails left in the city. Garland also sent back news that on 12 August he had found the rails between Jeda'a and Abu Na'am badly silted with sand, indicating that no trains had passed over that section of the line for some time.

116

Bimbashi H. Garland: Raids on the Railway, Istabl Antar-Hedia, Aug 1917

By 7 August Bimbashi Garland had, with characteristic vigour, set out again from Prince Abdullah's camp at Abu Markha. Heading south-west towards Jebel Antar, he was accompanied by a force of 36 Arab dynamiters and 200 tribesmen under Sherif Nassir. After feeding and watering at Helwan, a spring close to Jebel Antar, they made their way over a tortuous mountain path towards the railway. Before any attack could be mounted however, the advance scouts reported back that the Turks had become aware of their presence and were patrolling the line in heavy numbers. They were unable to carry out the intended raid, and returned to their camp at Helwan for the night.

The following morning, Garland was astonished to discover that their position was clearly visible from both Abu Na'am and Istabl Antar Stations. Believing the railway to have been on the other side of the range of hills, their

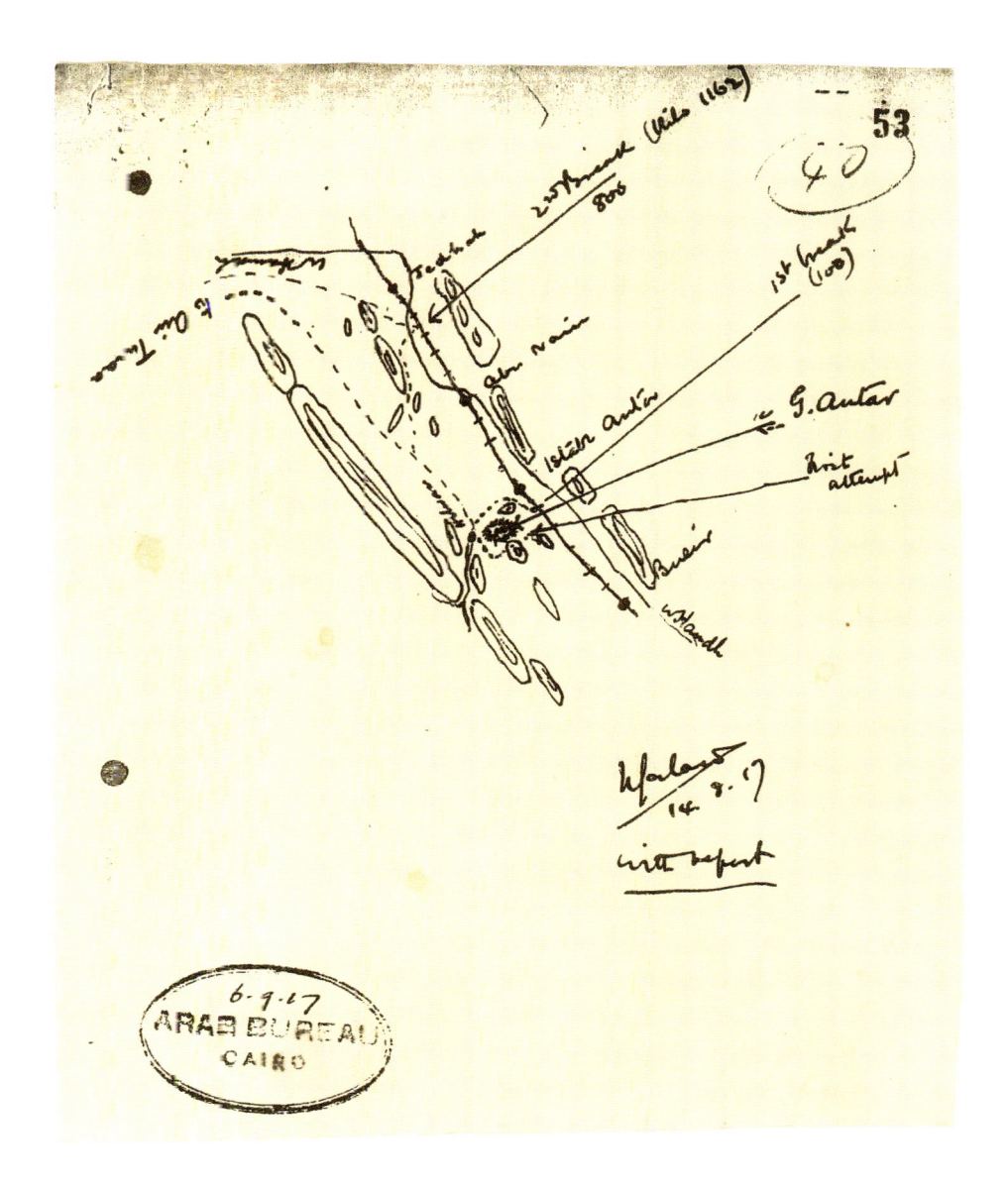

Left:
Hand-drawn sketch made by Bimbashi (Major) Garland of the attacks he carried out between Buwair and Jeda'a in August 1917.

Above:
Sherif Shakir carried out a number of attacks on the line in the Hejaz.

party had trotted quite happily up Wadi Hamdh in broad daylight, in full view of Abu Na'am Station for at least six kilometres. By evening, the Turks finished patrolling and withdrew to the stations, leaving a garrison on a hill about four kilometres south of Istabl Antar. Garland decided to attempt a small-scale night raid on the stretch of line between the station and this occupied hill. Leaving Helwan as darkness was falling, the party passed within 1,000 metres of Istabl Antar Station. The last part of the approach was made on foot, but seven of the group got lost and never reached the railway and as a result, only about 100 rails were demolished. While the charges were being detonated, a Turkish force attacked the men on the line. Although the party was able to withdraw safely to Helwan, the large numbers of enemy soldiers in the area persuaded Garland to move northwards to a point between Jeda'a and Abu Na'am.

On the evening of 11 August, the group advanced on the railway again and laid almost 900 charges. Garland became very frustrated by some of the dynamiters, who insisted on using large amounts of gun-cotton rather than clearing away the sand from the rails in order to achieve a good contact. About 800 rails were demolished and a long stretch of the telegraph was pulled down. Misfires were relit, but there was a good deal of faulty fuse, as well as some defective gun-cotton, which failed to detonate. The station at Jeda'a turned a search-light on them during the firing of the charges, but no Turkish soldiers ventured out to make an attack.

Withdrawing from the area at dawn, the party moved on to Ain Turaa, where a fresh supply of gun-cotton had been left for them. On 14 August they set out for the railway again with an extra 50 bedouin tribesmen in their escort. Arriving at a point between Jeda'a and Hedia Stations, they dismounted to complete their approach on foot. As they prepared their equipment however, a 'foolishly or traitorously inclined' member of the party fired off his gun and 'as the base where we were to leave our camels was over one hour's walk from the railway one fervently hoped no sleepless Turk had heard the rifle shot.'[27] They made their way quietly on foot over high hills of drift sand, each member of the demolition team carrying 24 lbs of gun-cotton, until eventually they entered the broad, flat floor of Wadi Hamdh.

Bedouin tribesmen were immediately stationed on both their flanks in order to secure a seven-kilometre stretch of line. Garland was at the northern end of the section, and moved up slowly towards a solid four-arch bridge, which he had been able to make out in the darkness. As he crept closer, a force of 30 Turks, concealed behind the brickwork, opened fire on them. There was no cover close to the line, so they turned and sprinted over soft sand to gain the refuge of the nearest hill, 600 metres away. Garland stumbled, but was helped to safety by an Arab soldier. The bedouin escort opened fire and eventually forced the Turkish troops to withdraw, leaving the way clear for the demolition teams to return and blow up the bridge and about 700 rails. Garland considered that his group had been saved by the enemy force's inability to hold its fire until they had moved in closer to the bridge. 'If the Turks had waited a few minutes more before opening fire, with their first salvo they could have knocked us over as easily as ninepins, but fortunately they fired before they could discern us properly in the darkness.'[28]

Results of the Railway Campaign in the Hejaz

Although the focus of the campaign in Arabia was to move northwards following the capture of Aqaba in July 1917, raids against the railway continued in the Hejaz throughout the war. Attacks were carried out mainly by Arab forces under Sherif Sharraf and Sherif Shakir (Prince Abdullah's principal commanders). They were well supported by Major Davenport with his force of Egyptian regulars, and a small French contingent. The Cairo-based Arab Bulletin reported in October 1917 that from July to September alone, 30 raids had been made on the line between Buwat and Ghadir al Hajj, destroying over 7,500 rails. The disruption to services caused great hardship for the garrisons of the stations and outposts on the railway. Prisoners taken during a raid near Abu Na'am by Davenport and Sherif Shakir at the beginning of September, for example were in a pitiful condition. 'The prisoners were ravenously hungry, and stated that they received only a water-bottle of water and one small loaf per day.'[29] Overall, the operations conducted in the Hejaz can be considered a strategic success. Through the efforts of a relatively small number of Arab, British and French fighters, as many as 25,000 Turkish troops, who would otherwise have been deployed against the main Allied forces in Palestine, were effectively tied down to the garrison posts along the railway.

The ability to keep the Turks permanently on the defensive also meant that Fakhri Pasha, the commander of the Turkish garrison at Madinah, was unable to launch a counter-attack against Makkah. In 1916 and 1917, foreign visitors were able to perform the pilgrimage, and the news that Amir Hussein had established effective rule over the area filtered back with the returning pilgrims to the rest of the Muslim community. This helped to confirm the existence of the Arab Revolt, and signified to the world that the great Padishah Abdulhamid II, Caliph and Sultan of the mighty Ottoman Empire, had finally lost control of Islam's holiest city.

Below:
A fortification was built on the black mound to the north of the Wadi Hamdh Bridges. In March 1917 Lawrence observed 'some dozen white tents with Turkish officers lounging in chairs' at the top of this hill.

8. The War along the Railway

II - Aqaba & Northwards

The March to Aqaba

On 9 May 1917 Lawrence set out from Wejh on an expedition through northern Arabia, which was, in the words of Ronald Storrs, 'to write his page, brilliant as a Persian miniature, in the History of England.'[1] There is some dispute as to whether it was Lawrence himself, Prince Faisal or Auda abu Taye who first devised the plan to surprise the Turks at Aqaba with an attack from the rear. What is certain, however, is that all three of them favoured the idea,

Below:
Auda abu Taye (on the left, holding the cane) about to set off on the journey from Wejh which would culminate in the capture of Aqaba.

and Lawrence was the only British officer to take part in the expedition. It is also clear that the whole venture had only been made possible by the arrival at Wejh of the legendary Auda abu Taye, who was, according to Lawrence, 'the greatest fighting man in north Arabia.'² Abu Taye was chief of the powerful Huweitat, and his support opened up the water-holes of the great Wadi Sirhan, the long desert approach to Aqaba. He also had the power to swing the tribes of the region against the Turks, and to provide a bedouin force capable of taking on their defensive garrisons.

The party that set off from Wejh consisted of only 40 men, led by Sherif Nassir of Madinah. They crossed the difficult volcanic terrain of the Hejaz and arrived at the railway just south of Disa'ad, 110 kilometres south of Tabuk, in the late afternoon of 19 May. Warned against the danger of enemy patrols, they crept to the top of a steep ridge of soft sand to observe the line. Having confirmed that all was peaceful and deserted, 'we ran to the edge of the rock-shelf, leapt out from it into the fine dry sand, and rolled down in a magnificent slide till we came to an abrupt and rather bruising halt in the level ground.'³ Meanwhile their Ageyl escort blew up a stretch of track, to the delight and astonishment of Auda, who had never seen dynamite used before. As they moved off eastwards into the dusk, they also cut the telegraph, attaching the loose wires to the saddles of six riding-camels to pull down the poles.

Above:
Unusually designed station building at Disa'ad, with only one storey and two entrances. Note the dried mud brick defences on the roof with loopholes.

T.E. Lawrence: Diversionary Attacks on the Railway, June 1917

By the middle of June, about 500 tribesmen had been assembled by Auda at Bair, ready for the advance on Aqaba. The force's main strategic asset was the element of surprise, for the Turks were expecting an attack from the sea and had set up all their defences accordingly. Lawrence was acutely aware that information carried quickly across the desert. In order to deflect Turkish

Below:
Lawrence crossed the line at this point on his way north with Auda abu Taye to attack Aqaba.

Above:
Lawrence called Auda abu Taye (in the black cloak) 'the greatest fighting man in northern Arabia.' Sitting second from the left with his face half-covered, is his nephew, Zaal, who accompanied Lawrence on a number of raids on the railway.

suspicions as to the real purpose of the assembled force, he took 110 men under Zaal, Auda's nephew, and moved northwards onto the railway. Reaching Zerqa on 22 June, they continued ten kilometres north to a large bridge close to the village of Dhuleil. When they arrived, they discovered that four of the arches were being rebuilt following flood damage. They decided that it would be pointless to risk casualties in an attempt to demolish it, and pushed on further northwards towards Minifir. As they made their way along the track in the darkness, they were surprised by a night-train. 'We pricked ears, wondering: and there came out of the north a dancing plume of flame bent low by the wind of its speed. It seemed to light us, extending its fire-tagged curtain of smoke over our heads, so near were we to the railway; and we shrank back while the train rushed on. Two minute's warning and I would have blown its locomotive into scrap.'[4]

The following night Lawrence laid a large automatic mine on a culvert at Minifir, north of Samra Station, and the group settled down on a nearby hill to wait for a train. A Turkish mule-mounted infantry company patrolling the line sorely tempted his bedouin, but he managed to persuade them to refrain from firing, as it was important to avoid needless casualties before the raid on Aqaba. They were running short of water, and eventually had to give up the idea of a train and settle instead for demolishing a stretch of track. They laid their gelignite charges against the curved rails, knowing that the Turks would have to bring special replacements all the way from Damascus. Later they were told that the train sent down to repair the track had triggered off the mine, damaging the engine and holding up traffic for three days.

Having ensured that the Turks were aware of their presence, they headed back towards the oasis of Bair, from where the main assault on Aqaba would be launched. On their return, they passed Suaka Station, which was little more than a crossing point; Lawrence calls it 'Atwi' after the name of the nearby settlement At-Tuwei. They decided that it was too good an opportunity to pass up. Just after dawn, the party approached on foot over a series of limestone ridges until the station lay beneath them. The Turks' day was just beginning and the blue smoke of a cooking fire could be seen curling up into the still air. The sound of singing rose from the two stone buildings, and one of the soldiers drove a flock of sheep into a nearby meadow to graze.

Zaal slipped quietly down with a small group, and crept along the valley until he was opposite the station. The main force up on the ridge had a perfect view as he settled himself into position, resting his rifle against a grassy bank. Lawrence described the scene: 'He took slow aim at the coffee-sipping officers and officials in shaded chairs, outside the ticket office. As he pressed the trigger, the report overtook the crash of the bullet against the stone wall, while the fattest man bowed slowly in his chair and sank to the ground under the frozen stare of his fellows.'[5]

Seconds later the whole of Zaal's group opened fire and rushed forward. They were only prevented from taking the station by a hasty Turkish retreat behind the heavy metal door of one of the buildings. After an exchange of rifle fire, both sides, realising their impotence, gave up. The tribesmen immediately turned to looting the undefended building. While they were busy grabbing whatever they could lay their hands on, an unsuspecting

Above:
Famous photograph taken by Lawrence of the entry into Aqaba, when the Arab force attacked the village from the rear, burst through the Turkish defences and rode triumphantly into the sea.

trolley patrol with four men was spotted swinging down the line from the south. An ambush was quickly set and, despite an attempt to escape into the valley, the Turks were easily picked off. The party then torched the deserted building, the petrol-splashed woodwork rapidly catching fire. Meanwhile the Ageyl tribesmen laid gelatine charges, destroying a culvert, some track and a length of telegraph. Their withdrawal was delayed while they chased the station's flock of sheep, which had scattered at the sound of the explosions. Having once more regained the security of the desert, the party sat down to a rare feast of roast mutton.

The Capture of Aqaba, July 1917

The excursion on the railway had been successful in diverting Turkish attention from the real aim of the expedition, and the main force now set off for the assault on Aqaba. Near Ghadir al Hajj, the first station south of Ma'an, an attack by the small garrison was easily repelled. At Abu Lissan, 20 kilometres to the west, there was more serious opposition. A relief battalion of Turkish infantry had dug in around the water hole. For once, the bedouin had no alternative but to stand and fight a more conventional form of pitched battle. In the terrible July heat they acquitted themselves well, routing the Turkish forces with a charge by 50 horses and 400 camels. The

Above:
Prince Zeid's army arriving at Aqaba in August 1917. The capture of the town allowed Arab forces to move up from Wejh into a position to attack the northern section of the railway.

remaining fortified outposts in Wadi Ithm capitulated, leaving Aqaba at their mercy. On 6 July Aqaba fell to the Arabs. They had managed to surprise the Turks from inland, where their defences were at their weakest.

The capture of Aqaba marked a turning point both for the Arab Revolt and for the war on the railway. Eight hundred kilometres north of Madinah and just over half way to Damascus, Aqaba shifted the whole centre of gravity of the Revolt northwards out of the Hejaz and into what is today Jordan and southern Syria. The Turks were denied the use of the port as a base to threaten the right flank of the British army in Sinai. It also enabled the Arab army under Prince Faisal and his half-brother Prince Zeid, to move up from Wejh into a more offensive position. The political implications were equally significant, for the move represented 'the tangible embodiment of the revolt'[6], bringing the tribes that controlled the lands along each side of the line over to the Allied side. This effectively enabled a continuation of the same form of guerilla warfare that had been pursued in the south.

Following the failure of two major offensives against the Turks at Gaza earlier in the year, the British commander-in-chief, Sir Archibald Murray, had been replaced by Sir Edmund Allenby. Arriving in Cairo at the end of June, the great general's historic meeting with Lawrence - 'a little bare-footed silk skirted man offering to hobble the enemy by his preaching'[7] - convinced him of the potential value of the Arab forces. His support signalled a shift in the official attitude to the Revolt, and henceforth the Arabs became a sort of irregular right flank of the British army. With official approval, large quantities of munitions, supplies and personnel began arriving at Aqaba, and 'presently the tiny hamlet took on the aspect of a large and variegated military beehive with wireless stations and an aerodrome, and jetties for the landing of supplies.'[8]

Raids were stepped up all along the railway, particularly in the long section between Qatrana and Tabuk. Although the arrival of the British had introduced armoured vehicles and even air support to the campaign, the tactics used during these operations were essentially the same as those employed in the Hejaz. The campaign remained dependent on the speed and mobility of the irregular bedouin forces, and on the inability of the better trained, well-equipped Turkish troops to follow the raiding parties into the desert. With the element of surprise, for a short time and at a particular point on the railway, the bedouin could exert a superiority in both numbers and equipment. They would then disappear into the empty wastes before Turkish reinforcements could be brought in. As Glubb Pasha (of later Trans-Jordanian Arab Legion fame) remarked, 'the whole Arab campaign provides a remarkable illustration of the extraordinary results which can be achieved by mobile guerilla tactics. For the Arabs detained tens of thousands of regular Turkish troops with a force scarcely capable of engaging a brigade of infantry in a pitched battle.'[9]

Above:
The appointment of General Allenby as commander of the Egyptian Expeditionary Force in 1917 was to mark a change in the fortunes of the Allies in the Middle East.

Left:
Stores at Aqaba Fort. The arrival of large amounts of supplies and munitions from British depots in Egypt meant a more effective campaign could be carried out against the railway.

Above:
A group of British officers relaxing on the beach at Aqaba. The two men with pipes are the railway demolition experts Bimbashi Peake (furthest from the camera) and Captain Hornby.

Air Attacks, August 1917

Once a British base had been established at Aqaba, the aeroplanes of the Royal Flying Corps (R.F.C.) were quickly returned to active duty in the region. One of their first tasks was to reduce the threat of a counter-attack on Aqaba by the main Turkish force in Ma'an. By the end of the summer, the Turks had strengthened their presence in the town, and with 6,000 infantry, 16 artillery pieces and a cavalry regiment, they presented a serious threat to the newly-arrived British and Arab troops. Lawrence approached the British air commander, Major General Salmond, for assistance. As ever, the railway was selected as a primary strategic target.

Capt. F. Stent, who had replaced Major A. Ross as commander of the Hejaz Detachment of No. 14 Squadron earlier in the year, was chosen to lead the mission. A forward landing ground was established at Quntilla, and from there a surprise attack was launched on Ma'an Station. Flying at a low altitude to make sure of their targets, the aircraft dropped 32 bombs. These included two on the barracks, killing 35 men, eight on the engine-shed, causing heavy damage to the rolling stock, four on a nearby aerodrome and one on the Turkish general's kitchen, which killed his cook. All the planes returned to the base camp safely, despite the low altitude of the mission. The following day, two further raids were carried out, dropping 74 bombs on an artillery battery and cavalry positions at Abu Lissan.

Arab Attacks, Autumn 1917

One of the first raids on the railway after the capture of Aqaba was carried out by Arab forces on the short branch line connecting Uneiza Station with Hisheh Forest. The forest was valuable to the overall Turkish war effort as a source of firewood for their armies in Palestine. It was also vitally important for the continued operation of the railway. The extreme shortage of coal meant that the Turks were dependent on wood in order to keep their trains running. Although wood was far inferior to fossil fuel, causing severe maintenance problems and reducing engine speeds, the wood supplies could at least sustain a basic service on the railway. By August 1917, reports coming out of Madinah told of private houses being stripped of their furniture and structural timber to provide fuel for the locomotives. It must therefore have added considerably to the Turks' difficulties when, in September 1917, a force of Arab regulars led by Maulud Mukhlis, together with 200 bedouin under Sherif Abdul Muin, tore up over 300 rails from the line. In January 1918, Abdul Muin returned with another force, and having driven the garrison off the railhead, completely destroyed the track between the forest and Uneiza Station.

Further south, a party of Beni Atiyya attacked a Turkish post north of Wadi Ithil Station on 18 September. Having captured it and taken 20 prisoners, the tribesmen demolished a section of about 650 rails. The Turks sent out a train with reinforcements, but the damage to the track prevented them from reaching the raiders. Next came a detachment of about 45

Below:
B.E.2c biplanes used by the British in the war on the railway.

THE HEJAZ RAILWAY

Circassian cavalry, but after a hard battle they too were driven off by the Arabs. Continuing up the line again towards Tabuk, the tribesmen attacked an outpost of 70 Turks, killing or capturing the whole garrison. A similar fate awaited another Turkish force, again around 70 men, who had been sent out from Tabuk to halt their progress. The raiding party then proceeded up the railway north of Tabuk, attacking any loose units of Turkish troops on the line. It advanced successfully as far as Mudawwara, where a train supported by machine-guns finally forced it to retire.

Other raids were also being carried out by bedouin forces in the same area. On 18 October an attack was made on 'Hill Post 4', a stronghold between Dhat al Hajj and Bir ibn Hermas Stations. A mixed force of 400 Beni Atiyya, Huweitat, Ruwalla and Sherarat tribesmen led by Sherif Merzuk al Takheimi, besieged the outpost for two days. On 20 October they overran its defences, killing or taking prisoner over half the Turkish force. A train sent to relieve the garrison was also attacked and derailed. However, owing to a lack of explosives, large-scale demolitions could not be undertaken. Nevertheless, the line was put out of action for three days, and a battalion from the 48th Division, stationed north of Ma'an, had to be sent down to the area to bolster the railway's defences.

In Prince Abdullah's southern sector, a major raid was carried out against Buwat Station. A large Arab force of 1,750 bedouin (mainly Al Harb) and four companies of regulars, together with a French artillery contingent of six mountain guns under Lt Kernag, launched the attack at dawn on 11 November. Following an artillery bombardment, the bedouin attempted to rush the defences, but were driven back. After further bombardment, the station caught fire. Two trains carrying reinforcements of Turkish infantry, machine-guns and artillery were brought in from both sides of the station. Although neither train could reach the scene of the action due to earlier demolitions on the line, the Turks quickly set about repairing the track under cover of their guns. By noon, the machine-guns had been moved up to the

Right:
A council of war between Lt Col. P. Joyce (sitting closest to the camera), head of the British mission to the Hejaz and Lawrence's commanding officer in the field, Prince Faisal (in the middle), and Ja'afar Pasha, the commander of the regular Arab forces. (August 1917)

THE WAR ALONG THE RAILWAY - II. AQABA & NORTHWARDS

Above:
A section of track lies twisted and deformed alongside the rail embankment at Akhdar Station.

garrison posts around the station and the Arabs were forced to withdraw.

On 12 December a party of 50 bedouin under Sheikh Mohammed al Ghasib mined and derailed a locomotive south of Akhdar. The train was carrying two Arab chiefs sympathetic to the Turks, Suleiman Rifada of the Billi tribe and Shehab of the Fuqara, each accompanied by a son. Both had been sent down from Damascus by Jemal Pasha to raise support among their followers. Suleiman Rifada was killed in the attack, but Shehab and his son managed to escape in the confusion. Although reinforcements were quickly sent in from both sides of the fighting, the raiding party managed to wipe out the escort of 60 men on the train. 'Having very short time at their disposal, the Arabs could not loot the whole train, which was loaded with supplies for Ibn Rashid among other things; but they succeeded in carrying off 300 rifles and L.T. 24,000 in gold.'[10] Other attacks, carried out by local tribesmen in the area of Tabuk between Al Hazm and Wadi Ithil, accounted for considerable numbers of Turkish dead and captured. Although the damage done to the line was generally small-scale and easily repaired, the raids kept up the pressure on the Turkish forces all along this section of the railway.

T.E. Lawrence: The Troop Train - Mudawwara, Sept 1917

By September 1917 the fierce summer heat had started to subside, and Lawrence decided that the time was ripe for another major raid on the railway. Tribal politics delayed his departure and reduced his bedouin escort to only 100 men. On 16 September the force was finally ready, and the expedition set off for Mudawwara Station, just north of the present Saudi border. Lawrence was well aware that although he had managed to put a

THE HEJAZ RAILWAY

Above:
Lawrence (on foot, centre) with members of his bodyguard at Aqaba in 1917.

Right:
Although the track was relaid at Hallat Ammar in the 1960s, the station still shows evidence of war damage.

raiding party together, tribal disputes and jealousies lay dangerously unresolved just below the surface. On this occasion, as well as the tribesmen under Auda's nephew Zaal, he took along two regular army sergeants, Yells and Brooke, soon to be nicknamed Lewis and Stokes after their 'jealously-loved'[11] weapons.

Arriving at Mudawwara as darkness was falling, Lawrence and Zaal crept slowly forwards across the flats in front of the station to reconnoitre. Although they were worried about the camp dogs giving away their presence, they managed to move in close enough to see the silhouettes of the unlighted tents and hear the men talking. Lawrence wrote, 'One came out a few steps in our direction, then hesitated. He struck a match to light a cigarette, and the bold light flooded his face, so that we saw him plainly, a young, hollow-faced sickly officer. He squatted, busy for a moment, and returned to his men, who hushed as he passed.'[12] Moving back to the safety of a nearby hill, they quickly decided that their force was neither strong enough nor sufficiently united to take on the station with its garrison of 200 men.

The next morning they marched southwards, looking for a suitable place to ambush a train. At Km. 587, between Mudawwara and Hallat Ammar Stations, in the area straddling the current Saudi-Jordanian border, they found a small two-arch bridge. It was an excellent position for the machine guns, set in a high embankment on a curved stretch of track, with a rocky ledge commanding the area. It took five hours to lay a 50 lb gelignite charge, including time to smooth over the disturbed sand. For the first time, Lawrence used an electric device fired by cables leading to a box with a plunging handle instead of the somewhat unreliable automatic mine. The next day, after avoiding one Turkish patrol and managing to divert another, he saw a large force of about 100 men leave Mudawwara Station and start slowly down the line towards their position. The group immediately prepared to withdraw, but before they had packed up their gear, one of the watchmen shouted down that he could see smoke rising from Hallat Ammar Station. Lawrence and Zaal quickly climbed the hill, and from the top saw the long, dark shape of a train moving slowly out of the station towards them.

As the train came closer, they heard the sound of random firing into the desert. It was so heavy that Lawrence wondered if they had enough men to carry out the ambush. 'However, at that moment' he wrote, 'the engines, looking very big, rocked with screaming whistles into view around the bend. Behind them followed ten box-wagons, crowded with rifle-muzzles at the windows and doors; and in little sand-bag rests on the roofs Turks precariously held on, to shoot at us.'[13] Momentarily taken aback by the fact that the train had two engines, Lawrence quickly decided to detonate the mine under the second of them. 'There followed a terrific roar, and the line vanished from sight behind a spouting column of black dust and smoke a hundred feet high and wide. Out of the darkness came shattering crashes and long, loud metallic clanging of ripped steel, with many lumps of iron and plate; while one entire wheel of a locomotive whirled up suddenly black out of the cloud against the sky, and sailed musically over our heads to fall slowly and heavily into the desert behind.'[14] The new electric mine had worked!

The first wagon tumbled into the gap made by the collapsed bridge, and the others were derailed and lay strewn along the track. Immediately, the machine-guns opened fire on the Turkish troops, cutting them down in droves as they scrambled for cover. At the same time the bedouin tribesmen poured in fire from the long spur above the valley, and the Stokes gun pounded those who had gained temporary shelter behind the curved embankment. The Turks broke in panic. Throwing down their rifles and equipment, they fled into the desert. The bedouin, seizing the opportunity, rushed forwards from the ridge and tore into the littered carriages in search of booty. The whole battle was over in less than ten minutes.

Above:
War damaged rolling stock can still be seen scattered along the Saudi section of the railway north of Medain Saleh.

THE HEJAZ RAILWAY

Right:
War Office diagram showing method of attaching explosive charges to the rails.

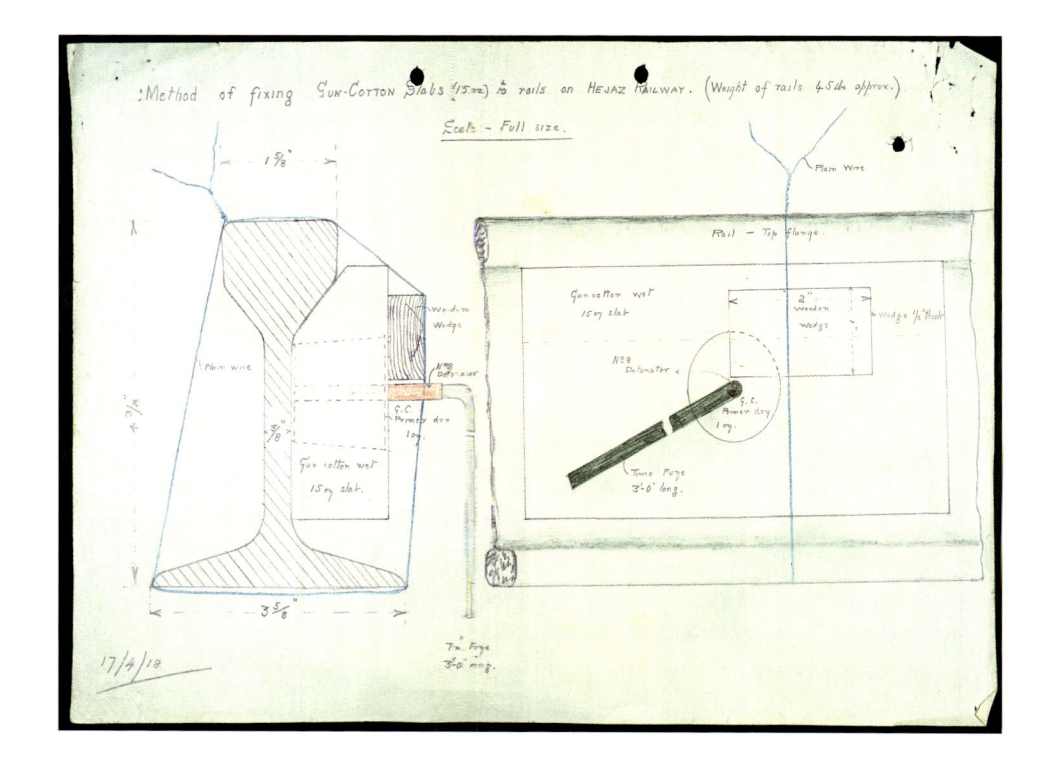

Below:
Initially reluctant to enter the war on the British side, Prince Faisal, Sherif Hussein's third son, was eventually to play a major part in the Allied victory as commander of the successful Arab Northern Army. He is best known in the west for his close relationship with T. E. Lawrence.

The second engine, which had taken the main brunt of the explosion, was completely destroyed. The first, derailed and lying on its side, was still in working order. Lawrence quickly fixed a charge of gun-cotton to the outside cylinder and detonated it before the reinforcements from Mudawwara could reach them. Meanwhile, the bedouin were swarming all over the train in a frenzy of plunder, throwing out the stores from the wagons and loading them onto their camels. In one of the carriages, among a large group of military prisoners, Lawrence discovered five Egyptians. They immediately recognised him and described how they had been captured during a night raid of Major Davenport's near Prince Abdullah's camp in the Hejaz. Before they were given the job of leading away their former captors as prisoners, they had time to tell Lawrence of Davenport's dogged persistence in carrying out operations against the railway in the southern sector. In another carriage he found a very old and dignified Arab lady. He reassured her that she would not be harmed and provided her with water. Months later, he wrote, he received a letter and a small Baluchi carpet from Damascus as a token of her gratitude.

Once the train had been completely looted, all semblance of military discipline was lost. The force broke into small groups, looking more like a straggling baggage caravan than a raiding party. Lawrence quickly had to withdraw, as the Turkish troops from Mudawwara arrived at the scene and attempted to cut off his retreat. The Turks lost 70 dead in the engagement. Thirty had been wounded and 80 taken prisoner. In contrast, only one Arab had been killed and a handful wounded. As well as destroying the two locomotives, the raid had served an important intelligence function, providing a survey of the terrain between Aqaba and Mudawwara. This information was to prove valuable: the ground was now known to be suitable for the use of armoured cars, opening up the possibility of swifter and more heavily-armed raids on the line south of Ma'an in the future.

T.E. Lawrence: Raid on Supply Train - Bir Shedia, October 1917

After a few days in camp discussing politics and military strategy with Prince Faisal, Lawrence was ready to carry out another raid on the railway. Accompanied by the French officer Captain Pisani, and about 150 bedouin, he set off at the beginning of October for the area between Ma'an and the Batn al Ghoul escarpment. Km. 475 was found to be too heavily defended by blockhouses, so the party moved further down the line to Km. 489. Here, Lawrence laid an automatic lyddite mine on one of three bridges in a valley south of Bir Shedia Station. They waited all day and night, but the train that finally passed was carrying only water. Much to the pleasure of the bedouin, who were primarily there for the booty, the explosive failed to detonate.

Lawrence returned to the bridge and laid an electric mine on top of the first one, running the wires to a detonator concealed under the middle bridge. Another 24 hours were spent in waiting, but on the morning of the third day, a pillar of smoke was seen leaving Ma'an. At the same time, the party noticed a patrol advancing slowly down the line towards their position. The group watched closely, wondering which of the two would arrive first. Although there were only six men in the patrol, Lawrence knew that they would be able to raise the alarm before the engine reached the site of the ambush. The train was travelling painfully slowly up a long, gentle slope, but the patrol was in no hurry either and halted several times. Finally, deciding that the train would win the race, Lawrence ordered his men into position. His judgment was correct, and as the engine rolled over the bridge, he stood up and waved his cloak as a signal to the men with the detonator box.

Below:
Captain Pisani's artillery detachment provided regular support for Allied attacks on the railway.

THE HEJAZ RAILWAY

The mine exploded with a huge blast of dust, and a cloud of sickly green-yellow lyddite smoke hung in the air. The locomotive was completely destroyed, but a quick-thinking Turk in the tail of the train jumped out onto the buffers and uncoupled the last four wagons, allowing them to roll back down the slope to safety. Lawrence made a half-hearted attempt to stop them by placing stones on the rails, and received a graze on the hip when a Turkish colonel opened fire at him from the window. The bedouin quickly set about looting the remaining eight wagons. These contained 70 tons of food-stuffs, 'urgently needed', according to the way-bill, in Medain Saleh. Turkish relief forces were within 400 metres of Lawrence's raiders by the time they had finished loading their camels, but the party made their escape without a single man killed or wounded. It was another typical railway attack of the kind described by Lawrence in a letter to his family as 'the usual Arab show, done at no cost to us, expensive for the Turks, but not decisive in any way, as it is a raid and not a sustained operation.'[15]

Right:
"Lawrence had discovered that the bridges on the Hejaz Railway were all built to one pattern, and that in every case the drainage gutter ran out at the spring of the arch, offering an ideal bed for an explosive charge." The Independent Arab - *Sir H. Young*

Effects of the Raids

At the same time as Lawrence was carrying out these raids in the autumn of 1917, a number of increasingly well-trained and experienced Arab fighters were engaged in similar operations on the railway. As part of a recently created force however, the Arabs lacked the vast infrastructure and framework of report-making which, through centuries of military practice, had become standard procedure in the British army. The details of their raids were therefore never documented, and for the most part have been lost to history. Much of their considerable contribution is known only through second-hand reports made by British officers operating alongside them in the field.

Lawrence estimated that as many as 17 locomotives were destroyed by raiding parties working out of Aqaba in the four months before the winter set

The Defence of the Railway

The ability to maintain services on the Hejaz Railway until the final stages of the war was a testimony to the outstanding defensive capabilities of the Turkish forces. Isolated in a harsh, barren environment, their steadfast resistance to the constant attacks made by the surrounding tribes and Allied raiding parties enabled the Ottoman Empire to retain its hold on the holy city of Madinah throughout the conflict.

The sustained operation of the railway was dependent on the Turks' capacity to repair the damage caused both to the track and rolling stock. At the outset of hostilities, they were helped by the fact that large quantities of rails had been stockpiled in Madinah for the planned extension to Makkah. However, these reserves were quickly depleted. Between June and August 1917 alone, the Cairo-based Arab Bureau estimated that the Turks were forced to replace as many as 7,500 rails on the section south of Ma'an. At the beginning of 1917, a deserter from Madinah reported that the station 'had three large stacks of spare rails.'[1] By September, only a remnant of one of these piles remained. To make up the shortfall, sidings were lifted at many of the stations, and track was removed from the Haifa branch (between Haifa and Afule) and the defunct Hisheh Forest line. Damaged rails were also collected and sent to Medain Saleh for reconditioning. Despite all the shortages however, breaks in the line were generally repaired within 24 hours.

The Turks were also extremely adept at keeping the rolling stock in operation. Extensive networks of stone fortifications were constructed in the hills overlooking the line, as well as at strategically important points such as stations and bridges. The garrisons were sent out into the surrounding countryside to cut trees for desperately needed fuel. By the end of the war, the houses of Madinah had been stripped of timber, and even the city gates and wooden sleepers from the track had been removed to keep the locomotives running. On the trains, reinforced carriages and wagons with armed escorts were used. Inspection teams were sent out from many of the stations, checking the line at regular intervals for hidden explosives. In April 1917, Lawrence witnessed these patrols at work every time a train was due to pass. A trolley would lead the team, followed by a group of 11 men on foot 'of whom three were on each side of the way, looking for tracks, and five on the way itself walking bent double, scanning the line for signs of disturbance.'[2] When a piece of rolling stock was damaged in an attack, it would be hauled back to safety, and repaired in the works yards. The remarkably few items abandoned on the line through war damage bear witness to the overwhelming success of the maintenance teams.

Perhaps the greatest achievement however, was that of the ordinary foot soldiers. Confined to their stations and a narrow strip of land along the railway, they were cast adrift in a vast and hostile country, far from the main centres of command. Desperately short of essential supplies, they depended on the railway for virtually all their food and much of their water. By 1918, many were close to starvation, clothed in rags and ravaged by scurvy and other diseases. Despite all the hardships however, they were able to keep the railway operating almost to the end of the war, when their main armies in the north finally collapsed. Their story, for the most part untold, is one of extraordinary resolve, and their accomplishment certainly upholds their long-standing reputation as one of the world's most determined and tenacious fighting forces.

Above:
The 14th bridge in the Yarmuk Valley was selected by Lawrence as the target for a major raid behind enemy lines.

in. As well as ruling out any chance of a Turkish evacuation from Madinah, the resulting pressure on rolling stock hampered the provision of supplies to their armies in Palestine at a critical point in the war. The effect on morale was also significant. As Lawrence put it: 'Travelling became an uncertain terror for the enemy. At Damascus, people scrambled for the back seats in trains, even paid extra for them. The engine-drivers struck. Civilian traffic nearly ceased; and we extended our threat to Aleppo by the mere posting of a notice one night on Damascus Town Hall, that good Arabs would henceforth travel by the Syrian railway at their own risk.'[16]

To defend against the remorseless and ever-increasing attacks from both British and Arab units along the railway, the Turks were forced to reorganise and strengthen their defences. As well as the 14,000 men with Fakhri Pasha in Madinah, four new separate areas of defensive responsibility were established. In the Al Ula sector, Basri Pasha, with 2,000 men at his disposal, patrolled the line southwards to Madinah. Between Al Ula and Tabuk the railway was under the protection of Atef Bey with 5,000 troops. Mohammed Jemal Pasha, based in Tabuk, commanded 5,000 men responsible for the line northwards to Ma'an. With headquarters in Ma'an itself, the 1st Composite force (VII Corps), under Mohammed Jemal Pasha Kuchuk ('The Lesser'), controlled the defence of the line all the way north to the strategically vital junction town of Deraa. Referred to as the 'Ma'an Command', by the end of 1917 its strength had increased to over 7,000 men. Lawrence's growing personal notoriety led to a reward being offered for his capture - 20,000 Turkish pounds alive, 10,000 dead.

T.E. Lawrence: The Raid on the Tel Shehab Bridge, Nov 1917

In the second week of October Lawrence was recalled to military HQ, where it was agreed with Allenby that he would attack a major target inside enemy territory to coincide with the Allied offensive against the Gaza-Beersheba line. The target selected was one of the large bridges in the Yarmuk Valley, on the strategically important Haifa-Deraa branch. Six years earlier as an aspiring young archaeologist, Lawrence had travelled up this line with his mentor, David Hogarth, and admired the splendid views from the bridges as the track twisted and turned its way up the gorge. Now his mission was to destroy one of them, thereby cutting the Turkish forces in Palestine off from their supply depots in Deraa and Damascus. The bridge they finally decided on was the great Yarmuk Valley Bridge No.14, situated below the village of Tel Shehab, 20 kilometres west of Deraa. Over 200 feet wide, its 165-foot central portion was spanned by enormous steel girders. Its destruction would be of a different magnitude altogether to the usual desert demolitions, and the Turks would neither be able to repair it quickly, nor run a diversionary line around the damage. The raid, if successful, would sever the main supply artery to the Gaza front, denying the Turks vital materials and troop reinforcements. It would also seriously impair their ability to retreat in good order.

Left:
British gold and good relations with many of the tribal chiefs enabled Lawrence to acquire some of the finest riding camels in Arabia.

From the beginning of the expedition, Lawrence ran into difficulties. In order to obtain the support of the exiled Algerians who had settled the villages along the north bank of the River Yarmuk, he allowed an Algerian amir named Abd al Kader to join their party. The newcomer immediately started a bitter feud with another member of the group, Sherif Ali ibn Hussein al Harthi (of the al Harith). The Algerian was jealous of Ali's popularity with the tribes and made little effort to conceal his contempt for Lawrence, whom he despised as a Christian. Warned by both the French colonel Edouard Brémond and Auda abu Taye that Abd al Kader might be traitorous, Lawrence kept a close eye on him and tried to calm his quarrels with Ali. However, when he suddenly disappeared with all his men at Azraq, it appeared that their warnings had been well-founded. Allenby wanted the bridge cut to coincide with his offensive in southern Palestine, and had asked for it to be done on 5 November or one of the three following days. It was now 4 November, and with the distant rumble of artillery already being heard far off to the west, Lawrence decided to press on.

The party included a section of Indian machine-gunners, as well as Captain Wood, a Royal Engineer with the demolition expertise necessary to bring down such a large bridge. The Indians, part of Captain Bray's volunteer force, were inexperienced in camel riding and possessed neither the skill nor the tenacious endurance of the bedouin. As time began to run out, Lawrence decided to send them back to base camp, keeping only the six best riders with one Vickers machine-gun. On 6 November they set out for the bridge, watching the lights of Deraa Station to the north as they plodded through the rich agricultural land. When rain began to fall, the soil of the ploughed fields turned to mud and the camels floundered on the slippery surface. Gradually however, the distant roar of the river grew closer until finally before dawn they reached the bridge.

The explosives were quickly handed out and the men picked their way slowly and carefully down the treacherous slope at the side of the valley. As they advanced, wrote Lawrence, they heard the sound of a train making its way up the line from Galilee, 'the flanges of its wheels screaming on the

Right:
Sketch from 1905 report showing the loops in the line beneath Tel Shehab.

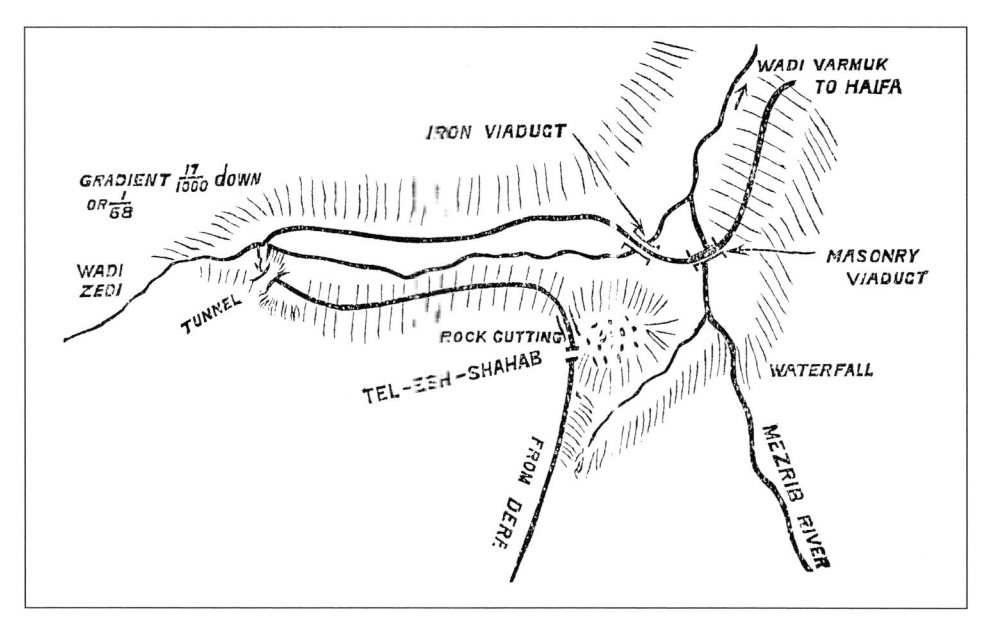

Above:
A German-made Krauss 0-6-0T abandoned on a siding at Hedia Station. The locomotive is now lying on its side.

curves and the steam of its engine panting out of the hidden depths of the ravine in white ghostly breaths.'[17] The rain had now stopped, and from a rocky ledge they could make out the silhouette of the bridge in the damp darkness, with a guard tent pitched at its far end. Lawrence and one of the Arabs crept in beneath the grey skeleton of the underhanging girders and watched a single sentry pacing up and down on the opposite side. Lawrence began climbing back up the slope to organise the munitions, but before he had reached the group, one of them dropped a rifle, which clattered noisily down the rocky bank. The sentry immediately shouted a challenge, fired off his weapon and yelled for the other guards. A gun battle broke out, both sides blasting away blindly into the darkness. The tribesmen, aware of the danger of holding gelignite with bullets flying around, quickly dumped their sacks of explosives over the edge of the gorge and fled. Lawrence had no alternative but to follow, and as they made their way back through the cold dawn rain, the distant rumble of Allenby's guns seemed to mock their failure.

Below:
Steam pipes on the Krauss 0-6-0T at Hedia Station.

T.E. Lawrence: Attack on Train at Km. 172, Nov 1917

Despite their cold and hunger, the men's sense of disappointment persuaded them to attack a train on the way back to Azraq. They stopped on the main Hejaz line at Minifir, where Lawrence had successfully operated with Zaal earlier in the year. Laying a mine on the same culvert as before, at Km. 172, they settled down to wait in the rain and bitter cold for an engine to pass. Finally, one of the watchmen reported that an unusually long train could be seen approaching from the south. Fuelled by an inefficient wood-fire boiler, the locomotive struggled up the gradient with its heavy load at a painfully slow pace. Lawrence, crouching behind a small bush, waited for the right

139

Above:
Lawrence spoke highly of the Ageyl as fighting men, and his personal bodyguard included many from the tribe.

moment to plunge down the handle of the detonator box, but when the time came, nothing happened. He was left sitting out in the open as the 24 wagons (the first ten of which were open trucks full of soldiers) crawled by. He felt the covering vegetation shrink 'smaller than a fig-leaf'[18], and could do nothing but sit there and grin inanely at the Turkish officers staring out at him from the train.

Bitterly disappointed at the missed opportunity, the group returned to their places to continue waiting. The next day, they were more fortunate. A double-engined train pulling 12 carriages was seen approaching from the north. This time the detonator box worked perfectly. The first engine careered off the rails, rolled down the embankment and fell on its side. The second engine toppled into the gap blown out of the culvert and ended up lying across the destroyed tender of the first. The leading three wagons then telescoped into the back of the engine. The other carriages were derailed and lay zigzagged along the track, buckled and broken. One of them was decorated with flags, and clearly contained someone important. Later, they found out that it was no less than the Turkish commander, Mohammed Jemal Pasha Kuchuk, on his way to Jerusalem to bolster the defence against Allenby.

There were about 400 men on board the train, and the absence of the Indian machine-gunners was sorely felt as the survivors scrambled for cover and set up a heavy return fire. Although the ground along the track was strewn with dead, the Turks, no doubt spurred on by the presence of their Corps commander, counter-attacked the Arab positions, trying to work around the sides to outflank them. As always though, the land beyond the railway was the Arabs', and as they gained the safety of the desert, their spirits were lifted by the knowledge that the attack on the train had to some extent made up for their failure at the bridge. 'Next day,' Lawrence wrote, 'we moved into Azraq, having a great welcome, and boasting - God forgive us - that we were victors.'[19]

Overleaf:
The German-made Krauss 0-6-0T was the original workhorse of the railway, with twelve being obtained during the early years of the line. This one can still be seen lying on its side at Hedia Station.

Left:
Iron rungs set into the walls gave the station garrisons easy access to the flat roof for defence purposes.

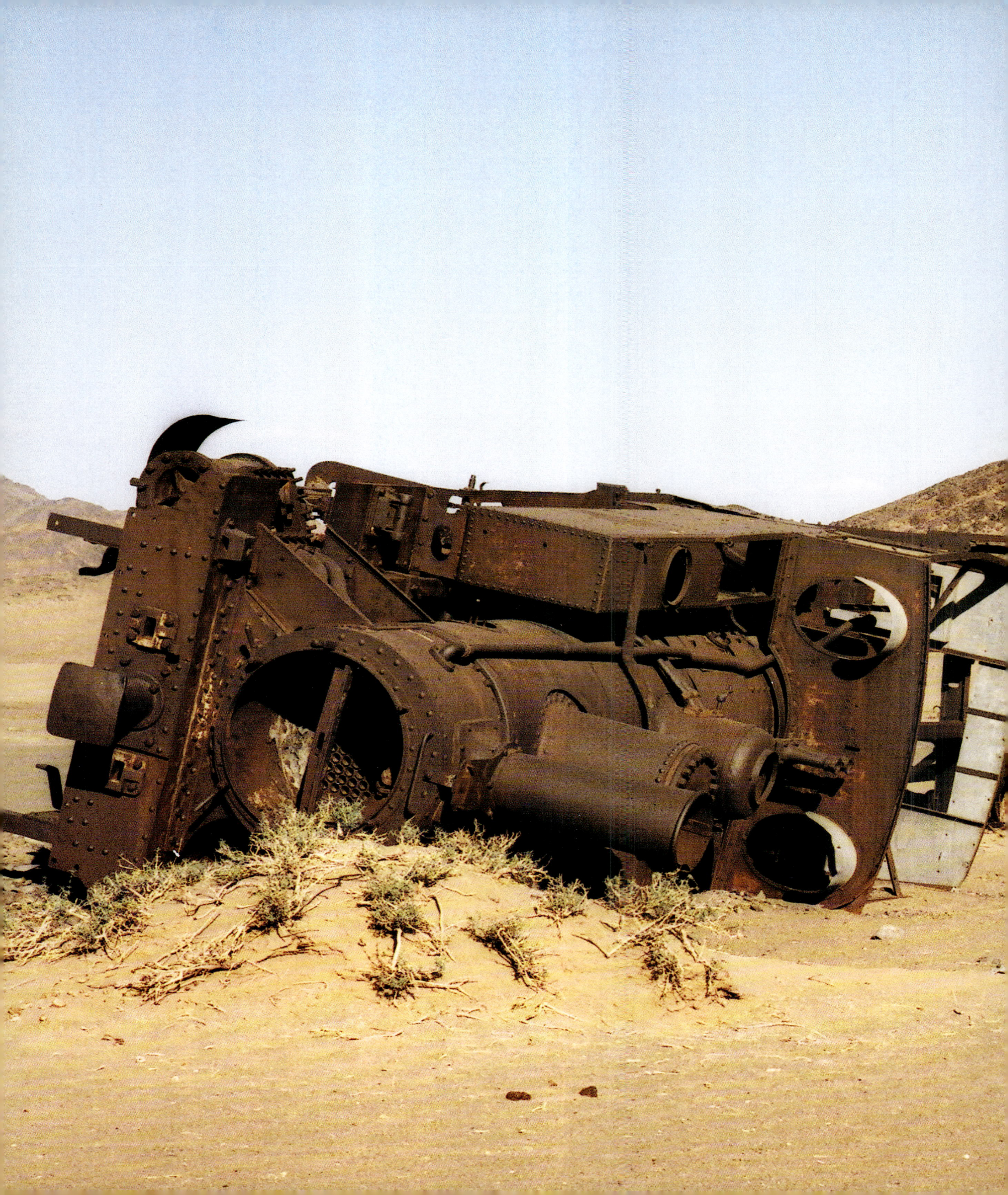

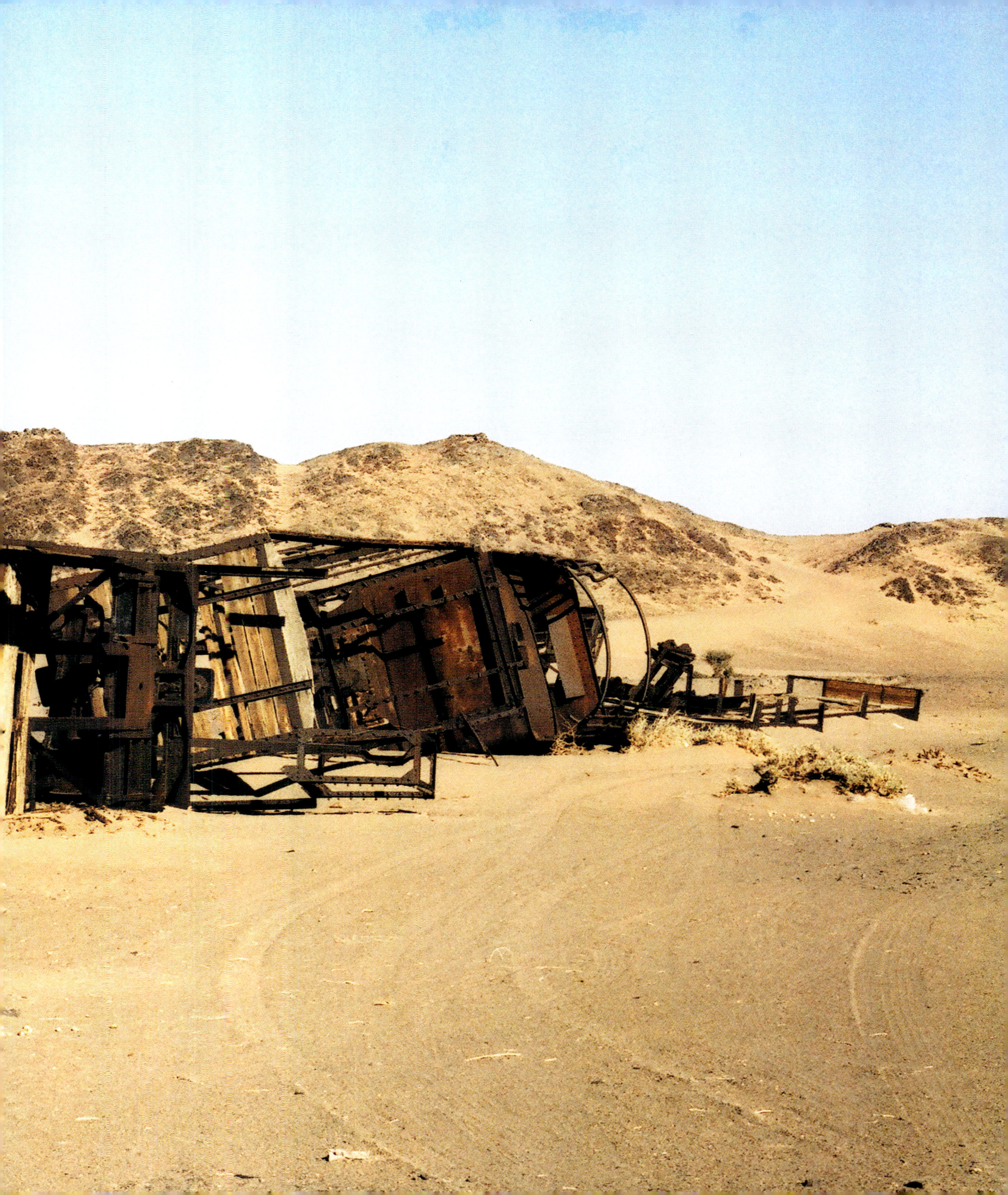

THE HEJAZ RAILWAY

9. The War along the Railway

III - The Road to Damascus

Allied Offensive - Palestine, Winter 1917

Allenby's massive winter offensive in Palestine, the opening shots of which Lawrence had heard during his raid on the Tel Shehab Bridge, met with much greater success than those carried out by his predecessor, Sir Archibald Murray. Beersheba was captured on 31 October 1917, and a week later Turkish forces evacuated Gaza and re-formed their defensive line around Jerusalem. The collapse of the Gaza-Beersheba front finally enabled the British, with an overwhelming force of 95,000 men, to break out of Sinai and push northwards into Palestine. At the same time, news of the Arab army's arrival in Aqaba, and its successful raids on the railway, provided a focal point for Arab dissatisfaction within the Ottoman ranks. The bedouin tribes that had fought on the Turkish side during Murray's unsuccessful attacks on Gaza in the spring now made up part of the British right flank as it occupied the city.

Below:
Meissner Pasha (fourth from the left, at the front) was brought in during the war to extend the Turkish supply lines to Palestine. This was the first train to reach Beersheba.

Left:
Lawrence took refuge for part of the winter of 1917 at Azraq Castle and "as the sky turned solidly to rain ... we learned the full disadvantages of imprisonment within such gloomy ancient unmortared places."
Seven Pillars of Wisdom

In 1914 the Turks had recalled Meissner to the region to help extend their strategic rail network. Now, as the Allied forces moved up through Palestine, they were able to consolidate their gains by taking over these lines. Most were converted to standard gauge to conform to the Egyptian network and to allow faster speeds and increased loads. Many were also increased to double track to avoid the delays caused by crossing points. By the end of 1917, the British had either built or captured a complete railway system, stretching from Egypt and covering the whole of southern Palestine. Although not part of the Hejaz Railway itself, these lines would later be connected up to the integral Haifa-Deraa branch. In the partition arrangements of the post-war period, they would be administered together under the British mandate as part of the 'Palestine Railways' network.

The Allies took Jerusalem on 9 December. To a large extent, the capture of the city changed the nature of the war on the Hejaz Railway. As Allenby's forces advanced across the River Jordan, the attacks from the western flank were carried out by regular British and Australian troops on more traditional military lines. From now on too, the regular section of Prince Faisal's army played a greater role in the Arab campaign. Still supported by a large 'irregular' bedouin contingent, the strategy increasingly revolved around conventional battles, often with the support of French artillery, British armoured cars and the Royal Flying Corps.

The successful Allied offensive in southern Palestine also lightened the response to Lawrence's failure at Tel Shehab. Having flown up to take part in the official entry into Jerusalem, he found Allenby so flushed with victory that his factual statement that he had failed to take the Yarmuk bridge was accepted without further question. Lawrence had spent part of November 1917 holed up in the old Byzantine castle of Azraq, which was to be the Arab's strategic base camp for the following year's push on Damascus. Situated far out in the eastern desert beyond the reach of the garrisons of the Hejaz Railway, the black basalt fortress provided a secure if cold, damp and draughty refuge. Lawrence took up residence in the southern gate tower, and as 'the sky turned solidly to rain... we learned the full disadvantages of

THE HEJAZ RAILWAY

Above:
Rolls Royce tender at Aqaba. The use of motor vehicles changed the nature of the war on the railway.

imprisonment within such gloomy ancient unmortared places.'[1] Despite the dismal weather, Lawrence received a steady flow of visitors, including chiefs of the surrounding tribes. Some were just curious, but others were prepared to give their allegiance to the Arab cause when the campaign restarted in the spring.

Raid on Tel Shahm, Jan 1918

The raid carried out against Tel Shahm Station on New Year's Day 1918 illustrates clearly the way in which the campaign on the railway was to change during the final year of the war. Lawrence had moved back to Aqaba at the beginning of December and found a growing British military infrastructure at his disposal. A track had been built through the rocky gorge of Wadi Ithm and now a full fleet of vehicles - Rolls Royce tenders and armoured cars - had been moved up from Aqaba to the forward camp at Guweira. On 30 December, eight imposing cars under the command of Lt Col. Joyce, raced out across the dried mud-flats towards Mudawwara, the scene of Lawrence's earlier successful ambushing of a train. This time however, Lawrence was involved more as a spectator, and the view from a nearby hill-top allowed him to appreciate fully the advantages of British armour.

The party arrived at the railway between the stations of Tel Shahm and Wadi Rutm on the morning of 1 January. A reconnaissance showed that the line was heavily defended by three outposts; two on hill tops and one dug in near a large seven-arch culvert, about six kilometres north of Tel Shahm. According to Lt Col. Joyce, 'owing to the nature of the country it would have been impossible to approach the line in order to lay a mine without being observed, and as there were no Arabs co-operating, the idea... had to be abandoned.'[2] Instead, it was decided that an attack would be made on the entrenched outpost close to the culvert. Behind steel-covered plating, the drivers were able to advance in total safety. Lawrence watched as three of the armoured cars 'crawled about the flanks of the Turkish earthwork like great dogs nosing out a trail.'[3] The Turks opened fire on them, but to no effect. Having machine-gunned the trenches and driven off a small Turkish relief force brought in from the south, the party moved down the line to attack Tel Shahm.

The engagement opened with an artillery bombardment, which damaged the station and destroyed a number of wagons. The armoured cars then moved up and fired on the windows and doors of the buildings, completely silencing any Turkish resistance. The lack of infantry support made it impossible for the small crews to get out and attempt to capture the station, and they decided to withdraw, content to have tested the suitability of their vehicles for this form of combat. While the amount of material destruction caused was limited, the raid had proved the vulnerability of the railway to the British bases at Aqaba and Guweira. Joyce immediately saw the potential of the armoured cars and reported back to the Arab Bureau in Cairo, asking for extra vehicles. 'It has now been proved that armoured cars can be utilised against the Hejaz railway line, and unless more important work on other fronts is already employing all available cars I suggest a battery be sent, where we can ensure their being utilised to good effect.'[4] Lawrence also recognised the significance of the raid. 'The certainty that in a day from Guweira, we could be operating along the railway, meant that traffic lay at our mercy.'[5] He called it 'fighting de luxe'[6]. The situation for the Turks, already bad, had now become hopeless. The days of the great Ottoman railway were numbered.

Below:
Extensive damage was caused to the station at Wadi Rutm by wartime attacks.

Arab Raids, Jan 1918

On 12 January 1918, as part of a three-pronged attack mounted by Arab forces, a column under Nuri Said and Sherif Nassir, and accompanied by Huweitat and Beni Sakhr tribesmen, attacked Jerouf (sometimes called Jurf or Jerouf al Darawish) Station to the north of Ma'an. It protected a large bridge just to the north, and had a garrison of two batallions and one artillery gun. In a short but bloody engagement the station was captured and nearly 200 Turks were killed or taken prisoner. After the bedouin had looted the station buildings, the regular soldiers demolished two locomotives, a number of trucks, the water tower and the points on the sidings. The important bridge just north of the station was also damaged, but not destroyed, the looting of seven wagons of delicacies intended for the officers' tables in Madinah taking precedence over the more serious work of demolition. One truck was found to be completely packed with cigarettes, and with its plunder the railway garrisons of the Hejaz were deprived of their precious tobacco ration. Prince Faisal, a dedicated smoker himself, was said to have felt so moved by their plight that, in an act of Saladin-like chivalry, he ordered some pack-camels to be loaded with cigarettes and driven in to Tabuk with his compliments.

Further south in the Hejaz, a successful operation was carried out by Sherif Abdullah's forces at Wagga, a long cutting through a ridge of black lava between Hedia and Jeda'a Stations. On 20 January, having destroyed over eight kilometres of track and 19 culverts, the Arab force fought a fierce battle with a Turkish defensive outpost. By the evening they were forced to retreat. 'A field gun fired on them from Hediyah, and two mountain guns arrived from that direction, while from the south came 400 infantry, 60 Camel Corps, four mountain guns and some machine guns.'[7] Ten days later the

Below:
This important bridge just outside Jerouf Station was damaged but not destroyed during the raid of January 1918.

track still hadn't been relaid, and raiding parties moved into position on both sides of the break, waiting for the anticipated repair teams. On 31 January, a French party mined a train carrying spare rails and wood between Abu Na'am and Istabl Antar. Two engines, a tender and three wagons were completely destroyed in the attack.

Spring Offensives, 1918: The Breaking of the Railway

In March 1918 a major Allied offensive was launched across the River Jordan aimed at Amman and the Hejaz Railway. Major General O'Shea and General Chauvel's Desert Mounted Corps crossed the river without difficulty and advanced eastwards, reaching the line on 26 March at a point ten kilometres south of Amman. Having demolished a section of track, one of the cavalry units attempted to run down a train. The driver managed to elude the horsemen by bursting through the breach in the line and escaping into the town. To the north of Amman another group demolished a bridge, effectively cutting it off from Deraa. On 28 March the main attack was carried out, but the Allied troops failed to take either the town or the station. By the beginning of April, they were forced to fall back across the river. The first battle of Amman achieved very little for the Allies, as the damage to the railway was quickly repaired. A further offensive carried out at the end of April met with similar results.

The raids carried out by the less conventional joint Arab-British 'right flank' of Allenby's forces met with greater success. Since the capture of Jerusalem, the Arab army's progress up the west side of the railway, and particularly the capture of Tafila, had increased the strategic pressure on the vital town of Ma'an. Raids on the line were becoming so frequent that traffic was reduced to one train a week. Faced with the prospect of being completely outflanked, the Turks finally decided that it was time to evacuate Madinah and bring the railway garrisons of the Hejaz north to join in the general defence. Prince Faisal received word of the intended evacuation in March, and together with Joyce and Lawrence, immediately set about devising a strategy to isolate Ma'an and thwart the Turkish plan.

On 11 April 1918 a force under Nuri Said and Lt Col. Alan Dawnay stormed Ghadir al Hajj Station, taking 27 prisoners and demolishing three culverts and 1,000 rails. Having wrecked the station, they moved up the line towards Ma'an. On 13 April a group led by Ja'afar Pasha, the Arab regular army's commander, captured Jerdun Station and advanced southwards, destroying up to 3,000 rails. At the same time an Arab column under Maulud Mukhlis captured Jebel Semna, a strategically important hill overlooking Ma'an Station. On 17 April the three prongs of the attack combined, and Nuri Said led a full-scale assault on the station. The attack opened well, and for a while his men gained the cover of some of the railway buildings. However, at the critical moment Captain Pisani's artillery stopped firing. The Arab troops had no alternative but to fall back. They regained the Semna hill, but sustained heavy casualties in the retreat. Arab historians have blamed the French captain for this failure, but he claimed that he had known

Above:
Hejazi medal awarded for bravery at the Battle of Ma'an.

THE HEJAZ RAILWAY

Above:
At Tel Shahm, after a short dash across open ground, Lawrence claimed the station bell.

all along that his ammunition was about to run out, and had implored Nuri Said not to attack at that particular time.

Although Ma'an itself could not be taken, the overall plan to isolate the town and prevent the Madinah evacuations continued south along the line. On 19 April a force under Dawnay, with a bedouin contingent led by Sherif Hazaa, attacked Tel Shahm Station. The operation was carried out with strict military precision, which caused Lawrence some wry amusement - his own successes, of course, having been gained in a much more haphazard fashion. The raid started at dawn, and the Turkish troops, caught sleeping in their trenches, surrendered to the armoured cars without a fight. Capt. Hornby (Royal Engineers) and Lawrence then moved in, and a number of bridges and a length of track were demolished. Following the capture of an outpost to the south, and an aerial bombardment by two planes of the Royal Flying Corps, the main assault on the station began. The Turks quickly surrendered when they saw the armoured cars advancing towards them. After a dash across open ground, Lawrence claimed the station bell, a fine old piece of Damascus brass work. 'The next man took the ticket punch, and the third the office stamp', he wrote, 'while the bewildered Turks stared at us, with a growing indignation that their importance should be merely secondary.'[8]

Having wrecked the station buildings, the party moved south to Ramleh. They found the station abandoned by the Turks and immediately set about demolishing long stretches of the unguarded track. They then continued further southwards with the intention of attacking Mudawwara, but by this time most of the bedouin tribesmen had left, heavily laden with booty. Confronted by accurate artillery fire, Dawnay decided to withdraw, opting instead for blowing up another bridge near Ramleh. On 22 April the party moved north and attacked Wadi Rutm. The enemy quickly retreated from the station to the safety of a redoubt on the Batn al Ghoul escarpment. The station was occupied and more than a kilometre of line destroyed. According to an Arab Bureau bulletin, the fight continued till dusk, the enemy suffering severe casualties from our accurate artillery fire, but pursuit was impossible in the dark owing to the precipitous nature of the passage up the escarpment.'[9] At about the same time, a party of Tuwaiha tribesmen under Sheikh Mohammed al Dheilan rampaged down the line, destroying the track and attacking the stations of Ghadir al Hajj, Bir Shedia, Aqaba Shamia, Batn al Ghoul and, at the bottom of the great escarpment, Wadi Rutm.

In all, about 125 kilometres of track and seven stations south of Ma'an fell in the offensive. Although Ma'an itself wasn't captured, the strategic stronghold of Jebel Semna was held, despite several strong counter-attacks by the Turks. The last through train of the war between Damascus and Madinah ran in early April 1918. With all the damage, and the reserves of spare rails now finally used up, Ma'an was effectively isolated. Any idea of evacuating Madinah and the railway garrisons of the Hejaz had to be abandoned. As the historian George Antonius has pointed out, the success of these operations can be gauged by looking at the numbers of Turkish troops tied up in defending the railway. In the spring of 1918 there were more Turkish troops deployed in Ma'an and the Hejaz than there were facing the main British army in Palestine.

THE WAR ALONG THE RAILWAY - III. THE ROAD TO DAMASCUS

Cutting the Railway: Ma'an to Qatrana, May 1918

Although the threat of reinforcements being brought up from Madinah and the Hejaz had been averted, a large Turkish force in Amman was still waiting to move southwards down the line to bolster the defence of Ma'an and open counter-attacks against the new Allied bases. Following the great German thrust on the Western Front in France, Allenby was temporarily hamstrung by the transfer of two of his divisions, and the responsibility for preventing the redeployment of the Turkish troops in Amman therefore fell to the Royal Flying Corps and the Arab army. As always, the railway held the key to the Allied strategy. Having effectively broken the line to the south of Ma'an, the focus of operations now turned to the section of track north of the town, with the aim of severing communications with Amman, and therefore with Damascus itself.

The first major attempt to cut the railway was carried out by an Arab force under Sherif Nassir at Qatrana. Over a period of five days from 8 May, three separate attacks were made on the station. Although they were all repulsed, a Turkish company was captured and considerable damage was caused to the line. On 11 May three battalions of regular Arab troops under Nuri Said carried out a raid on Jerdun, the first station to the north of Ma'an. Supported by artillery and three planes from the R.F.C., the Arabs overwhelmed the garrison after a brief engagement. Thirty Turks were killed and 150 were captured, and some machine-guns and an artillery piece were seized. After demolishing a long stretch of track, the Arabs pulled out on 14 May. The Turks immediately re-occupied the station, and an Arab attempt to retake it three days later was beaten back by a Turkish bayonet charge. As

Below:
As Chief of Staff of the Arab regular forces, Nuri Said took part in many of the raids on the railway. He later became Prime Minister of Iraq, and was killed by a mob in Baghdad during the military coup of July 1958.

Above:
Before heading north for the wells of Jefer, Buxton's Imperial Camel Corps blew up the station's water installations.

reinforcements started to arrive from Uneiza, the party was forced to withdraw.

On 23 May, Sherif Nassir, with a party of Huweitat and Beni Sakhr tribesmen, and accompanied by Capt. Hornby and Capt. F. Peake (Egyptian Camel Corps), kept up the pressure on this section of the railway by attacking and capturing Al Hasa Station. Following an initial charge by the bedouin, the two British officers moved in and reduced the buildings to rubble. As well as the station itself, they demolished the well, the tanks and pumps, some rolling stock, three bridges and about six kilometres of track. The next day the party moved north and destroyed Faraifra Station and its sidings. The attacks then continued along the line for several days, with extensive demolitions causing heavy damage to Sultani (a crossing between Menzil and Faraifra), Jerouf, and sections of the track between Jerdun and Ma'an. The Germans in the area admitted that over 25 bridges had been destroyed in these raids, effectively preventing the movement of a large-scale force southwards to Ma'an.

The Advance on Damascus, Sept–Oct 1918

During the hot summer months of 1918, a slow war of attrition was waged along the railway, with the Arab army and the R.F.C. maintaining steady pressure on the Turks through persistent raiding. By August, Indian troops had arrived in Palestine to replace the two Allied divisions transferred to

France. Following a radical reorganisation of his forces, Allenby was ready to reopen a major front. Before battle was joined, there was time for one last raid against the station of Mudawwara, which was still being resolutely defended, holding out defiantly amidst all the destruction. For this operation, the newly-arrived battalion of Major Buxton's Imperial Camel Corps was used. On 8 August, with the support of the Royal Flying Corps and an artillery battery, an attack was made at dawn in three columns. Against such overwhelming odds the Turkish garrison finally capitulated, with 21 men killed and 150 taken prisoner. The captured Turks were set to work providing water for the camels, while Buxton's engineers demolished the wells, the pumps and about 2,000 metres of track. Before the party finally moved off towards the wells of Jefer at dusk, the great water tower was blown to pieces in a mighty explosion.

The concluding phase of the campaign in Arabia finally brought together the two main elements of the Allied war machine, as Allenby's regular army converged with Prince Faisal's forces in a single push towards Damascus. Allenby's offensive of September 1918 has gone down in the annals of military history as a tactical masterpiece. Even taking into consideration his clear superiority in numbers and equipment, the speed with which his forces overwhelmed the well-entrenched Turkish defences was remarkable. The principal element of his strategy was surprise, achieved through the dissemination of false intelligence and a build-up of decoy troops. In the end, his lightening cavalry strike of 19 September up the Mediterranean coastal strip enabled him to completely outflank, surround and annihilate the core of the Turkish 4th and 7th Armies.

On Allenby's right flank, Prince Faisal's army, including the British contingent under Joyce and Lawrence, was given the strategically vital role of isolating the junction town of Deraa. They were to prevent the movement of reinforcements up to the main Palestine front and impede the withdrawal of the large garrison from Ma'an. Prince Zeid, Faisal's half-brother, together

Above:
Allied troops preparing the charges for the water tower at Mudawwara Station during the successful raid of 8th August 1918.

Left:
Prince Faisal (seated, front right) with Auda abu Taye and Lowell Thomas, Lawrence's first biographer, driving through Wadi Ithm in a Talbot.

THE HEJAZ RAILWAY

Above:
Jemal Pasha commanded the Turkish forces in Syria, Palestine and the Hejaz from his headquarters in Damascus.

with some of the bedouin forces, was detailed to keep up the pressure on the railway between Ma'an and Amman, while a large mobile column of troops under Nuri Said and Sherif Nassir assembled at Azraq ready for the main assault on Deraa.

The British offensive was scheduled to commence on 19 September. However, the railway operations were opened a few days in advance, with the aim of severing communications at Deraa and drawing in vitally needed Turkish troops to reinforce the junction station. On 13 September an attempt by Peake to cut the line at Mafraq, between Amman and Deraa, was called off due to hostility from the local tribes: even at this late stage, local Arab support for the Allied cause could not be taken for granted. The following night, moving north towards Nessib, Peake achieved his objective, finding an area of the railway open to attack and demolishing a bridge.

On 16 September, the severing of the line between Amman and Deraa was made certain. Joyce and Lawrence, using two armoured cars, attacked and captured the garrison of a guard-house protecting a large bridge, also on the section between Mafraq and Nessib. The 80-foot-long structure, with its shining white marble slab inscribed with a dedication to the now deposed Sultan Abdulhamid II, was blown up, but intentionally left standing. This method of demolition shattered the arches of the bridge but kept its skeleton intact, giving the enemy the additional task of clearing away the wreckage before rebuilding it.

Having effectively cut Deraa off from Amman and the possibility of reinforcement from the south, the attacks now moved to the section of line north of the town. On 17 September an Arab force under Nuri Said, accompanied by Major H. Young (Indian Army) and Captain Pisani's French artillery battery, attacked and captured a defensive Turkish outpost on the line near Tel Arar. Despite being straffed and bombed by enemy planes from Deraa, Peake's demolition teams managed to destroy about 600 pairs of rails using the 'tulip' method. The track had now been cut on both sides of Deraa, effectively severing the Turkish lines of communication two days before the launch of Allenby's great offensive. Lawrence commented: 'It was the only railway to Palestine and Hejaz and I could hardly realize our fortune; hardly believe that our word to Allenby was fulfilled so simply and so soon.'[10]

The focus of the attacks then shifted to the west of Deraa, where the final arm of the railway branched off through the Yarmuk Valley towards Haifa and Palestine. At Muzeirib Station, following a bombardment by Captain Pisani's artillery, Nuri Said and Sherif Nassir quickly forced the surrender of the garrison. While the station buildings were being smashed up and looted by the local peasantry, Lawrence and Young cut the telegraph and demolished the points. Finally at sunset, having found two large petrol tanks and some wagons full of firewood, they set the whole place on fire. The party then continued down the line to the bridge at Tel Shehab, the scene of Lawrence's earlier failed raid. Although the garrison had been strengthened, the capture of the bridge seemed possible when the young sheikh of Shehab village approached to tell them that the Armenian commander of the guard was prepared to betray his post. However, as they waited at the top of the ravine, Young 'heard an engine puffing heavily up the steep gradient on our left. It

'Tulips'

It was in the summer of 1918, as the Allied forces were converging on Damascus, that Lawrence and Capt. Peake 'hit upon the plan of blowing up rails by the method called by Lawrence the 'Tulip'.'[1] The customary technique of detonating a charge directly under the rails was of limited benefit 'as the Turks merely joined the broken ends together, if pressed for time; or, in great emergency ran the train over the broken rails.'[2] With the tulip method however, more extensive damage could be caused. It was found that a 2 lb. charge placed under the central sleeper would blow the metal upwards 'into a tulip-like shape without breaking; by doing so it distorted the two rails to which its ends were attached.'[3] When the charge was properly laid, the Turks were unable to repair the damage, and had to replace the whole section of track. As Lawrence described it: 'The lift of it pulled them six inches together; and as the chairs gripped the bottom flanges, warped them inward seriously. The triple distortion put them beyond repair. Three or five sleepers would be likewise ruined, and a trench driven across the earthwork: all this with one charge, fired by a fuse, so short that the first, blowing off while the third was being lighted, cast its debris safely overhead.'[4]

came to a stand-still just below us, and sounds of booted feet and hoarse words of command came up to us through the night mist.'[11] It was a trainload of Turkish and German reserves sent up from Afule to reinforce Deraa. Their arrival destroyed any chance of an attack. Instead, they moved south towards Nessib, where, following some fierce fighting, Lawrence demolished a large bridge using 800 lbs of gun-cotton.

Above:
A 'tulip' charge exploding on the railway near Deraa.

THE HEJAZ RAILWAY

The Final Offensive, Sept 1918

With Deraa isolated, and after a feint towards Nablus, Allenby's forces launched the main thrust of their offensive up the weakly-defended coastal plain on 19 September. The speed of their advance was devastating and an account of the campaign reads very much like a list of captured towns. By the second day of the offensive, having overwhelmed Jenin, the Allied forces powered up the Nablus branch line taking the junction station of Afule with ten engines and 50 wagons. They then swung east towards Deraa, following the Haifa branch, and captured Beisan. On 21 September, the Turks abandoned Jisr al Mejami Station, and an advance Allied unit took up position beside the River Jordan to block the line.

On 22 September the German commander, Liman von Sanders, withdrawing up the Hejaz Railway from Deraa to Damascus, suffered the indignity of having to disembark from the train and continue his journey on foot, owing to the demolitions on the line. The following day, trains carrying about 3,000 Turkish troops between Amman and Deraa were also forced to halt, the men having to march alongside the damaged track between Mafraq and Nessib. On 25 September Major-General Chaytor's Anzac troops

Below:
Locomotives captured from the Turks lined up in the sidings at Haifa Station.

entered Amman, blocking the retreat of the Ma'an garrison. This beleaguered force 'harassed by Arabs, reached the vicinity of Zize [Jiza], where it was surrounded by the Beni Sakhr and the people of Kerak. The whole force, numbering rather over 5,000, was in great straits, owing to want of food and water, and surrendered to a detachment of British cavalry on September 29.'[12] At the same time, the station at Jiza was taken, with three engines and 25 wagons captured. An Allied brigade also moved north from Amman, taking Zerqa Station on 26 September and Mafraq Station two days later.

On the western flank Allenby's forces had pushed up the coast as far as Haifa and Acre. These two ports, with their short connecting branch around the bay, were in Allied hands by 24 September. On the Haifa-Deraa line the advance reached the village of Samakh on 25 September. After some heavy fighting around the sidings, the station was taken. An Allied unit then continued eastwards along the railway, taking control of the first bridge in the Yarmuk Valley. The Turkish and German forces began moving back rapidly towards Deraa, demolishing the second and third Yarmuk bridges to cover their retreat.

By 26 September the Turks had carried out sufficient repairs to the line to enable trains to run between Deraa and Damascus. By this time Lawrence had moved back into the area and, after watching three full trains pass unmolested, he took his men down onto the railway and blew up a three-kilometre section of track. The task of cutting Damascus off from the south was then completed by Sheikh Tallal and Auda abu Taye. While Tallal seized Ezra, Auda took Ghazala Station, capturing 200 men, a train and a large cache of guns. On the same day, Allenby issued orders for the advance on Damascus. As the Australian Desert Mounted Corps and the Indian 5th Cavalry Division moved in from the west, the Indian 4th Cavalry Division joined Prince Faisal's forces for the final thrust up the Hejaz Railway.

Above:
S.L.M. (Swiss Locomotive and Machine Works) 2-8-0 standing on the line three kilometres south of Wayban Station. Its derailment was almost certainly the result of an attack by an Arab raiding party in November 1918, ten days after the armistice was signed (see p.110).

Below:
Hartmann 2-8-2 (No. 260) on the Syrian section of the line north of Ezra.

Above:
Arab forces entering Damascus along the rail track in October 1918. At the same time Turkish prisoners are being led out of the city in the opposite direction.

On 27 September Terad Shaalan, together with a force of Ruwalla tribesmen, entered Deraa, capturing 500 prisoners. The arrival of Sherif Nassir and General Barrow's Indian cavalry the following day put a halt to the customary looting and made the town secure enough for Prince Faisal to move in on the 29th and set up his headquarters. The station was taken in reasonable condition; most of the damage to the buildings had been caused by an Allied air attack four days earlier. Among the captured rolling stock were some new Hartmann 2-8-2s. Two heavily-loaded trains were found standing in the sidings - one of the wagons contained a full set of brass musical instruments. Meanwhile, the shattered Turkish forces were desperately trying to retreat towards Damascus. As they straggled back through hostile country, the Arab army, and in particular the bedouin contingent, harried them every inch of the way. Auda abu Taye, the hero of Aqaba, fell upon what was left of the crushed and exhausted Turkish troops, decimating a column of over 4,000 men as they attempted to make their way north to safety. 'In that night of his last battle the old man killed and killed, plundered and captured, till dawn showed him the end.'[13]

On 1 October 1918, elements of the Allied and Arab forces arrived in

THE WAR ALONG THE RAILWAY - III. THE ROAD TO DAMASCUS

Right:
The Turks set fire to Qadem Station before retreating from Damascus. The locomotive shed (the large structure on the left) and the smaller administrative building in front of it escaped damage.

Below:
Famous photograph of Lawrence, taken at Damascus in November 1918, when the full strain of his long term of wartime duty was clearly visible on his face.

THE HEJAZ RAILWAY

Right:
Damaged rolling stock, evidence of the heavy fighting that took place at Abu Na'am.

Below:
Fakhri Pasha's determined leadership prevented Madinah from falling into Allied hands during the war. Even after the armistice was signed in October 1918, he refused to relinquish the Holy City.

Damascus to a tumultuous reception. Sherif Nassir, a mainstay of the revolt from its earliest days, fittingly led the Arab forces through the celebrating crowds. Two days later, Prince Faisal's triumphal entry confirmed the end of 400 years of Ottoman rule. Before the Turks retreated however, they made one last attempt to destroy part of the great railway which only ten years earlier they had been so proud to have built. Abandoning the city, they demolished the telegraph centre, blew up their supply depots and finally set Damascus Qadem Station on fire. As Lawrence approached over a ridge at dawn the following morning, he looked down at 'the silent gardens... blurred green with river mist, in whose setting shimmered the city beautiful as ever, like a pearl in the morning sun. The uproar of the night had shrunk to a stiff, tall column of smoke, which rose in sullen blackness from the store-yard by Kadem, terminus of the Hejaz line.'[14] Although the fighting was to continue up through Syria until an armistice was signed on 30 October, as far as the Hejaz Railway was concerned, the war in the north was over.

The Surrender of Madinah, Jan 1919

As a final footnote to the conflict, one last scene had yet to be played out on the railway. Far off to the south, behind all the manoeuvering of great armies, the city of Madinah was still resolutely holding out. Tabuk fell to the Arabs on 20 October, with 200 Turks and several machine-guns captured. The garrisons of the stations between Akhdar and Tabuk then evacuated their posts and retreated northwards, harried relentlessly by the local bedouin as they withdrew. Medain Saleh was taken by Sheikh Sultan al Faqir 'who was given two old guns from Teima. He succeeded in surrounding the town and an unsuccessful sortie of the garrison was heavily punished, 33 Turks being killed and 21 taken prisoner.'[15] Abu Na'am fell to Farhan al Aida and his Anaiza, with 30 of the garrison captured. However, despite having been under constant siege since 1916, the garrison of Madinah, led by its redoubtable commander Fakhri Pasha, still stood firm.

When the Armistice of Mudros was signed at the end of October, it was expected that even Fakhri Pasha, like all the other Ottoman officers in the field, would surrender his forces 'to the nearest Allied commander'. However, he deemed it his solemn duty to continue his defence of the Prophet's tomb until a personal order from the Sultan relieved him of the responsibility. He also considered it dishonourable to have to surrender to Bimbashi Garland, whom he did not regard as a genuine 'Allied commander'. Captain Bassett explained his rationale: 'In battle, he said, a subaltern may take prisoner a Field Marshal but when it was a question of the surrender of an unbeaten garrison under the terms of an armistice such a position seemed to him impossible.'[16] He held out for over two months further, and only on 10 January 1919, when a group of his less determined fellow officers mutinied and handed him over to the enemy, did the city finally surrender. With its fall, the whole of the Hejaz line passed out of Ottoman hands. The 'sick old man of Europe' had finally expired, and the Arab provinces of the once-great empire, through whose lands the railway ran, were to be formed into three new nation states. Although a few trains would still struggle south to Madinah, with the collapse of political unity, for all practical purposes the great Ottoman Hejaz Railway, linking Damascus to the Holy Land of Islam, had come to an end.

Below:
Fakhri Pasha shaking hands with Prince Abdullah, after a group of his fellow officers mutinied and finally forced him to surrender Madinah in January 1918.

THE HEJAZ RAILWAY

10. *The Railway after the First World War*

The End of Hostilities - Damage Assessment

With the capture of Fakhri Pasha in Madinah, Ottoman control of the Hejaz Railway came to a complete end. By the 'Agreement for the Surrender of Madinah', all Turkish forces still on the railway in the Hejaz were ordered to evacuate their garrisons and assemble at the southern terminus. A committee of notables and tribal sheikhs was formed to prevent attacks on the retreating soldiers and to avoid further demolitions being carried out on the line. A few of the railway staff, as well as some of the technicians operating the telegraph and the city's electrical installations, were retained on full pay. King Hussein also paid subsidies to the tribes to prevent unnecessary damage being caused to the track. Having sponsored some repair work, by 1920 a limited service for pilgrims had been re-established.

In the immediate aftermath of the armistice, the area north of Ma'an fell under British military control. In January 1919, an expedition led by Major D. Heslop was sent from Haifa to assess the damage done (both by the Allies and the retreating Turks) to the track south of Deraa. Using a small tank

Below:
Original photograph of the train Major Heslop used on his 1919 expedition to assess the damage caused to the railway.

162

Left:
A wrecked train at Ghadir al Haj Station, 16 kilometres south of Ma'an.

engine sent down from Damascus, the group proceeded to Nessib without difficulty. Beyond this point, numerous stops were made to clear telegraph poles and wire from the line. On two occasions abandoned wagons had to be hauled off the track. At Amman the roof of the engine shed had been damaged, but the expedition was able to continue southwards as far as Qatrana, where three days were spent carrying out temporary repairs to a wrecked bridge.

Beyond Qatrana extensive damage had been caused to the line and the expedition could proceed only very slowly by clearing debris from the track. Some of the bridges also had to be repaired, including a large one at Uneiza. Between Amman and Ma'an, all the stations except Qatrana had been wrecked and the wells and cisterns filled in. Heslop's comment on the damage caused to the track by the 'tulip' method of demolition was a clear indication of its destructive power. 'Lawrence's most effective demolitions, however, were when he destroyed several hundred yards of permanent way by blowing up the joints. These we could not repair, and much delay was caused by taking up the track behind the train and relaying it in front.'[1]

About five kilometres south of Ma'an, two kilometres of the line had been completely demolished and the expedition had to be abandoned. Leaving the tank engine with a damaged fire-box at Ma'an, the men set off on foot across the desert to Aqaba, where they arrived safely after a three-day march. Some months later it was reported that Hejazi soldiers had managed to push the engine all the way back to Deraa, where they repaired it and returned it to Damascus!

Other inspections showed that the track between Damascus and Deraa was in a good state of repair. Despite the damage done to Qadem Station by the retreating Turkish forces, the line could be brought back into service almost immediately. The Haifa-Deraa branch was also found to be in a reasonable condition. However, two bridges in the Yarmuk Valley between Samakh and Hamme had been destroyed by the Turks and had to be temporarily rebuilt - one by the Royal Engineers, and the other by an Australian team. At the beginning of 1919, when the members of Heslop's expedition made the

Below:
The Sultan's private carriage now provides the focal point for a bustling café at Damascus Kanawat Station.

Above:
The large bridges of the Yarmuk Valley were rebuilt after the war.

journey up to Deraa on this line, trains were being operated, but 'with some difficulty.'[2]

The Afule to Massoudiah branch, which during the war had been linked up to the rest of the Palestine network via Tel Keram, was found to be in a usable condition. The Deraa to Bosra branch however, had been lifted by the Turks in 1915, as the rails had been urgently needed for military supply lines in Palestine. It was rebuilt in the early 1920s. The 18-kilometre Haifa-Acre branch, also taken up in 1915, was replaced by the British in 1919, and a steel bridge over the River Na'amein near Acre, destroyed by a French battleship, was rebuilt using wooden trestles.

Post-War Arrangements

The southern section of the railway in the Hejaz now lay within King Hussein's new realm. The administrative arrangements for the area north of Ma'an however, were more complicated. Following negotiations in Europe, the Allies set up three separate sectors, with the British in Palestine, the French in Lebanon, and the Arabs under Prince Faisal controlling the interior from Damascus to Ma'an. Despite travelling to London and Paris, Prince Faisal was unable to secure the lands which the Arabs believed had been pledged to them at the beginning of the war. In a meeting with Clemenceau in November 1919, under threat of military confrontation with the French, he was forced to accept the arrangements as they stood, pending a final settlement at the peace conference. The nationalists were incensed by the perceived Allied duplicity, and following his return to Damascus, declared

THE RAILWAY AFTER THE FIRST WORLD WAR

Syria an independent state. Faisal became its first constitutional monarch on 8 March 1920.

The policy of declaring the railway a waqf (religious endowment) had been employed by the Turks in 1914 to frustrate French attempts to gain control of it. As a religious institution it could not be administered by non-Muslims, and a concession to the French for its operation had therefore been out of the question. By 1920 the British had developed long-term ambitions to build a pipeline and railway to link the oil fields of Iraq with the Mediterranean Sea at Haifa. In order to implement the plan it was essential that they held control of the Haifa-Deraa branch. Aware of British intentions, the Arab government in Syria declared that the whole Hejaz Railway system, including its branches, was waqf. Officials from the British government in Palestine responded by claiming (erroneously) that the Haifa branch had never been an integral part of the railway.

As the officials of various government agencies argued over the meaning, extent and implications of waqf, the issue was further complicated by the seizure of Damascus by the French. A month after the declaration of Syrian independence, the San Remo Conference confirmed the Allies' division of territory into what were now called 'mandates', with Britain taking Palestine, Transjordan and Iraq, and France gaining Lebanon and parts of Syria. Arab frustration boiled over into violence, and there were a number of attacks against French military outposts. This was exactly the pretext the French had been waiting for to move against King Faisal. By July, the king's position in Damascus had become impossible. To the end he clung to the belief that Allenby would intervene on his behalf, and his final removal by force after such a glorious entry to the city less than two years earlier 'was a pathetic, almost tragic episode.'[3]

Above:
The wood has slowly decayed on this carriage standing by the line north of Medain Saleh.

Left:
All that remains of the station building at Muzeirib on the now defunct D.H.P. Muzeirib to Damascus line.

THE HEJAZ RAILWAY

Right:
Tubize 0-6-0T abandoned at Madinah Station. Built in Belgium in 1893, it was originally intended for the French D.H.P. Damascus-Muzeririb line.

Below:
Container for carrying documents and plans, used during the post-war period, when the Jordanian section of the railway came under British administration.

Ironically, Faisal's departure from Damascus was to be on the same railway that had provided the focal point for his inspired leadership and the campaign of his victorious Arab army. The telegram from Colonel Toulat, Chief of the French Mission, confirming his expulsion, was composed in the same fine diplomatic language that had accompanied the agreements made with the British at the beginning of the war:

'I have the honour to communicate to Y.R.H. a decision of the French Government requesting you to leave Damascus as soon as possible by way of the Hejaz Railways, with Y.R.H.'s Family and Suite.
A special train will be at the disposal of Y.R.H. and Suite.
This train will leave the Hejaz Station at 5 hours tomorrow, July 28th 1920.
I beg Y.R.H. to accept the expression of my high consideration.' [4]

The 'special train' took Faisal to the coast at Haifa. Anxious to reach Egypt before Allenby left for England, he requested to proceed south by rail through Palestine. Ronald Storrs, who had played such a large part in the negotiations to bring Sherif Hussein and his family into the war on the Allied side, organised a guard of honour as the train passed through Lydda. One can imagine his feelings as he watched the beleaguered Amir now making his way out of the country as an exile. 'He carried himself with dignity… though the tears stood in his eyes and he was wounded to the soul. The Egyptian Sultanate did not 'recognise' him, and at Qantara station he awaited his train sitting on his luggage.'[5] Although at the Cairo Conference of 1921, Churchill and Lawrence managed to install Faisal on the throne of Iraq, his departure from Damascus was a sad epitaph for Arab aspirations to achieve a great and unified independent state.

The French takeover of Syria did not solve the issue of the railway's legal status. 'The violent seizure of Damascus… introduced a new complication into an already complex problem.'[6] In the discussions that preceded the

Treaty of Sèvres (August 1920), the Turks abandoned their previous claim that the line was a religious endowment. They argued instead that it was state property, and that as such it should be included in the assessment of reparations. They were negotiating from a position of weakness, and ultimately had no option but to accept the terms dictated by the British and French. In Article 360 of the treaty, the Turkish government relinquished all rights to possession of the railway. Nevertheless, having given up the claim to ownership, the Sultan's representative was able to secure recognition of its 'special position... from the religious point of view.'[7]

Following the invasion of Damascus, the French military authorities had taken over the running of the Hejaz Railway from an Arab directorate. Preference was immediately given to the D.H.P.'s Damascus to Beirut line, with the Haifa-Deraa branch receiving only a limited share of the available freight. In spite of this, between 1920 and 1923 the French military was able to make a profit of almost half a million Syrian pounds from its operation. In 1921, during riots in Damascus, a fire destroyed one of the administrative buildings, causing the loss of all the Arabic records relating to the construction, financing and running of the railway.

The Treaty of Sèvres confirmed the division of Arab territory and the railway was formally carved up between the British and French mandated areas of control. In a convention signed in December 1920, the French were awarded the Damascus-Nessib main line section, and the portion between Samakh and Deraa on the Haifa branch. The British received the remainder of this branch, from Samakh to Haifa, as well as the extension to Acre, and the Afule to Nablus line (which was now linked up to the rest of the British-administered system in Palestine). On the main line they controlled the whole stretch between Nessib in the north and Qatrana in the south. The

Above:
Popular local support and Allied gratitude for his wartime role ensured that Prince Abdullah became the first ruler of Transjordan.

Below:
Train crossing a bridge north of Amman. The locomotive is a Nippon 4-6-2 (No. 82)

THE HEJAZ RAILWAY

Above:
Sleepers from the original track are still used by the bedouin of the Hejaz to mark their land.

Right:
The works yard at Amman Station still maintains the old steam locomotives for the Hejaz Railway in Jordan.

southern section, incorporating Ma'an and Mudawwara, remained a part of the Hejaz until June 1925.

In November 1920, Prince Abdullah, accompanied by several Arab notables and a force of 500 men, travelled by train from Madinah to Ma'an. On arrival, he declared that he had come to support the struggle against the French, and called on the Syrians to rise up in revolt. The potential for unrest alarmed the British, and their concern was increased when, in March 1921, Abdullah moved to Amman and received a tumultuous reception. Churchill had just opened the Cairo Conference and the resulting creation of the new state of Transjordan, with Abdullah as its first ruler, served to relieve the situation. Together with the acquisition of the throne of Iraq for Faisal, this measure to some extent appeased British consciences over the wartime debt to the Hashemites.

From the ashes of the Ottoman Empire, the Turkish nationalists led by Mustafa Kemal (Atatürk) soon re-established Turkey as an independent sovereign state. By 1923 they were a force that could no longer be disregarded, and when they renounced the harsh terms of the Treaty of Sèvres, the Allies were left with no option but to return to the conference table. At the talks preceding the Treaty of Lausanne, the Turkish representative, Ismet Pasha Inonu, refused to accept Article 360 of the Sèvres Treaty. He declared that the railway was a religious endowment, and that as such its ownership and administration should be restored to the Caliph. The British and French, reluctant to give up any part of their newly-gained possessions in the Middle East, avoided the issue of ownership. However, they were prepared to compromise on the question of administration, and agreed to the setting up of a Muslim advisory council at Madinah, with members from Syria, Palestine, Transjordan and the Hejaz, charged with safeguarding the special religious character of the railway.

The issue of ownership came up again as part of the final assessment process of war reparations. If the Hejaz Railway was legally deemed to be a

THE RAILWAY AFTER THE FIRST WORLD WAR

Above:
De Dion railcar ACMI standing outside the works shed at Deraa Station in 1979.

religious endowment, then its value would not be included in the settlement. The Turkish position therefore shifted again, away from the one held by Inonu Pasha at Lausanne. It was now argued that, rather than being the possession of the Sultan in his capacity as Caliph, the line was in fact Ottoman state property, paid for through national taxation. Professor Eugène Borel, brought in as an arbiter by the League of Nations, accepted the Turkish claim. He ruled that the Sultan's role of Caliph could not be considered as distinct from the Ottoman state, and that the railway was therefore part of the empire's legal possessions. While this opened the way for it to be included in Turkey's reparation settlement, it also implied that the line would automatically become the property of the new nation states created after the war. In effect, the Borel Decision of 1925 gave the Mandate powers the ability to dispose of the railway as they saw fit.

The Inter-war Years

The partitioning of the Hejaz Railway between Britain and France led to several administrative complications. The British controlled two separate areas of the railway, from Haifa to Samakh (Palestine), and from Nessib to Ma'an (Transjordan). The French section, from Samakh to Nessib, lay in the middle of these two British portions, and passengers travelling from Haifa to Amman had to pass through all three segments to complete their journey. To

THE HEJAZ RAILWAY

Above:
Another view of the Hartmann 2-8-0 at Buwair Station, with its tender and wagons.

avoid disruptions and delays, it was therefore agreed that there would be a free interchange of rolling stock, with equipment being used and returned in accordance with operational requirements.

The Palestinian section was administered directly by Palestine Railways (P.R.). The Transjordanian portion came under the control of the British Representative in Amman, H. St J. Philby. However, mindful of Arab claims that the railway was waqf, he arranged for three officials from Palestine Railways to be brought in to run it. A British general manager was appointed to oversee operations. Between 1921 and 1923, expenditure on the section stood at £35,860, while only £31,460 was received in revenues. By the spring of 1924 the section was bankrupt, and the Palestinian government decided to send in the auditors to check the accounts.

One of the first things that came to light was that the general manager had advanced himself nearly three years' salary. Several other members of staff had followed his example, but for shorter periods. The advances were all above board - properly recorded and supported by receipts - and there was no way of obtaining redress, except by retaining the staff until they had worked off their debts. It was also discovered that one of the heaviest items of expenditure was for special trains to Uneiza. This was the result of an attempt by Philby to promote tourist trips to the Nabataean site of Petra. The trains had been prepared with no expense spared, including sleeping berths and restaurant cars. Fleets of cars had also been laid on to meet the passengers when they arrived at Uneiza Station. Unfortunately however, the venture was unable to pay for itself, and only served to worsen the overall economic position of the railway. In 1924, before leaving Transjordan, Philby attempted to resolve the situation by handing the whole section over to Prince Ali, King Hussein's eldest son. The British government however, had not been a party to this decision and refused to endorse it.

In addition to re-establishing operations to Ma'an in 1921, Philby had attempted to reopen a regular through service to the Hejaz. A few trains

THE RAILWAY AFTER THE FIRST WORLD WAR

Left:
Hohenzollern 0-6-0T (No. 37, built 1908) at Damascus Qadem Station.

managed to run all the way south to Madinah, but the journey took twelve days, the track was in very poor condition, and constant repair work had to be carried out to keep the line open. In October 1924, under pressure from the rising power in the region, Abdulaziz ibn Saud, Amir of Nejd (later King of Saudi Arabia), King Hussein abdicated in favour of his eldest son, Ali. By December, Abdulaziz had advanced into the Hejaz, taking Makkah and besieging the new ruler in Jeddah. With the situation for Ali looking increasingly hopeless, the British persuaded King Abdullah of Transjordan to annex the district of Ma'an in June 1925, thus extending his control of the railway as far south as Mudawwara. Owing to the political upheaval, only a small number of pilgrims arrived for the Hajj in June and July 1925. With Jeddah under seige, most were brought in through the captured ports of

Left:
1936 Ford road vehicle converted for use on the Hejaz Railway.

171

Rabigh, Al Lith and Al Qunfudah. A few travelled on the Hejaz Railway to Madinah, which was still under Ali's control. Following the pilgrimage, Abdulaziz's forces continued their advance and in the autumn surrounded Madinah. In October, three trains from Ma'an brought in supplies to the beleaguered city, the last through services to reach the Hejaz. In December, the garrison commander, Abdulmajid al Mifaie, and the controller of the railway, Azzat Effendi, negotiated for the city's surrender. In the winter of that year, torrential rain caused extensive damage to the track, and the southern section finally became permanently inoperable.

By 1925, just 20 out of 72 locomotives under French control at Damascus Qadem Station were in good working order. In addition, there were nearly 200 wagons awaiting repair. At the same time the British were being forced to curtail some of their services due to a shortage of rolling stock. In order to rationalise the situation, an agreement was reached in 1926 between Palestine Railways and the Chemin de Fer Hedjaz (C.F.H.) of Syria. A full assessment of the locomotives, carriages and goods wagons was made, and under the settlement, the rolling stock was officially apportioned between the two organisations.

Following a revolt by the Druze against the French in 1925, a 45-kilometre line was built between Ezra and Suweida. The narrow-gauge track of 60 cm. was the only one of its kind in Syria. From Ezra, the line proceeded southeast across the Hauran to the first of two intermediate stations at Herak (15 kms). It then turned east to Um Waled (at 33 kms), before heading into the foothills of Jebel Druze and on to Suweida, the mountain stronghold of the Druze.

By the late 1920s, operations on the Hejaz Railway had settled into a fairly

Below:
Meissner Pasha's house at Ma'an Station in Jordan is now a museum.

THE RAILWAY AFTER THE FIRST WORLD WAR

fixed pattern. Extra locomotives and coaching stock were purchased to meet the demands of traffic, and regular services were run over the usable sections of the railway. There was a weekly operation from Amman to Ma'an, and on the more populous section between Haifa and Damascus trains ran three times a week. As well as additional services provided on the shorter, solely P.R., section between Haifa and Samakh, operations from Deraa to Amman were run to connect with the Haifa-Damascus train. Passengers for Amman would change at Deraa.

Throughout the 1920s and 1930s, services continued to operate between Damascus and Haifa. The trains would generally include carriages belonging to both the P.R. and the C.F.H., but the locomotives and all the staff, except for the passport officer, would be changed at the border. In 1929, Cynric Mytton-Davies described the process: 'The cars running into Palestine are painted grey, with H.R. and the class number in gold lettering on their sides, while those for internal use in Syria are brown, with C.F.H. and the class number in black... At Samakh, the British engine is detached and a French one substituted... and, with the exception of the Passport Officer, the train staff descend and French, or rather Syrian, guards and conductors take their places.'[18] Goods wagons were added at the rear of the train, and although there was no restaurant car, if there were sufficient numbers travelling first-class, pre-cooked food would be taken on board and served in a special saloon car.

In 1932 the line between Afule and Massoudiah was discontinued owing to a lack of passenger demand. At about the same time, the Haifa-Deraa branch experienced a temporary surge in traffic, due to the transportation of large quantities of building material for the Iraq Petroleum Company's long-

Above:
A lone modern-day bedouin cuts through the wide flood plain between Muazzam and Disa'ad.

Below:
Although the Haifa branch is now impassable beyond Zeizoun, parts of the track are still visible at Hamme at the western end of the Yarmuk Valley.

THE HEJAZ RAILWAY

Above:
H.S.P. (Haine St. Pierre) 2-8-2 No. 71 was one of three supplied to Jordan by the Belgian Forges, Usines et Fonderies company in 1956.

awaited pipeline from Iraq to Haifa. Two La Meuse 0-10-0Ts were brought back into service to cope with the additional traffic. In 1932, extra railway workshops for Haifa were built in neighbouring Qishon, and the following year a new harbour was constructed. Although the completion of the Iraqi pipeline in 1934 resulted in a loss of freight traffic, this was to a large extent offset by the rapid industrial and urban development of the city.

The Railway in the Modern Era: Attempts at Reconstruction

At the beginning of the Second World War, the allegiance of the Vichy French in Beirut and Damascus was unclear. However, in 1941, when the Germans were permitted to use Syrian air bases to attack Allied troops, a mixed force of Australian, British, Indian and Free French troops was ordered to invade. Although the Vichy French cut the Haifa-Deraa branch by demolishing one of the bridges in the Yarmuk Valley, the Allied troops swept into Syria and Lebanon. After five weeks of bloody fighting, the Vichy French forces surrendered, and an armistice was signed at Acre on 14 July. Under the terms agreed by the two sides, the railway, together with all the rolling stock, was handed over intact to the Allies.

In 1941 Australian troops began work on a new supply line, intended to link the harbour at Aqaba to the Hejaz Railway. To obtain rails, over 60 kilometres of track were lifted from the unused area of the railway south of Ma'an. Fifteen derelict locomotives and 40 wagons were also renovated and brought back into service. Opened in March 1942, the new line covered 42.6 kilometres from Ma'an to Naqb Ashtar. The next stage of construction would have entailed taking the line down a steep escarpment, but Allied military successes removed the need for an Aqaba supply route, and the project was discontinued.

On the night of 16 June 1946, the 2nd Yarmuk Bridge on the Haifa-Deraa branch was demolished by Jewish saboteurs. Services between Palestine, Transjordan and Syria were cut, and when an attempt to rebuild the damaged bridge was abandoned, the Hejaz Railway lost its Mediterranean port outlet. Following the British withdrawal from Palestine in May 1948, the dislocated branch line fell largely into disuse, and the few remaining services were completely discontinued in 1954.

Proposals to rehabilitate the defunct part of the railway between Ma'an and Madinah had been made as far back as 1925, when the heavy rains of that year finally rendered the southern section impassable. However, it was not until 1948 that Syria, Jordan and Saudi Arabia formed a joint committee to look into the question of reconstruction. An agreement was signed in Riyadh in January 1955, and the three governments undertook to make equal contributions to the cost of the restoration work. The following year, a preliminary survey was carried out by the International Resources Engineering and Exploration Group. This showed that, while the original masonry work was still in good condition, wartime demolitions, flash floods and general weathering had caused extensive damage to the rail embankment and track.

Following the failure of negotiations, first with Polish representatives, and then with an American firm, Intrafi, the contract was put out to tender in 1960. More than 50 companies submitted proposals. Eventually, a consortium made up of Maribeni (Japan), Bin Laden (Saudi Arabia) and Ferrovial (Spain) was awarded the project. A provisional deal was signed in August 1962, but due to contractual difficulties, was withdrawn a year later on the grounds that Maribeni had not lodged its performance bond.

In 1963 the project was awarded to the British firms, Alderton Construction Co. Ltd. and Martin Cowley Ltd. The supply of points and crossings was subcontracted to Thomas Summerson and Sons. In preparation for the work, a more detailed survey of the line between Ma'an and Madinah was carried out. The report stated that as much as 85 per cent of the line had suffered some form of damage! Fifty kilometres of the embankment had been completely washed away by flash floods, 250 kilometres of track had been affected by blown sand, and another 16 kilometres completely buried in deep drifts. Between Mudawwara and Ma'an, over 60 kilometres of track had also been lifted by the Allies to build the Naqb Ashtar branch in 1941.

The existing rails were in a very poor condition. Only 44 per cent of what remained was found to be serviceable, although some of the old track could be used for goods yards and sidings. In all, just over 300 kilometres of the line could be considered as potentially usable, with minor reconditioning. The stations had also fallen into disrepair. While virtually all the heavy stonework was found to have survived intact, the utilities and water points were in need of total rehabilitation.

Below:
A modern metal tank has been erected to supplement the original stone Ottoman water tower.

THE HEJAZ RAILWAY

Above:
Jung 2-6-0 (No. 60, originally No. 31), built in Jungenthal bei Kirchen, Germany, in 1906, was restored at the same time as Medain Saleh Station, where it is now on display.

The quantity surveyor's assessment of the materials needed to carry out the work is a good indication of the monumental scale of the undertaking. The original computation for the earthworks amounted to a colossal 1,684,600 cu.yd, with the ballast required for the track-bed estimated at 784,770 cu.yd. In addition, 764,000 rails, 1,600,000 sleepers, 306,000 nuts, bolts and washers, 3,130,000 base plates and 1,800 spikes would be needed. For water provision, 11 diesel pumps, three electric pumps and 24 new tanks were required to ensure an adequate supply.

Work began in 1966, with large deliveries of equipment and materials being brought in through Aqaba. The rails were supplied by British companies and the sleepers were shipped in from Australia. The rebuilding of the earth embankment, bridges and culverts was completed from the Saudi-Jordanian border almost as far as Tabuk, while the track was laid to six kilometres south of Dhat al Haj. Other miscellaneous work was also carried out along the length of the railway; damaged bridges and culverts were repaired or replaced with reinforced concrete as far south as Buwat. In contrast to the original building of the line, when a huge workforce toiled in harsh conditions without mechanical aids, the modern mobile work camp, with a labour force of just 200, was provided with all the latest heavy engineering machinery. 'In addition, regular and daily radio contact with base is maintained and two private aircraft bring in mail and key supplies. There are lorries adapted for desert movement and each night a snug, mobile, caravan-village with its own generating station - able to supply power for electric light, refrigeration, fans, cooking and all associated services - awaits the weary railway builder.'[9]

The line was scheduled to be completed by 1968, with trains expected to make the journey in 'about half the time taken by the old steam engines.

THE RAILWAY AFTER THE FIRST WORLD WAR

During the peak Hajj season, 12 trains will carry 15,000 passengers each day'¹ Completion was delayed however, and by the early 1970s an extensive road network had been built in Saudi Arabia. This, together with the rapid development of international airline facilities, meant that the pilgrims were well provided for with fast and convenient alternatives to rail travel. The costs of reconstruction were rapidly escalating, and a decision was taken to suspend the work. Although there have been occasional calls for the project to be reopened - as recently as 1980 a full inspection was carried out to check the condition of the line - no serious attempt has been made to restart the construction.

The Railway Today

In 1977 a 40-kilometre branch was built between Damascus and Qatana in Syria, constructed to modern standards, with automatic level crossings and colour light signalling. The line follows the main Hejaz Railway track for 12 kilometres before branching off to the west for 28 kilometres. The service runs out of Damascus Kanawat Station, and has four intermediate stations. It is currently operated with Romanian railcars.

The exploitation of Jordan's phosphate reserves in 1972 led to the building of a short branch line leading to a mine five kilometres east of Al Hasa. A new line, linking the Hejaz Railway to Aqaba was opened in 1975 to transport the phosphate to the coast for export. Although this was not considered part of the Hejaz network, the construction of the line entailed the rehabilitation of the original railway between Al Hasa and Batn al Ghoul. The work, carried out by Held and Francke Bauaktien Gesselschaft of Munich, used the main Hejaz line to the top of the plateau beyond Batn al Ghoul Station. It then branched east on the new track, before swinging westwards to negotiate the

Above:
Traditional Ottoman station building at Kiswe, with a satellite dish installed on the roof.

Below:
This line of locomotives at Damascus Qadem makes up part of the station's 'graveyard' of derelict rolling stock.

THE HEJAZ RAILWAY

Opposite:
A 4-wheel drive convoy following the old rail embankment through the spectacular mountain scenery of the Hejaz.

great Batn al Ghoul escarpment at a moderate gradient. At the bottom of the slope, it cut through the embankment of the old Hejaz line before continuing on westwards to Wadi Rumm and Aqaba.

Another short phosphate branch line, to a mine at Wadi al Abyad (White Valley) in 1979, required the refurbishment of the Hejaz Railway between Menzil and Al Hasa. These new sections of the line remain in operation today, employing 24 diesel locomotives and over 300 goods wagons. The long phosphate trains can still be seen winding their way down the Batn al Ghoul escarpment, cutting through the scar of the long-deserted Hejaz embankment and disappearing across the vast, empty sand basin of Wadi Rutm into the distant western hills.

South of this point, and down through Saudi Arabia, the full length of the railway can only be properly covered off-road, using four-wheel drive vehicles. Although the rails have long since disappeared, the earth embankment, with its solid stone bridges and culverts, provides a reliable path through the desolate landscape of the Hejaz. The spectacular desert mountain scenery, together with the old Ottoman stations and the occasional piece of abandoned rolling stock, is enough to attract regular groups of intrepid expatriates, following in the footsteps of T.E. Lawrence. The rebuilt station complex at Medain Saleh, in the same area as the Nabataean antiquities, includes an engine shed with a 1906 Jung 2-6-0. There has also been a recent project to restore Madinah Station (see Appendix 1).

In the north, there are museums at the stations in Damascus (Qadem), Amman and Ma'an, as well as a section in the Railway History Museum at Ankara. At Damascus Kanawat, the Sultan's private carriage now serves as the station's café bar. Its plush leather, polished wood and glass tulip-shaped lampshades give an insight into the railway's past elegance. The area where the old locomotives are stored by the works yard at Damascus Qadem, nicknamed 'the graveyard' by railway enthusiasts, is a veritable treasure-house of ancient rolling stock. In the station's repair shops, teams of engineers work constantly to restore items taken from the long lines of derelict locomotives. The old steam trains are brought back into temporary service for the groups of railway tourists who come here from around the world, providing a rare glimpse into the way the line must have looked nearly 100 years ago.

A regular passenger service still runs twice weekly between Amman and Damascus. The journey takes nine hours (including a change of train at the border), compared with three hours by road. As well as being slow, the carriages are old and draughty, and provide an inviting target for stone-throwing children along the line. However, the romantic appeal of the railway is such that it still attracts a steady trickle of travellers, willing to endure these minor hardships in order to journey over the same tracks on which Lawrence laid his mines. The railway is not just for the use of tourists though. In February 2002, while travelling between Amman and Damascus, I was surprised to meet two Turkish pilgrims on their way back to Istanbul from Saudi Arabia. Preferring, wherever possible, to take the train rather than the more common alternative of bus or plane, they were happily unaware that by their choice of transport they were still fulfilling the long-faded hopes and dreams of Abdulhamid II, the last great Sultan of the Ottoman Empire.

THE RAILWAY AFTER THE FIRST WORLD WAR

THE HEJAZ RAILWAY

Appendix 1.
Project for the Restoration of Madinah Station

Opposite (clockwise from top):
Staff rest-house;
One of the windows in the main station building;
Detail of one of the 17 arches making up the facade of the main station building.

Below:
The facade of the main station building at Madinah.

In 2001 the Saudi Arabian Deputy Ministry for Antiquities and Museums (Ministry of Education) initiated a three year project for the complete rehabilitation of Madinah Station. Within the programme the station buildings have been restored to their original condition. At the same time, the site has been developed as a tourist attraction, with the outbuildings and courtyard converted into an open museum for the display of rolling stock and railway equipment. As part of the same scheme, the main station building has been refurbished to house an Islamic Museum, where archaeological and ethnographic items relating to the history of Madinah will be exhibited.

APPENDIX 1

THE HEJAZ RAILWAY

Above:
Line of derelict rolling stock at Madinah Station standing very much as it was left in 1925 when the railway fell into disuse. The locomotive is a Hartmann 2-8-0.

Below:
Interior of restored Baume et Marpent 3rd class carriage (built 1905).

The whole complex covers an area of 540,000 square metres, and includes 12 separate architectural units. The main station building, overlooking the Al Anbaria Mosque (originally called the Hamidia Mosque by the Ottomans), has an impressive facade incorporating 17 pointed archways. There are three principal entrances. The eastern one was used by the passengers and led to the station's courtyard and platforms. The central area consists of a large hall, the ceiling of which is supported by an arcade of arches resting on square stone buttresses.

The upper level was built using basalt and limestone. The central section comprises three vertical rectangles, each containing a window surrounded by an ornate semi-circular arch of black and white stone. On both sides of the central section there are four smaller rectangles with arched windows of a similar design. At the top of the upper level, a white marble panel is inscribed with the name 'Al Madinah al Munawara'. On each side of the plaque there are two decorative five-point stars, symbolising the Ottoman state. Early photographs of the station show that the upper level had not been constructed at the time of the official inauguration ceremony in 1908.

The other buildings renovated within the project are the station master's residence, the operations centre, the staff rest-house, the passenger rest-house, the toilets and washroom, the main storehouse, the locomotive workshop, the maintenance supervisor's residence, the goods office, the water tower and the Suqia Mosque. The Mosque is of particular historical interest as it was built during the early Islamic period. Remains of plaster used in the original construction have been dated back to the time of Omar bin Abdulaziz (706-712 A.D.). In addition extensive track works were carried out by Al-Turath (Heritage) Establishment of Saudi Arabia.

APPENDIX 1

Above:
Restored Hartmann 2-6-0 and Baume et Marpent 3rd class carriage (built in Belgium, 1905) in the locomotive workshop.

There is also a considerable amount of rolling stock within the complex. This includes six locomotives, abandoned in 1925 when the southern section of the railway fell into disuse, as well as a variety of carriages, wagons and flatbed trucks. Inside the locomotive workshop there are three engines: a Hartmann 2-6-0, a Swiss Locomotive & Machine Works (S.L.M.) 2-8-0 and a Hartmann 2-8-0. Standing outside in the yard are an S.L.M. 2-8-0, a Hartmann 2-8-0 and a Tubize 0-6-0T, built in Belgium in 1893, originally for the French D.H.P. Damascus - Muzeirib line.

Projects to restore the Hejaz Railway stations at Tabuk and Al Ula are also to be carried out by the Ministry of Education, Deputy Ministry for Antiquities and Museums, in the near future.

Left:
The station name plaque following restoration.

Appendix 2 - Hejaz Railway Stations

Damascus - Madinah Line

Station　　　　　　　　　　Distance - from Damascus Qadem Station (kms.)

Syria

1	Damascus Kanawat	-3
2	Damascus Qadem	0
3	Kiswe	21
4	Dair Ali	31
5	Mismia	50
6	Jebab	63
7	Khebab	69
8	Mehaye	78
9	Shakra	85
10	Ezra	91
11	Ghazala	106
12	Deraa	123
13	Nessib	136

Jordan

14	Mafraq	162
15	Samra	185
16	Zerqa	203
17	Amman	222
18	Kassir	234
19	Libban	249
20	Jiza	260
21	Deba'a	279
22	Khan Zebib	295
23	Suaka	309
24	Qatrana	326
25	Menzil	348
26	Faraifra	367
27	Al Hasa	378
28	Jerouf	397
29	Uneiza	423
30	Jerdun	441
31	Ma'an	459
32	Ghadir al Haj	475
33	Bir Shedia	487
34	Aqaba Shamia	514
35	Batn al Ghoul	520
36	Wadi Rutm	530
37	Tel Shahm	545
38	Ramleh	554
39	Mudawwara	572

Saudi Arabia

40	Hallat Ammar	594
41	Dhat al Haj	608
42	Bir ibn Hermas	632
43	Al Hazm	655
44	Muhtahab	677
45	Tabuk	692
46	Wadi Ithil	720
47	Khashm Birk	731
48	Dar al Haj	743
49	Awjariya	752
50	Mustabgha	756
51	Akhdar	761
52	Khamis	780
53	Disa'ad	806
54	Muazzam	828
55	Khashm Sana'a	853
56	Dar al Hamra	880
57	Mutalli	903
58	Abu Taqa	923
59	Mabrak al Naga	939
60	Medain Saleh	955
61	Wadi Hashish	968
62	Al Ula	980
63	Bedaya'	1002
64	Mashad	1015
65	Sahl Matran	1037
66	Zumurrud	1052
67	Bir Jadeed	1075
68	Towaira	1092
69	Wayban	1104
70	Mudarraj	1116
71	Hedia	1133
72	Jeda'a	1155
73	Abu Na'am	1173
74	Istabl Antar	1191
75	Buwair	1211
76	Bir Nassif	1231
77	Buwat	1251
78	Hafira	1272
79	Muhit	1290
80	Madinah	1302

Appendix 2 – Hejaz Railway Stations

Haifa - Deraa Branch Line

Station — Distance - from Haifa Station (kms.)

	Station	km		Station	km
	(Acre)	-18	11	Ash Shajara	119
1	Haifa	0		8th Yarmuk Bridge	121
2	Shemmamia	11		9th Yarmuk Bridge	121.5
3	Tel Shemmam	22	12	Mukarram	124
4	Afule	36		10th Yarmuk Bridge	127
5	Shatta	51		2nd Yarmuk Tunnel	128
6	Beisan	59		11th Yarmuk Bridge	128.5
7	Jisr al Mejami	76		12th Yarmuk Bridge	130
	Jisr al Mejami Bridge	77		3rd Yarmuk Tunnel	131
	1st Yarmuk Bridge	79		4th Yarmuk Tunnel	132
8	Samakh	87	13	Zeizoun	136
	2nd Yarmuk Bridge	92		5th Yarmuk Tunnel	137
	3rd Yarmuk Bridge	93		6th Yarmuk Tunnel	138
9	Hamme	95		13th Yarmuk Bridge	140
	4th Yarmuk Bridge	96		14th Yarmuk Bridge	140.5
	5th Yarmuk Bridge	100		15th Yarmuk Bridge	142.5
	1st Yarmuk Tunnel	105		7th Yarmuk Tunnel	143
	6th Yarmuk Bridge	106	14	Tel Shehab	145
10	Wadi Kilit	107	15	Muzeirib	149
	7th Yarmuk Bridge	114	16	Deraa	161

Deraa - Bosra Branch Line

Station — Distance - from Deraa Station (kms.)

	Station	km		Station	km
1	Deraa	0	4	Haisem	29
2	Gassim Junction	6	5	Bosra (al Sham)	38
3	Taibe	15		Bosra Citadel	40

Afule - Nablus Branch Line

Station — Distance - from Afule Station (kms.)

	Station	km		Station	km
1	Afule	0		Ramin Tunnel	49
2	Jenin	17	5	Massoudiah	60
3	Arrabeh	28	6	Nablus	78
4	Sileh	40			

Chapter Notes

Abbreviations:

BL (IOR)   British Library (India Office Records)
FO   Foreign Office
PRO   Public Record Office
IWM   Imperial War Museum

Chapter 1   Introduction

1 PRO FO78/5452 W.Richards (British Consul, Damascus) to Sir Nicolas O'Conor (British Ambassador, Constantinople) 30.4.00
2 PRO FO78/5452 Richards to O'Conor 20.6.00
3 Shaw, S.J. & Shaw, E.K. *History of the Ottoman Empire and Modern Turkey* (Vol.III), Cambridge, 1997

Chapter 2   Building the Railway - I. The Main Line

1 PRO FO78/5452 Richards to O'Conor 4.12.01
2 PRO FO78/5452 Richards to O'Conor 8.2.02
3 PRO FO78/5451 Report. Lt Col. F. Maunsell (Military Attaché, Constantinople) 1905
4 PRO FO78/5452 Richards to O'Conor 12.3.02
5 Wasti, Syed Tanvir, 'Muhammad Inshaullah and the Hijaz Railway', *Middle East Studies*, Vol. 34, No.2, April 1998
6 PRO FO78/5452 Wilkie Young (Beirut) to R. Drummond-Hay (Damascus) 23.3.04
7 Ibid.
8 Ibid.
9 BL (IOR) L/PLS/10/12 Report. Auler Pasha 1906
10 PRO FO78/5451 Report. Lt Col. F. Maunsell 1905
11 Ibid.
12 BL (IOR) L/PLS/10/12 Telegram. Rahmi Pasha (The Sultan's Aide-de-Camp) to Izzat Pasha al Abid (The Sultan's Second Secretary) 20-8-06
13 Doughty, Charles M. *Travels in Arabia Deserta*, Cambridge, 1888
14 Ibid.
15 University of Durham Sudan Archives (Wingate Papers) Report. Agent 'G' - Cairo Intelligence Department, 1907
16 Wavell, A.J.B. *A Modern Pilgrim in Mecca and a Siege in Sanaa*, Boston 1913

Chapter 3   Building the Railway - II. The Branch Lines

1 PRO FO78/5451 Telegram. O'Conor to Foreign Office 15.3.02
2 PRO FO78/5451 W. Hills to A.J. Balfour (Foreign Office) 9-4-03
3 PRO FO/785451 O'Conor to Marquess of Lansdowne 18-8-03
4 Storrs, R. *Orientations*, London, 1937

Chapter 4   Paying for the Railway

1 FO 881/7655/352A Sir Maurice be Bunsen (Chargé d'Affaires, Constantinople) to Marquess of Salisbury 10-10-00
2 PRO FO78/5452 De Bunsen to Marquess of Lansdowne 23-11-00
3 PRO FO78/5451 Report. Lt Col. F. Maunsell 1905
4 Ochsenwald, W. *The Hijaz Railroad*, Virginia, 1980

Chapter 5   Running the Railway

1 Antonius, George, *The Arab Awakening*, London, 1965
2 Wavell, *A Modern Pilgrim in Mecca and a Siege in Sanaa*
3 Ibid.
4 Sykes, Lt Col. M. *The Caliphs' Last Heritage*, London, 1915
5 Wavell, *A Modern Pilgrim in Mecca and a Siege in Sanaa*
6 BL (IOR) L/PLS/10/12 Report. Lt Col. F. Maunsell (Military Attaché, Constantinople) 1907
7 Wavell, *A Modern Pilgrim in Mecca and a Siege in Sanaa*
8 Lawrence, T.E. *The Home Letters of T.E. Lawrence and His Brothers*, Oxford, 1954
9 Ibid.
10 Sykes, Lt Col. M. *The Caliphs' Last Heritage*
11 PRO FO882/3 (1916) Musil, Alois, The North of Hegaz - A Preliminary Report of the Exploring Expedition of 1910
12 BL (IOR) L/PLS/10/12 Report Auler Pasha 1906
13 Sykes, Lt Col. M. *The Caliphs' Last Heritage*
14 Maunsell, Lt Col. F. 'The Hejaz Railway' *Geographical Journal*, 32 (6), 1908
15 Hamilton, Angus *Problems of the Middle East*, London, 1909
16 BL (IOR) L/PLS/ 10/12 Report. Lt Col. F. Maunsell 1907
17 Abdullah, King of Transjordan *Memoirs of King Abdullah of Transjordan*, London, 1950
18 Ibid.
19 Ibid.

Chapter 6   The Outbreak of the First World War

1 Quoted in Monroe, E. *Britain's Moment in the Middle East 1914-1956*, Baltimore, 1956
2 Kedourie, E. *In the Anglo-Arab Labyrinth*, Cambridge, 1976
3 MacMunn, Lt Gen. G. & Falls, Capt.C. *Military Operations. Egypt and Palestine. From the Outbreak of War with Germany to June 1917*, Official War History, 1928
4 Rush, Alan de L. (ed.) *Records of the Hashemite Dynasties*, 1995
5 PRO FO-882/4 Report Lt Col. S. Newcombe 1917
6 Lawrence, T.E. *Seven Pillars of Wisdom*, London, 1926
7 Baker, R. *King Husain and the Kingdom of Hejaz*, Cambridge 1979

Chapter 7   The War on the Railway - I. The Hejaz

1 El Edroos, Brig. Syed Ali *The Hashemite Arab Army 1908-1979. An Appreciation and Analysis of Military Operations*, Amman, 1980
2 Lawrence, *Seven Pillars of Wisdom*
3 PRO FO882/4 Report Bimbashi H. Garland 1917
4 Ibid.
5 Ibid.
6 PRO FO882/26 Arab Bureau (Cairo) Bulletin 49

Chapter Notes

7 Lawrence, *Seven Pillars of Wisdom*
8 Ibid.
9 Ibid.
10 PRO FO882/6 'Extract from Reports of Captain Lawrence' 1917
11 Lawrence, *Seven Pillars of Wisdom*
12 PRO FO882/6 Report Captain T.E. Lawrence April 1917
13 Lawrence, *Seven Pillars of Wisdom*
14 Ibid.
15 Ibid.
16 Ibid.
17 Ibid.
18 PRO FO882/6 'Extract from Reports of Captain Lawrence' 1917
19 Lawrence, *Seven Pillars of Wisdom*
20 Ibid.
21 IWM Document Archive, Henderson, Capt. T., *The Hejas Expedition 1916-1917*
22 Ibid.
23 Ibid.
24 Ibid.
25 Ibid.
26 PRO FO882/4 Report Lt Col. P Joyce 1917
27 PRO FO882/4 Report Bimbashi H. Garland 1917
28 Ibid.
29 PRO FO882/26 Arab Bureau (Cairo) Bulletin 63

Box Text - 'Lawrence's Trains'?

1 Lockman, J.N. *Scattered Tracks on the Lawrence Trail*, Michigan, 1996
2 PRO FO882/7 Report Bimbashi H. Garland 1918
3 PRO FO882/6 Report T.E. Lawrence April 1917
4 PRO FO882/27 Arab Bureau (Cairo) Bulletin 96

Chapter 8 The War on the Railway - II. Aqaba & Northwards

1 Storrs, *Orientations*
2 Lawrence, *Seven Pillars of Wisdom*
3 Ibid.
4 Ibid.
5 Ibid.
6 Antonius, *The Arab Awakening*
7 Lawrence, *Seven Pillars of Wisdom*
8 Antonius, *The Arab Awakening*
9 Glubb, J.B. *Britain and the Arabs*, London, 1959
10 PRO FO882/26 Arab Bureau (Cairo) Bulletin 74
11 Lawrence, *Seven Pillars of Wisdom*
12 Ibid.
13 Ibid.
14 Ibid.
15 Lawrence, *The Home Letters of T.E. Lawrence and His Brothers*
16 Lawrence, *Seven Pillars of Wisdom*
17 Ibid.
18 Ibid.
19 Ibid.

Box Text - The Defence of the Railway

1 PRO FO882/26 Arab Bureau (Cairo) Bulletin 65
2 PRO FO882/6 Report T.E. Lawrence April 1917

Chapter 9 The War on the Railway - III. The Road to Damascus

1 Lawrence, *Seven Pillars of Wisdom*
2 PRO FO882/4 Report Lt Col. P. Joyce 5-1-18
3 Lawrence, *Seven Pillars of Wisdom*
4 PRO FO882/4 Report Lt Col. P. Joyce 5-1-18
5 Lawrence, *Seven Pillars of Wisdom*
6 Ibid.
7 PRO FO882/27 Arab Bureau (Cairo) Bulletin 78
8 Lawrence, Seven Pillars of Wisdom
9 PRO FO882/27 Arab Bureau (Cairo) Bulletin 87
10 Lawrence, *Seven Pillars of Wisdom*
11 Young, Major H. *The Independent Arab*, London, 1933
12 PRO FO882/27 Arab Bureau (Cairo) Bulletin 105
13 Lawrence, *Seven Pillars of Wisdom*
14 Ibid.
15 PRO FO882/27 Arab Bureau (Cairo) Bulletin 107
16 PRO FO882/20 Capt. Bassett to Lt Col.C. Wilson 17.1.19

Box Text - 'Tulips'

1 IWM Document Archive DS/MISC/16 Report Capt. F. Peake 1918
2 Ibid.
3 Kirkbride, Alec. *An Awakening: The Arab Campaign 1917-18* Frome, 1917
4 Lawrence, *Seven Pillars of Wisdom*

Chapter 10 The Railway after the First World War

1 Heslop, Major D.G. 'Railways of the Near East. II- After Lawrence in Arabia' *Railway Magazine*, April 1934
2 Ibid.
3 Storrs, *Orientations*
4 Quoted in Storrs, *Orientations*
5 Storrs, *Orientations*
6 Ochsenwald, W.L. 'A Modern Waqf: the Hijaz Railway, 1900-48' *Arabian Studies III* 1976
7 Carnegie Endowment for International Peace, *The Treaties of Peace, 1919-1923*, New York, 1924
8 Mytton-Davies, C. 'Railways of the Near East I- The Hedjaz Railway' *The Railway Magazine*, No.440, Vol. LXXIV, Feb 1934
9 Hurren, B.J. 'Pilgrim Railway into Arabia Part Two' *Railway Magazine*, July 1965
10 Carter, W. 'The Pilgrim Railway' *Geographical Magazine*, Vol. 39, 1966

Bibliography

Abdullah, King of Transjordan, *Memoirs of King Abdullah of Transjordan*, Jonathan Cape 1950
Aboura, Ahmed Khair, *Al Khatt al Hadeedi al Hejazi Al Asala wa Al Hadatha*, 1998
Ahmad, Feroz, *The Young Turks: The Committee of Union and Progress in Turkish Politics 1908-1914*, Oxford University Press 1969
Aksay, M. & Akyuz, O., *Hicaz Demiryolu*, Al Baraka Turk 1999
Al-Amr, Saleh Muhammad, *The Hijaz under Ottoman Rule 1869 - 1914: The Ottoman Vali, the Sharif of Mecca, and the Growth of British Influence,* Dissertation Leeds University 1974
Al-Hameed, Abdullatif Muhammad, *The Hejaz Railway 1900-1918: Policy Objectives and Consequences*, Ph.D. Thesis University of Essex 1989
Alborough, B. 'To the Hedjaz Railway for Steam' *Railway World*, July 1980, pp.374-78
Aldington, R. *Lawrence of Arabia: A Biographical Enquiry*, Collins 1955
Anon, 'The Pilgrims' Railway to Medina', *The Railway Gazette*, Oct 1927, p.458
Anon, 'The Hedjaz Railway', *The Railway Magazine*, Sept 1934, p.208
Antonius, George, *The Arab Awakening*, Hamish Hamilton 1965
Asher, Michael, *Lawrence: The Uncrowned King of Arabia*, Penguin 1998
Baker, Randall, *King Husain and the Kingdom of Hejaz*, The Oleander Press 1979
Bell, Gertrude Lowthian, *Syria: The Desert and the Sown*, William Heinemann 1907
Blake, G. & King, R., 'The Hijaz Railway and the Pilgrimage to Mecca' *Asian Affairs. Journal of the Royal Central Asian Society*, Vol. 59 Part 3, October 1972
Bliss, W. Tyler, 'The Sultan's Dummy Railway', *Harper's Weekly* (50) 1906, pp.733-36
Bray, N.N.E., *Shifting Sands*, Unicorn Press 1934
Brémond, General Edouard, *Le Hedjaz dans la guerre mondiale*, Payot 1931
Brown, Malcolm & Cave, Julia, *A Touch of Genius: The Life of T.E. Lawrence*, Dent 1988
Carruthers, Douglas, 'A Journey in North-Western Arabia' *The Geographical Journal* Vol. XXXV No.3, March 1910
Carter, W., 'The Pilgrim Railway' *Geographical Magazine* Vol. 39 1966, pp.422-33
Clemow, Frank G., 'A Visit to the Rock-Tombs of Medain-I-Salih, and the Southern Section of the Hejaz Railway', *Geographical Journal* Vol. XLII, Dec 1913, No.6 pp.534-40
Clayton, Sir Gilbert, *An Arabian Diary*, University of California Press 1969
Cotterell, Paul, *The Railways of Palestine and Israel*, Tourret Publishing 1984
Da Cruz, D., 'Pilgrim's Road' *Aramco World* Vol. 16(5) 1965, pp.23-33
Dawn, C. Ernest, *From Ottomanism to Arabism: Essays on the Origins of Arab Nationalism*, University of Illinois Press 1973
Dayton, John E., 'Tracking the Train Lawrence Wrecked', *The Times* 4-12-64
De Gaury, G., *Rulers of Mecca*, Harrap 1951
Doughty, Charles, M., *Travels in Arabia Deserta* (2 vols.), CUP 1888
El Edroos, Brig. Syed Ali, *The Hashemite Army 1908-1979: An Appreciation and Analysis of Military Operations*, Amman 1980
Falls, Cyril & Becke, A.F. (eds.), *Military Operations in Egypt and Palestine, Vol. II*, His Majesty's Stationery Office 1930
Fraser, Neil., 'Hedjaz Jordan Railway Locomotives' *The Stephenson Locomotive Society* vol. XLI No. 480, July 1965 p.191
Fromkin, David, *A Peace To End All Peace: The Fall of the Ottoman Empire and the Creation of the Modern Middle East*, Avon Books 1989
Granger, Keith, 'The Hijaz: Saudi Arabia's Other Railway', *Aramco World*, March 1990
Graves, Robert, *Lawrence and the Arabs*, Cape 1927
HDVMT (Abbreviation): *Hicaz Demiryolu (Hejaz Railway) Varidat ve Masarifi ve Terakki Insaati ile Hattin Ahvali Umumiyesi Hakkinda Malumat Ihsaiye ve Izahat Lazimegi Muhtevidir*, Istanbul Contemporary Documents 1334/ 1916
Haddad, W. & Ochsenwald, W. (eds.), *Nationalism in a Non-National State: The Dissolution of the Ottoman Empire*, Ohio State University Press 1977
Hamilton, Angus, *Problems of the Middle East*, Eveleigh Nash 1909
Henderson, Capt. T., *The Hejas Expedition 1916-17: A narrative of the work done by the Arabian Detachment of No.14 Squadron R.F.C. while attached to the Hejaz Expedition*, Imperial War Museum G(41)18 (X59483-2)
Heslop, Major D. G., Railways of the Near East II After Lawrence in Arabia, *Railway Magazine* April 1934, pp.235-40
Hogarth, David George, *Hejaz [Before World War I] A Handbook*, Falcon-Oleander 1917
Holman, James Knox, *Sacred Line to Madina: The History of the Hejaz Railway*, B.A. Degree Thesis Princeton University 1967
Hourani, Albert, *The Emergence of the Modern Middle East*, Macmillan 1981
Howard, P. J., 'The Hedjaz Railway' *Trains and Railways* Vol.2 No.5, 1975, p.148
Hughes, H.C., 'Hedjaz Locomotives', *The Railway Magazine*, Vol. III No. 774 Oct 1965 p.603
Hughes, H., *Middle East Railways*, Continental Railway Circle 1981
Hurren, B. J., 'Pilgrim Railway into Arabia. Part One' *Railway Magazine*, June 1965, pp.346-51
Hurren, B.J., 'Pilgrim Railway into Arabia. Part Two' *Railway Magazine*, July 1965, pp.408-12
Inalcik, Halil & Quataert, Donald. (eds.), *An Economic and Social History of the Ottoman Empire Volume 2: 1600-1914*, Cambridge University Press 1994
Inshallah, Mohammed., 'The Hedjaz Railway', *The Spectator* 29-7-05 pp.148-49
Karsh, E. & Karsh, I., 'Myth in the Desert or Not the Great Arab Revolt', *Middle East Studies* Vol. 33 No. 2 April 1977, pp. 267-312
Kedourie, Elie, *England and the Middle East*, Bowes & Bowes 1956
Kedourie, Elie, 'The Surrender of Medina', *Middle East Studies* Vol. 13 No.1 1977, pp.124-43
King, Russell, 'The Pilgrimage to Mecca: Some Geographical and Historical Aspects', Erkunde Vol. 26 1972, pp.61-73
Kirby, A.F., 'Rebuilding the Hedjaz Railway', *The Railway Gazette*, Aug 1945, p.218
Kirkbride, Sir Alec, *A Crackle of Thorns*, John Murray 1956
Kirkbride, Sir Alec, *An Awakening: The Arab Campaign 1917-18*, University Press of Arabia 1971

Bibliography

Knightley, Phillip & Simpson, Colin, *The Secret Lives of Lawrence of Arabia*, Nelson 1969

Landau, Jacob M., *The Hejaz Railway and the Muslim Pilgrimage: A Case Study of Ottoman Political Propaganda*, Wayne State University Press 1971

Lawrence T.E., *Seven Pillars of Wisdom*, Jonathan Cape 1926

Lawrence T.E. et al., *The Home Letters of T.E. Lawrence and His Brothers* Basil Blackwell 1954

Leach, Hugh 'Off and On the Tracks to Atwi' *The Journal of the T.E. Lawrence Society* Vol. 1 No. 2, Winter 1991-2

Leclerc, Christophe, 'The French Soldiers in the Arab Revolt' *The Journal of the T.E. Lawrence Society* Vol. IX No. 1, Autumn 1999

Leroux, Ernest (ed.), *Revue du Monde Musulman Vols. 3, 4, 5, & 6*, La Mission Scientifique du Maroc 1907/1908

Liddell Hart, Basil H., *T.E. Lawrence: In Arabia and After*, Cape 1934

Liman von Sanders, Otto, *Five Years in Turkey*, The U.S. Naval Institute 1927

Lockman, J.N., *Scattered Tracks on the Lawrence Trail*, Falcon Books 1996

Mack, John. E., *A Prince of Our Disorder: The Life of T.E. Lawrence*, Weidenfeld & Nicholson 1976

MacMunn, George & Falls, Cyril (eds.), *Military Operations in Egypt and Palestine Vol. I*, His Majesty's Stationery Office 1928

Maunsell, Lt Col. F.R., 'The Hejaz Railway' *Geographical Journal* 32(6) 1908, pp.570-85

McKale, Donald M., 'Germany and the Arab Question in the First World War', *Middle East Studies* Vol. 29 No. 2 April 1993, pp. 236-53

McLoughlin, Anthony, 'The Hejaz Railroad' *The Geographical Journal* Vol. CXXIV, June 1958 Part 2, pp.282-83

Ministry of Education (Saudi Arabia), *Mahattat Sikka: Hadeed al Hejaz bil Madinah Al Munawerah* (undated)

Monroe, E., *Britain's Moment in the Middle East 1914-1956*, Chatto & Windus 1963

Monroe, Elizabeth, *Philby of Arabia* Faber & Faber 1973

Mousa, Suleiman *T.E. Lawrence: An Arab View*, Oxford University Press 1966

Musil, Alois *The North of Hegaz - A Preliminary Report of the Exploring Expedition of 1910*, Public Records Office FO882/3 1916

Mytton-Davies, Cynric, 'Railways of the Middle East: 1. The Hedjaz Railway', *The Railway Magazine* Vol. LXXIV No. 440 Feb 1934, pp.109-15

Ochsenwald, W. L., 'A Modern Waqf: the Hijaz Railway, 1900-48' *Arabian Studies III*, 1976

Ochsenwald, William, *The Hijaz Railroad*, University Press of Virginia 1980

Ochsenwald, W., 'The Commercial History of the Hijaz Vilayet 1840-1908' *Arabian Studies VI* 1982

Ochsenwald, William, *Religion, Society and the State in Arabia: The Hijaz under Ottoman Control, 1840-1908* Ohio State University Press 1984

Palmer, Alan, *The Decline and Fall of the Ottoman Empire*, M. Evans & Co. Inc. 1992

Peters, F.E., *Mecca A Literary History of the Muslim Holy Land*, Princeton University Press 1994

Pierard, Patrick & Legros, Patrick, *Off-Road in the Hejaz*, Motivate 1997

Quale, F.A., 'Hedjaz Railway Locomotives' *The Stephenson Locomotive Society*, Vol. XLI No. 482 Sept 1965, p.255

Raw-Rees, Owain, 'The Ottoman Empire Hejaz Railway Medal' *Journal of the Orders and Medals Society of America*, Vol. 49 No.1 Jan-Feb 1998

Raw-Rees, Owain, 'The Order of Al Nahda of the Kingdom of the Hijaz' *Journal of the Orders and Medals Society of America*, Vol. 42 No.1 March 2003

Rolls, S.C., *Steel Chariots in the Desert*, Jonathan Cape 1937

Schoenberg, P.E., 'The Evolution of Transport in Turkey (Eastern Thrace & Asia Minor) under Ottoman Rule, 1856-1918' *Middle East Studies*, Vol.13 No.3 Oct 1977, pp. 359-72

Scrivener, R. F., 'The Hedjaz Railway' *Railway Magazine*, Sept 1934, p.208

Seikaly, May, *Haifa. Transformation of an Arab Society*, 1918-1939 I.B. Taurus 1995

Shaw, S.J. & Shaw, E.K., *History of the Ottoman Empire and Modern Turkey (Vol. III)*, Cambridge 1997

Shepstone, Harold J., 'To Jerusalem and Mecca by Train' *The Railway Magazine*, Sept 1913, pp.219-23

Stevenson, John, 'The "Lawrence of Arabia" Line' *Steam Railway*, No.17 Sept 1981, pp.28-31

Stewart, Desmond, *T. E. Lawrence*, Hamish Hamilton 1977

Stirling, W.F., *Safety Last*, Hollis & Carter 1953

Stitt, George, *A Prince of Arabia*, Allen & Unwin 1940

Storrs, Ronald, *Orientations*, Nicholson and Watson 1937

Swanberg, J.W., 'Jurf Ad Darawish' *Trains*, Vol.62 No.7 July 2002, pp.64-66

Sykes, Lt Col. Sir Mark, '*The Caliphs' Last Heritage*', Macmillan & Co. 1915

Thalaker, Lieutenant, 'The Hijaz Railway 1918-19, A German Report' *The Journal of the T.E. Lawrence Society*, Vol. XII No.2 Spring 2003

Times of India ('The Special Correspondent'), 'Hejaz Railway: Some Interesting Information' 1907

Tourret, R., *Hedjaz Railway*, Tourret Publishing 1989

Waugh, Sir Telford, 'A Translation of the German Account of the Stotzingen Mission from the "Orient Rundschau"' *Royal Central Asian Journal* Vol. XXIV Part II April 1937, p.313

Wasti, S.T., 'Mohammed Inshaullah and the Hijaz Railway' *Middle East Studies* Vol.34 No.2 April 1998, pp.60-72

Wasti, S.T., 'The Defence of Medina 1916-19' *Middle East Studies* Vol. 27 No. 4 Oct 1991, pp.642-53

Wavell, A.J.B., *A Modern Pilgrim in Mecca and A Siege in Sanaa*, Small, Maynard & Co. 1913

Westrate, Bruce, The Arab Bureau: British Policy in the Middle East 1916-1920 The Pennsylvania State University Press 1992

Wilson, Jeremy, *Lawrence of Arabia. The Authorised Biography of T.E. Lawrence*, Heinemann 1989

Wright, P. & Bragger, R., 'Lawrence's Air Force', *Cross & Cockade International*, Vol.34 No.2 2003

Yardley, Michael, *Backing into the Limelight: A Biography of T.E. Lawrence*, Harrap 1985

Young, Major Sir H., *The Independent Arab*, Murray 1933

Zaidi, Z. H., 'Hidjaz Railway' *The Encyclopaedia of Islam* Vol. III 1971

Zeine, N. Zeine, *Arab-Turkish Relations and the Emergence of Arab Nationalism*, Greenwood Press 1958

Index

Page numbers in **bold** refer to illustrations

A

Abbas II, Khedive of Egypt, 65
Abd al Haq, 65
Abd al Kader, Amir, 138
Abdul Muin, Sherif, 127
Abdulaziz, Sultan, 8
Abdulhamid II, Sultan, 4-7, **7**, 11, 14-18, 24, 45-46, 59, 63-64, 67, 70, 73, 80, 119, 154, 178
Abdullah ibn Hussein, Sherif, 84-85, 87-88, 91, 94, 97, 105-7, 114, 116-17, 119, 128, 132, 148, **161**, **167**, 168, 171
Abdulrahman Pasha Yousif, 17
Abrak, 116
Abu Lissan, 123, 126
Abu Markha, 105, **105**, 107, 108, 117
Abu Na'am, **6**, 46, 93, 104-6, **104**, **106**, 116-19, 149, 160, **160**
Abu Raqa, 103-4
Abu Taqa, 43
Abu Taye, Auda, 120-22, **120**, **122**, 130, 138, 157-58
Abu Taye, Zaal, 122, 122, 130-31, 139
Abyssinia, 90
Acre, 55, 157, 164, 167, 174
Aden, 12
Afule, 53, 57, 135, 155-56, 164, 167, 173
Ageyl, 101-3, 121, 123, **140**
Aida, Farhan al, 110, 160
Ain al Fije, 79
Ain Turaa, 118
Akhdar, 32, 41-2, 129, **129**, 160
Al Harb (Harbi), 45, 91, 116, 128
Al Hasa, 152, 177-78
Al Hazm, 129
Al Lith, 91, 172
Al Qunfudah, 91, 172
Al Ula, **16**, 20, 33, **41**, 41, 43-6, **88**, 89, **90**, 91, 101, 112-14, **113**, 136
Albania, 5
Alderton Construction Co. Ltd., 175
Aleppo, 9, 95, 136
Algeria, 6
Ali ibn Hussein, Sherif, 46, 58, 70-1, 84-9, 91-4, 119, 162, 164, 166, 170-71
Allenby, General Sir Edmund, 124, **125**, 137-39, 141, 144-45, 149, 151, 153-54, 156-57, 165-66
American Steel Trust, 28-9
Amman, 24-6, 26, 59, 59, 149, 151, 154, 156-57, 163, 168-70, **168**, 173, 178
Anaiza, 160
Anatolia, 28, 89
Anatolian Railway, 8, 39
Ankara, 8, 178
Anti-Lebanon Mountains, 9
Antonius, George, 150
Aqaba Shamia, 150
Aqaba, 37, 59-61, 119-27, **123-26**, 132, 134, 144, 146-47, 158, 163, 174-78
Arab Revolt, 88-91, 93-6, 101, 104, 111, 119, 124-25
Armistice of Mudros, 161
Asir, 7
Atef Bey, 136
Atwi (At-Tuwei), 122
Auda abu Taye – see Abu Taye
Auler Pasha, 37
Australia, 176
Austria, 28
Awqaf (Waqf), 12, 80, 83, 165, 170
Aydin, 8
Azraq, 138-39, 141, 145, **145**, 154
Azzat, Effendi, 172

B

Baghdad, 8, 46
Bair, 121-22
Balad al Sheikh, 56
Balkans, 5, 7, 83, 86
Bangladesh, 65
Barada Gorge, **9**
Baramke, 57
Barrow, General, 158
Basri Pasha, 136
Bassett, Captain, 161
Batn al Ghoul, 36-8, 133, 150, 177-78
Baume et Marpent, 29, 79
Beersheba, 137, 144
Beirut, 9, 18, 26, 50-2, 63-4, 71, 77, 82, 84, 89, 167, 174
Beisan, 50, 52, 156
Belgium, 28-9
Beni Atiyya, 77, 81-2, 110, 127-28
Beni Sakhr, 77, 148, 152, 157
Berlin, 5-6, 8, 90
Billi, 129
Bin Laden, 175
Bir al Mashi, 45
Bir Ali, 57
Bir ibn Hermas, 128
Bir Jadeed, 116
Bir Rubiaan, 109, **109**
Bir Shedia, 133, 150
Black Sea, 37
Boghaz al Akhdar, 41
Bombay, 65
Borel, Prof. Eugène, 169
Borsig, **55**, 78
Bosra (al Sham), 55, **55**, 164
Boyle, H., 87
Bray, Captain, 138
Brémond, Colonel Edouard, 138
Britain, 59, 65, 87-8, 165, 169
Brooke, Sergeant, 130
Bukhara, 65
Bulgaria, 5
Bunsen, Sir Maurice de, 62
Burma, 65
Buwair, **77**, 107, 110, **170**
Buwat, 58, 93, 119, 128, 176
Buxton, Major N., 153

C

Cairo Conference, 14, 44, 61, 87, 93, 94-6, 119, 124, 135, 147, 166, 168
Cairo, 166, 168
Cardiff, 37
Caspian Sea, 37
Cassell, 54
Caucasus, 7, 25, 86
Central (Constantinople) Commission, 16, 24, 28, 52, 58, 80
Chapman, Thomas, 95
Chauvel, General, 149
Chaytor, Major-General, 156
Chemin de Fer Hedjaz (C.F.H.), 172
Chemnitz, 29
China, 65
Churchill, Winston, 166, 168
Clayton, General Gilbert, 96
Clemenceau, Georges, 164
Cockerill, 28-9
Congress of Berlin, 5-6
Constantinople, 2, 4, 7-8, 11, 14-17, 23, 28-9, 38-9, 45, 60-3, 66, 71, 83-8, 90
Crimean War, 4, 8
Cromer, Lord, 87

D

Damas, Hama et Prolongements (D.H.P.) Railway, 9

INDEX

Damascus, 2, 4, 7, 9, 11-12, 14, 16-8, 22, 24, 26-8, 32-3, 37-41, 45, 50-1, 56-8, **56**, 71-3, 77, 79-84, 89, 91, 95, 110, 122, 124, 129, 132, 136-7, 144-45, 150-61, **158**, 163-67, 172-74, 177-78
Dar al Hamra, 42-3, **43**, 103-4
Darb Sultani, 94
Davenport, Major, 115-16, 119, 132
De Dion, **169**
Deraa, 9, 18-19, **19**, 24, 27, 39, 50-3, 55, 57, 59, 71-2, 74, 79-80, 82-3, 136-38, 145, 149, 153-58, 162-65, 167, **169**, 173-75
Dhat al Haj, 128, 176
Dheilan, Sheikh Mohammed al, 150
Dhuleil, 122
Dieckmann, Peter, 77, 81
Disa'ad, 104, 121, **121**
Donawitz, 28
Doughty, Charles, 42-3

E

Egypt, 6-7, 12, 19, **61**, 65, 73, 81, 86-7, 101, 114, 145, 166
Elias, Joseph, 50
England, 61, 94, 120, 166
Enver Pasha, 85-6, 90-1, 104
Ezra, 55, 157, 172

F

Faisal ibn Hussein, Sherif, 89, 92-3, **93**, 95-6, 104, 106, 114, 120, 124, **128**, **132**, 133, 148-9, 153, 158, 164-66, 168
Fakhri Pasha, 91-2, 96-7, 104, 119, 136, **160**, 161-2, **161**
Faqir, Sheikh Sultan al, 160
Faraifra, 152
Faruqi, Sami Bey al, 55
Ferrovial, 175
Firaun Island, 61, **61**
First World War, 46, 57-8, 70-3, 83-169
Ford, **171**
France, 151, 153, 165, 169
Frankfurt-am-Main, 29
Franz Ferdinand, Archduke, 85
Fuqara, 129

G

Gallipoli, 86
Garland, Major Herbert, 94, 96, 101, **102**, 102, 104, 110, 116-18, 161
Gaudin, Paul, 81

Gayadah, 101, 112-13, **112**, **114**, 116
Gaza, 124, 137, 144
Germany, 29, 70, 77
Ghadir al Haj, 119, 123, 149-50, **163**
Ghasib, Sheikh Mohammed al, 129
Ghazala, 157
Glubb Pasha, John, 125
Goltz, General C. von der, 14
Gothaer Wagon Fabrik Fritz Bothmann & Gluck, 29
Greece, 5
Gutte-Hoffnung-Hutte, 28
Guweira, 146-7

H

Hada, Abu al, 14
Haidar Ali, Sherif, 93, **94**
Haifa, 9, 27, 50-7, **54**, 59, **59**, 71-2, 77, 79, 81-2, 95, 135, 137, 145, 154, 156-57, **156**, 162-67, 169, 173-75
Hail, 81
Haine St Pierre, **25**, 29, **174**
Hallat Ammar, 110, **130**, 131
Hamdi Pasha, Vice-Admiral, 17
Hamidia (Al Anbaria) Mosque, 46, **85**
Hamme, 163
Hamra, 96
Hanomag, 78
Harb, Sheikh ibn Mohammed, 82
Harthi, Sherif Ali ibn Hussein, 138
Harthi, Sherif Fauzan al, 105, 116
Hartmann, **15**, 29, **37**, 45, **52**, **58**, **67**, 77-8, 110, **110**, **157**, 158, **170**
Hauran, 4, 19, 55, 74, 77, 81, 172
Hazaa, Sherif, 150
Hedia, 14, 45-6, 108-10, 113, 116-18, **139**, 148
Helwan, 117-18
Henschel & Sohn, 54, 78
Herak, 172
Heraklia, 37, 63
Heslop, Major D., 162
Hills, W., 50-1, 59
Hisheh Forest, 57, 127, 135
Hodeida, 58, 89
Hogarth, David, 72, 95, 137
Hohenzollern, 29, 54, 78, 171
Homs-Hama-Aleppo Railway, 9
Hornby, Captain H., **115**, **126**, 150, 152
Hussein ibn Ali, Sherif, Amir of Makkah, 46, 58, 70-1, **70**, **83**, 84-6, **86**, 87-9, 91, 93-4, 119, 162, 166, 171
Huweitat, 121, 128, 148, 152

I

Ibn Rashid, 129
Ibn Saud, Abdulaziz, King of Saudi Arabia, 171
Imperial Camel Corps, 153
India, 7, 65
Insha Allah, Mohammed, 14, 65
Intrafi, 175
Iraq Petroleum Company, 173
Iraq, 88, 165-66, 168, 174
Ismet Pasha, Inonu, 168-69
Istabl Antar, 117-18, 149
Izmir, 8
Izzat Pasha, Ahmed, 12
Izzat, Pasha al Abid, 7, 12, 14, 16, 24, 41, 66, 80

J

Ja'afar Pasha al Askari, 115, **128**, 149
Janissaries, 5
Jebel Antar, 46, **98-99**, 105, 107, 117
Jebel Druze, 55, 172
Jebel Semna, 149-50
Jeda'a, 116, 118, 148
Jeddah, 12, 58-9, 65, 84, 91, 94, 171
Jefer, 153
Jemal Pasha, Ahmed, Governor of Syria, 86, 89, **94**, 104, 129, **154**
Jemal Pasha, Mohammed Kuchuk, 136, 141
Jemal Pasha, Mohammed, 136
Jenin, 57, 156
Jerash, 25
Jerdun, 149, 151-52
Jerouf (al Darawish), 148, **148**, 152
Jerusalem, 57, 141, 144-45, 149
Jisr al Mejami, 52-3, 156
Jiza, 157
Jordan Valley, 52-3
Jordan, 124, 175
Jordan, River, 52-3, 145, 149, 156
Joyce, Lt Col. P., 114, 116, **128**, 146-47, 149, 153-54
Juhanni, 101, 105, 108, 116
Jung, **24**, 29, 78, 110, **176**, 178

K

Kanawat Station (Damascus), 56-7, **163**, 177-78
Kapp, Otto von, 58
Karakum Desert, 37
Kassir, 24-5, 38
Kazim Pasha, 17, 19-20, **19**, 23, 45, **59**, 70, 82

191

Kemal, Mustapha (Attaturk), 168
Kerak, 74, 77, 157
Kernag, Lieutenant, 128
Khadhi, Mohammed al, 105-6, **106**, **108**
Khairi Bey, 89, 91
Khamis, 104
Khashm Sana'a, 43, 104
Khuraiba, 44
Kiswe, **177**
Kitchener, Lord, H., 87-8
Krauss, **26**, 29, 38, 54, 78, 110, **139**, **142-43**
Kut, 86
Kuwait, 12, 65

L

La Meuse, 29, 78, 174
La Motte, M., 115
Labella, Signor, 18, 20
Lake Tiberias, 52-3
Law of Vilayets, 84
Lawrence, Sarah, 95
Lawrence, T.E. (Lawrence of Arabia), 72, 93-7, **95**, 101, **101**, 104-10, 116, 119-24, 126, 129-41, **130**, **137**, 144-47, 149-50, 153-55, 157, **159**, 160, 166, 178
League of Nations, 169
Lebanon Mountains, 9
Lebanon, 164-65, 174
Leipzig, 23
Liddell Hart, Sir Basil, 105
Liège, 29
Liman von Sanders, General Otto, 86, 156
Limpus, Rear-Admiral Sir Arthur, 86
Local (Damascus) Commission, 16-17, 19
Lockman, J.N., 110
London, 8, 88, 164
Lydda, 166

M

Ma'an, 29, 33, 37-9, 43, 59, 61, 72, 77, 79, 81, 94, 123, 126, 128, 132-33, 136, 148-54, 157, 162-64, 168-73, **172**, 174-75, 178
Mabrak al Naga, **11**, 43
Macedonia, 5, 28
Madahrij – see Mudarraj
Madinah, 4, **5**, 7, 11, 14, 17-18, 24, 31, 39, 44-6, **44**, **47**, 50, 52, 57-60, 64, 71-4, **74**, 79, 84, **85**, 89, 91-4, 97, 100, 102, 104, 108, 110-12, **112**, 116, 119, 121, 124, 127, 135-36, 148-51, 160-62, 168, 171-72, 175, 178

Mafraq, 154, 156-57
Makkah, 2, 4, 7, 11, 14, 44-6, 58-9, 63, 70, 84, 91, 93-4, 97, 100, 111, 119, 135, 171
Maribeni, 175
Martin Cowley Ltd., 175
Maryland, 28
Mashad, 32, 58
Massoudiah, 57, 164, 173
Mastur, Sherif, 116
Maunsell, Lt Col. F., 23, 29, 38-9, 66, 72
McConaghy, Major W., **96**
McMahon, Sir Henry, 88
Medain Saleh, 8, **33**, 42-4, **42**, 71, 79, 81, 102-04, 110, 112, 131, 134-35, 160, 176, 178
Mediterranean Sea, 9, 61, 153, 165, 175
Mehmed Ali Pasha, 19-20
Meissner, Heinrich August, 8, 18-20, **20**, 23-4, 33, 37, 46, 52, 59, **59**, **144**, 145
Menzil, 152, 178
Mesopotamia, 73, 86
Miclevich, Mr, 39
Midhat Pasha, 7
Mifaie, Abdulmajid al, 172
Minifir, 122, 139
Mohammed Rashid V, Sultan, 70
Mokhtar Bey, 14-15, **39**, 53, 58, 81
Moller, Captain von, 91
Montenegro, 5
Mosul, 37
Muayin, Lieutenant Hassan, 15
Muayyad, General Sadiq Pasha al, 14, 17
Muazzam, **10**, **31**, **34**, 42-3, **84**, 104
Mudarraj (Madahrij), 46, 107-8, 110, **116**, 116
Mudawwara, 38, 40, 128-32, 146, 150, **152**, 153, **153**, 168, 171, 175
Muhit, **62**, **91**, 92
Mukhlis, Maulud, 115, 127, 149
Munich, 29, 177
Murabba, 116
Murray, General Sir Archibald, 86, 104, 124, 144
Musil, Alois, 79
Mutalli, 43
Muzeirib, 9, 18-19, 24, 51-3, 57, 83, 154, **165**
Mytton-Davies, Cynric, 173

N

Na'amein, River, 56, 164
Nablus, 57, 156, 167
Naqb Ashtar, 175
Nassir, Sherif, 102-3, **102**, 117, 121, 148, 151-52, 154, 158, 160

Naval Arsenal, 16-17, 28-9
Nazim Pasha, Vali, 17
Nazmi, Adib, 17
Nedim Bey, 31
Nessib, 154-56, 163, 167, 169
Newcombe, Lt Col. S., 72, 93, 102-4, **103**, 114-16, **115**
Nippon, **80**, **167**

O

O'Conor, Sir Nicolas, 2, 60-1, 64
O'Shea, Major-General, 149
Ochsenwald, William, 67
Orient Express, 8
Otaibi, 105, 108
Ottoman Empire, 2, 4, **6**, 8, 23, 62-3, 70, 74, 86, 119, 135, 168, 178

P

Pakistan, 65
Palestine Railways, 57, 145, 170, 172
Palestine, 7, 57, 81, 86, 104, 119, 127, 136-38, 144-45, 150, 152-54, 164-69, 173, 175
Palmer, Herr., 57
Paris, 8, 83, 164
Peace of Paris, 4
Peake, Captain, F., **126**, 152, 154-55
Persia, 73
Petra, 57, 81, 170
Philby, H. St J., 170
Pilling, Robert, 50
Piraeus, 61
Pisani, Captain, 133, 149-50, 154
Pressel, Wilhelm von, 14
Providence-Russe, 28
Punjab, 14

Q

Qadem Station (Damascus), 56-7, 79, **159**, 160, 163, 172, **177**, 178
Qadi, Dakhil Allah al, 116
Qantara, 166
Qatana, 177
Qatrana, 24, 29, 35, 77, 125, 151, 163, 167
Qishon, 174
Qishon, River (Nahr al Mokatta), 28
Quntilla, 126

R

Rabigh, 45, 58, 91, 93-4, 97, 111, 172
Rahmi Pasha, 40-1
Rako, Captain, 105, **107**
Ramin Tunnel, 57, **57**
Ramleh, 150
Ratib Pasha, Ahmed, 45
Red Sea, 12, 37, 44, 58-9, 91, 96-7
Reshid, Major Ahmed, 12
Richards, W., 2, 4, 22-3, 66
Rifada, Sheikh Suleiman, 129
Ross, Major, A., 97, 112, 126
Royal Engineers, 94, 102, 150, 163
Royal Flying Corps (R.F.C.), 112, 126, 145, 150-51, 153
Romania, 5
Russia, 4-5, 28, 65, 73, 86
Ruwalla, 128, 158

S

Sabah, Sheikh Mubarak al, 65
Sabastiya, 57
Sahl Matran, 58, 115
Said Bey, 84
Said, Nuri, 148-51, **151**, 154
Salmond, Major-General, 126
Salonica, 11, 18, 45
Salt, 59
Samakh, 52, 157, 163, 167, 169, 173
Samara, 122
San Remo Conference, 165
Sana'a, 58
Sarajevo, 85
Saudi Arabia, 28, 37, 171, 175, 177-78
Schlieffen, Countess, 90
Second World War, 174-75
Serbia, 5
Shaalan, Terad, 158
Shakir Bey, **39**
Shakir Pasha, Mehmet, 12
Shakir, Sherif, 106, **107**, **118**, 119
Sharraf, Sherif, 115, 119
Sharwish Aziz, 103
Shehab, Sheikh, 129
Sherarat, 128
Shobek, 57
Shuk al Ajouz, 43
Sileh, 57
Sinai, 60-1, 72-3, 124, 144
Singapore, 65
Smyrna, 8
Somaliland, 90
South Africa, 65
St Leonard, 29, 78

Stent, Captain, F., 126
Storrs, Sir Ronald, 61, 88, 94, 120, 166
Stotzingen, Baron Freiharr von, 89-91
Suaka, 122
Sublime Porte, 5
Sudan, 6, 12, 90
Suddeutsche Wagon Fabrik-Kelsterbach, 29
Suez Canal, 6, 12, **12**, 65, 86, 89
Sultani, 152
Suweida, 55, 172
Swiss Locomotive & Machine Works (S.L.M.), **9**, 78, 110, **157**
Sykes, Sir Mark, 72, 74, 79, **86**
Sykes-Picot Agreement, 88
Syria, 7-8, 17-18, 22, 28, 73, 81-2, 86, 88-9, 124, 160, 165-66, 168, 172-75, 177

T

Taba, 59, 60
Tabuk, 32-3, 36, **38**, 40-1, 43, 73, 79, 81, 121, 125, 128-29, 136, 148, 160, 176
Tafila, 149
Taif, 91
Takheimi, Sherif Merzuk al, 128
Talaat Pasha, Mehmet, 84
Tallal, Sheikh, 157
Tanzimat, 5
Tel Arar, 154
Tel Keram, 57, 164
Tel Shahm, 146-47, 150
Tel Shammam, 53
Tel Shehab, 53, 137, **138**, 144-45, 154
Thomas Summerson & Sons, 175
Thrace, 5
Topusian, Mr, 39
Toulat, Colonel, 166
Tewaira, 101, 116
Trans-Caspian Railway, 37
Transjordan, 165, 168-71, 175
Treaty of Lausanne, 168-69
Treaty of Sèvres, 167-68
Trucial States, 12
Tubize, **166**
Tunisia, 6
Tur, 73
Turkey, 73, 86-8, 168
Tuwaiha, 150

U

U.S.A., 28, 65
Um al Amal, 81
Um Jarad, 112
Um Lejj, 91
Um Waled, 172

Um Zuraiba, 116
Uneiza, 57, 127, 152, 163, 170

V

Vehib Bey, 84
Vienna, 6, 8
Vignoles, Charles, 28

W

Wadi Ais, 105, 108-9
Wadi Akhdar, 42
Wadi al Abyad, 178
Wadi Hamdh, 46, 108-9, 112, 118, **119**
Wadi Ithil, **35**, 36, 127, 129
Wadi Ithm, 124, 146, **153**
Wadi Jizzil, 114
Wadi Rutm, 36, 146, **147**, 150, 178
Wadi Safra, 93-4, 96
Wadi Sirhan, 121
Wagga, 148
Waqf (Awqaf), 83, 165, 170
Wavell, A.J., 46, 71-2
Wayban, 101, 110, 116
Wejh, 44, 91, 97, **97**, 100-2, 104, 111-12, **111**, 114, 120-21, 124
Wilson, Lt Col. C., 94, **96**
Wood, Lieutenant, 138

Y

Yahya, Imam of Yemen, 14
Yanbu, 45, 74, 84, **89**, 91, 93-4, 96
Yanbu al Nakhl, 93
Yarmuk, 52-4, **51**, **52**, 72, **136**, 137-38, 145, 154, 157, 163, **164**, 174-75
Yells, Sergeant, 130
Yemen, 7, 14, 58, 74, 89, 91
Yildiz Palace, 17
Young Turks, 66, 70, 77, 84, 87
Young, Major Hubert, 134, 154
Young, Wilkie, 26-7

Z

Zaki, Captain Omar, 15
Zehringer, Mr, 81
Zeid ibn Hussein, Sherif, 124, 153
Zeizoun, 53, **58**
Zerqa, 24-5, 29, 35, 122, 157
Zimpel, Dr Charles, 12
Zumurrud Fort, 114-15, **114**
Zumurrud Station, 31, 45, 114-16